GOLF IS NO ORDINARY GAME

14 EXTRAORDINARY TALES OF GOLF, LIFE, DEATH...AND EVERYTHING IN-BETWEEN

G. GUILFORD BARTON

Booktrope Editions
Seattle WA 2015

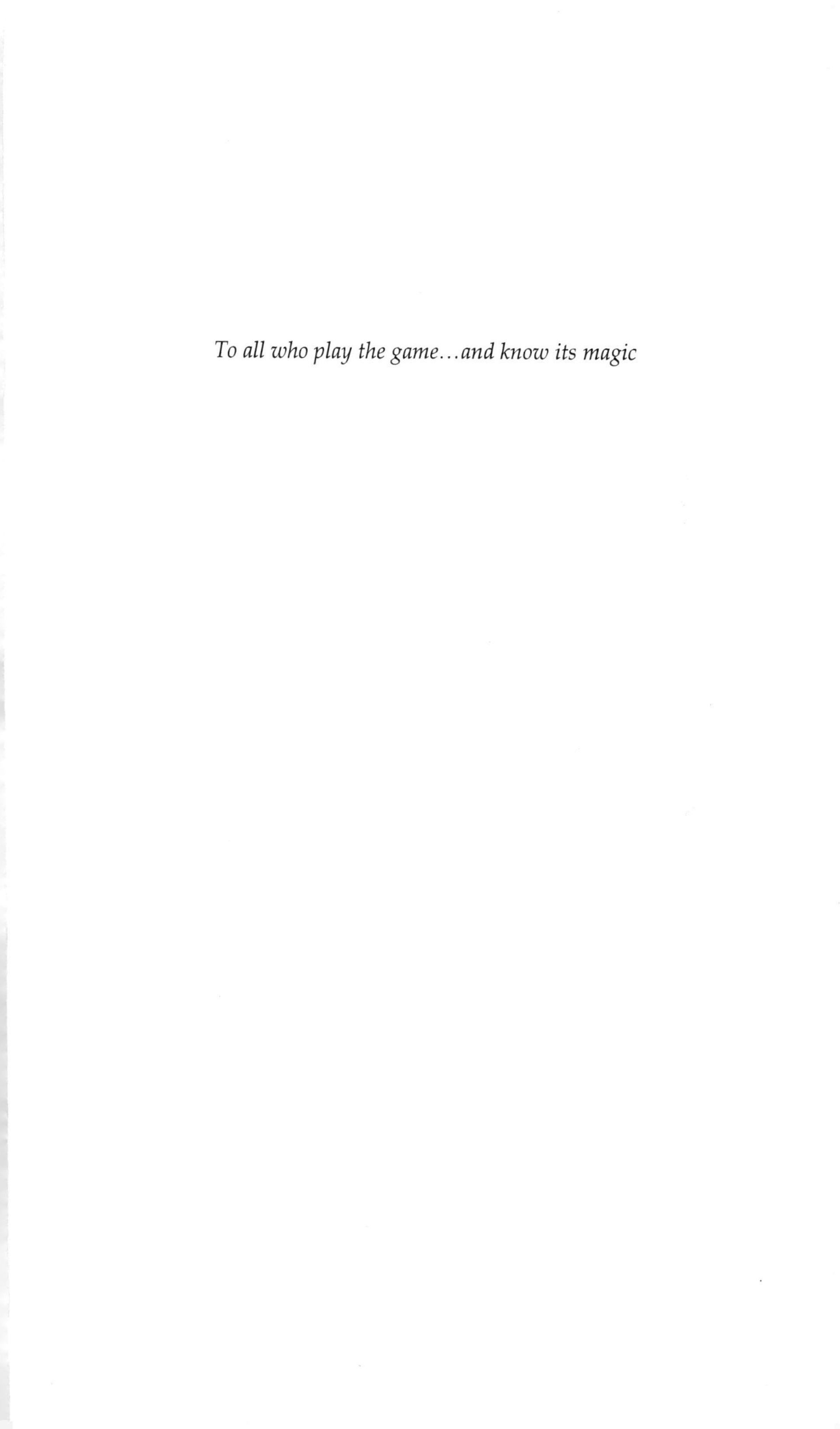

To all who play the game…and know its magic

ACKNOWLEDGMENTS

Many thanks to our illustrator, Majanka, for her wonderful work on the cover. To Mary, our proofreader, and her eagle eyes. To our book manager, Ruth, for keeping us ducks in a row and pulling it all together. And most of all to our editor, Judith, whose many hours of diligence have made the stories all the better.

TABLE OF CONTENTS

The Nimble Men 10

The Girl With The Swing 28

The Flying Scotsman 52

Local Knowledge 92

Glencoe 118

On the Fringe 130

Old Tom 150

Big Bertha 166

A Gentlemen's Game 186

They Play Golf in Heaven 222

Ganymede Golf & Country Club 242

At the Turn 254

The Magic Niblick 290

Four For Fore 324

About the Author 331

Golf Is No Ordinary Game. Who hasn't watched the flight of a
well-struck ball with a sense of wonder, or shaken their head after
witnessing an impossible sixty-foot putt snake into the cup, or stood
on a twilight-shrouded links and felt the magic of the place? There's
more to the game than meets the mortal eye.

When reading *Golf in the Kingdom* so many moons ago I became
intrigued with the idea of the inner game of golf. Man is, after all, both
body and soul, just as the world around us is made up of the material
and the spiritual. Golf, when played correctly, is the embodiment of
such subtle harmonics, a union of the physical and nonphysical.

Fore!

G. G. Barton

The
Nimble
Men

By
G. Guilford Barton

Introducing the Series

·GOLF IS NO ORDINARY GAME·

Years ago I was rummaging around a bookstore when I came across a volume about Scotland. Inside I found a photograph of the Aurora borealis blazing above the moorlands. Below the photo was a short blurb describing a bit of ancient Scottish folklore, attributing the Northern Lights to a mythical tribe of creatures called the Nimble Men. What follows is the tale that myth inspired, one that weaves the colorful spirit of the game with the equally colorful legend.

The Nimble Men

High above the scottish islands of the Hebrides the night skies often blaze with color. It's called the "Aurora borealis," or the "Northern Lights," and the islanders tell the myth of a tribe of shining fairies that course through the summer sky carrying great, shimmering banners of light and magic.

They call this tribe the Nimble Men.

She came across the cap while rummaging through an antique shop one cold rainy day in Traverse City. What drew her attention to it she could never say. The hat dangled high on the wall from a set of deer antlers, and when the proprietor noticed her staring up at it he grinned with pleasure.

"That hat has a story that goes along with it, young lady," he said from behind a roll-top desk. "Quite a tale if you care to hear it."

She was skeptical of any and all sales pitches. But the weather was bad and she was bored and depressed, so she sat down in a nearby rocking chair. "Fire when ready."

Taking a long wooden pole from behind the counter, the shopkeeper retrieved the hat from its place on the wall. It was made of old gray tweed and was rather formless in shape, its brim tattered and showing signs of unraveling.

"Have you ever been to the Hebrides Islands?" he asked her.

She thought this a very odd way to begin a sales pitch and admired the man's ingenuity.

"No, but both my husband and I are of Scottish descent. Most of his family still live there.

His…our last name is Drummond," she added sadly, thinking how likely it was that their life together would soon end.

The shopkeeper's eyes popped open wide at this and he scratched the top of his head. "My, but this is a coincidence. One of the protagonists in the story happens to go by that very name."

"Really?" she said with a wry grin, not buying it for an instant.

"Yes, indeed. Andrew Drummond. The other man's name was Christy Graham."

Now it was her turn for surprise. "But that's my maiden name!"

The antique dealer stared at her for a long moment, then pulled a small flask from his hip pocket and quickly downed a nip before replacing it and pulling up a chair next to hers.

"This is really almost too much." He nervously twirled the cap in his hands. "Kind of gives me the willies, if you know what I mean." He looked at the young woman, who had pulled both feet up onto the rocking chair and was resting her chin on her knees while waiting for him to continue.

"Have you ever seen the Northern Lights?" he asked her.

"Yes, once, when I was a very little girl. It was a weak display," she said, "at least according to my father, who's seen the lights many times. He said it's like heaven itself is in flames, as if maybe we've gotten our directions all mixed up regarding the afterlife and that hell is really up instead of down."

"Yes," mused the shopkeeper, "I suppose it can appear like that. Especially during a particularly strong show like the one Drummond and Graham were said to have witnessed on the island of South Uist in the summer of 1883.

"First off let me tell you that Andrew and Christy were the worst of enemies. The Drummonds and the Grahams had been feuding for decades."

She raised her dark eyebrows at this, not in surprise but in irony: after ten years of marriage she and her husband were thinking of calling it quits. The weekend in Northern Michigan had been her idea, a last ditch effort to patch things up between them. But the previous night's shouting match still rang in her ears, and she could not rid herself of the taste of the bitter argument they'd had just before he'd stalked off and left her to roam the shops alone.

"Take my word for it," she said softly, "they're still at it."

"Well," continued the shopkeeper, "both men were out playing a late round of golf—on separate parts of the links, mind you—during the long summer twilight when the sky suddenly exploded in sheets of electric fire. And as they stood and watched they saw a ball of energy detach itself from the midst of the torment and drift toward the earth somewhere west of their location. It could mean only one thing: the Nimble Men."

She was hooked now. "Who are the Nimble Men?"

"There is an ancient Hebrides myth that tells the tale of a tribe of shining fairies that course through the summer sky, carrying great shimmering banners of light and magic," the shopkeeper replied. "The islanders call this tribe the Nimble Men, and legend has it that from time to time some of these creatures lose their celestial balance and come hurtling to earth. If you are lucky enough to capture one he has to grant you a wish before being allowed to return to the skies and rejoin the tribe."

"But that's nonsense." She waved a hand in the air. "Everyone knows the Aurora borealis is just the result of sunspot activity."

"Maybe so," the shopkeeper said, "but this took place in the 1800s, and there was not a child raised on the Outer Hebrides who did not know the tale of the Nimble Men. Christy and Andrew were no exception. The both of them were running all out for the close horizon before the tiny ball of light had fallen halfway to the ground. Drummond approached from the 15th fairway, Graham raced from the green at seventeen, and they converged at the point of impact just as the fairy was dusting itself off from the long tumble."

The young woman leaned forward. "What did it look like?"

"Well, it was very short, only a little over two feet in height, with long silken wings and a distinctly girlish face. On the dark moor it glowed a bright blue."

* * *

"Bother these new wings," he mumbled to himself trying to straighten out the butterfly-like appendages. "And why do I always have to be blue? I'd like very much to be red someday."

"Hold right there, ye beasty!" they both cried in unison, brandishing their irons at the fairy.

Then they scowled at each other from opposite sides of their quarry.

"What are ye doing 'ere, Andrew Drummond?" shouted Graham. "Be off with ye now, this is me Nimble Man and nae other."

"Aye," spat Andrew back at his shorter rival, "ye'd like nothing more than fer me to leave ye with me prize, Graham."

Though hesitant by nature, no one could say that Christy Graham lacked spunk. "I was 'ere first, Drummond. Don't make me hurt ye; I'd only be too glad to oblige."

Andrew let out a booming laugh. "Ye were a distant second and ye'll be the one that's hurting when I'm through with ye!"

"Come now, gents," the Nimble Man said. "Me name is Gorm and it seems to me that ye were both on the scene at the same moment."

"Then grant us both a wish," demanded the barrel-chested Drummond.

"Nae," said the fairy with a wave of a glowing finger, "I can nae grant but one wish per fall."

"Then grant it to me!" insisted Christy.

"I don't think that he would allow it," the fairy said, glancing at the suddenly lethal-looking mashie that the bigger Scot held in his beefy hand.

"Aye," Andrew said menacingly, "ye have a nimble mind, Nimble Man."

"Ye will have to vie fer the wish," Gorm declared.

"How?" asked Graham.

The strange creature pointed to Christy's tweed cap. "Take your hat off and give it to me." Christy did so, and Gorm reached back into the folds of his wings and came away with a handful of blue flame. He placed this in the open cap and flew off into the night, leaving a bright trail in his wake. The fairy returned a few moments later and landed on the limb of a gorse shrub.

"I have placed a charm on the hat and set it atop a flagstick," he said. "First one o' ye into the hole gains the prize. Agreed?"

"Aye," Christy said, eyeing the hated Drummond suspiciously.

"Aye," agreed Andrew. "Which hole?"

Gorm grinned a bright flash of glowing teeth.

"The par-six 12th?" Christy asked.

The fairy shook his head. "Guess again."

Andrew pointed up the fairway. "Number eight and the double dogleg?"

Gorm's grin grew wider and full of mischief.

"Not the Devil's Claw!" Christy cried.

"Ye can nae play The Claw in the dark," protested Drummond.

"Aye," agreed Christy. "It would be foolhardy."

But the creature merely looked up at the fiery night sky and said, "It's nae completely dark."

*　*　*

The Devil's Claw is a long, curving, rocky promontory that juts for 300 yards out into the North Sea. Only 30 yards wide at its throat, it narrows to a treacherous thirty feet, sloping steeply the whole length before rising again and ballooning into a relatively luxurious, 20-yard-wide plateau that holds a long, finger-like green. Little grass grows on the headland, and where the fairway ends the cliffs begin, falling precipitously to the sea. A century earlier some madman had the notion of placing a golf hole on the headland, and legend has it that he lost his life while playing it. While the hole is no longer officially part of the course, many an adventurous soul attempts it merely for the challenge it offers.

But no one dares play it in the dark.

"It's too difficult I tell ye," insisted Christy, "Las' week I carded a 10—in broad daylight!"

The fairy shrugged. "That's the deal, lads. If ye wish the wish ye'll have to play The Claw to get it."

The two men glanced at each other, dreading to have to play the perilous hole in the dark but dreading even more the thought of the other getting the priceless charm. Reluctantly they shouldered their bags and trudged to the ill-groomed patch of grass that served as tee for The Claw. Andrew and Christy gazed down toward the tiny green below them. It was not a long hole, just a shade over 300 yards, but the bottlenecking fairway created a perspective illusion that made it appear much longer. No detail could be seen in the dark, but they could clearly make out the tweed cap glowing blue on top of the flagstick.

As they contemplated their task the Nimble Man flitted about their heads, alternately offering encouragement and impediment. "Who will hit first?…Better to hit last, I think…But first on the fairway has the advantage…Then again, if ye end up in the drink…Use your play club; I think ye can reach it…Nae, best to lay up."

"Will ye close your impish trap?" shouted Andrew irritably. "I'll play first." He glared into his bag and finally settled on his brassie.

"Bold," challenged Gorm, "very bold."

Andrew scowled at the fairy and took his stance, aiming for the eerie glow in the distance. He swung and the ball shot off the wooden clubface and into the night sky. For a brief moment they could see it silhouetted against the Aurora before it fell toward the fairway.

Gorm clapped his hands and wings together. "Well struck!"

The big Scot grinned haughtily at his longtime enemy. "See if ye can better that, then."

Christy pretended to ignore the challenge. He tested the wind and chose to go with a jigger; his shot stayed low and straight.

"Equally well done," applauded the fairy.

"We'll just see about that." Andrew stomped off the tee. Christy picked up his bag and was beside the bigger man in an instant. "Ye best stay away from me, Graham," threatened Andrew.

"Ye'll nae be leaving me sight 'til the hole is settled, Drummond."

Andrew rounded on him in anger. "And what's *that* supposed to mean?"

"It means that I don't trust ye, Drummond."

"Are ye insinuating that I might engage in foul play?" Andrew loomed over him.

Christy backed away slightly, then remembered who he was speaking to. "Ye'd cheat your own mother if it served your purpose."

Andrew took a menacing step forward but Gorm flew between them before he could strike out. "If there be any violence ye'll both lose the wish," scolded the fairy. "Nor will there be any cheating. Whoever does so forfeits the prize to the other."

The two mortals glared at each other as they carefully made their way down the steep slope to their balls. They found them lying next to each other in the middle of the fairway at its narrowest point—so close they almost touched.

"Now what do ye make o' that?" Gorm said as he hovered hummingbird-like over the two balls. "Different approaches, same result."

"A coincidence plain an' simple," spat Andrew. "Watch me approach, Graham. It'll make your heart faint fer sure." The big man addressed his ball and took a mighty swing, but instead of flying toward the green the ball sliced off his open clubface and sailed to the right. "Blast!" he cried in disgust and tossed his club to the ground.

Christy laughed. "Me heart is still beating, Drummond. Now stand aside and let me show ye how it's done." But he fared no better than his rival, pulling his shot well to the left and short of the target.

It was Andrew's turn to chuckle. "Ahhhhh, so that's how it's to be done, is it?" His toothy smile shone with the light of the Aurora. "When the time comes perhaps I should just wish fer your swing?"

"Bah!" Christy shouted sourly and stalked off to look for his ball. He found it lying precariously close to the edge of the bluff, with the fairy standing nearby watching the light show with his wings and arms folded.

"I must say the red team is putting on a splendid display tonight," Gorm remarked admiringly. A bright flash of deep crimson flared high in the sky and slowly rippled its way across the horizon. "That'll be Gimbe," sighed the fairy. "He always was a bit o' a show-off."

With a quick flap of his translucent wings the Nimble Man was airborne again and hovering over Christy's ball. "You're lucky to still be in the running."

"Luck has nothing to do with it," Christy responded confidently. He pulled a niblick from his bag and casually lofted a shot onto the center of the green.

"Most impressive," smiled the fairy, his wings generating a low hum of satisfaction. "Now let us see how your big friend is making on."

Andrew had the more difficult lie, his ball hard up against the twisted trunk of a stunted, wind-sculpted pine. Christy and the fairy arrived to find him wrestling with how to best play the shot up to the waiting green. Before they could say a word he turned a scornful eye on Christy's smug look. "I suppose that Graham is already on the putting surface?"

"Aye," replied Gorm, flying low and circling the tree to examine the unfortunate lie, "and unless ye can produce a prodigious effort, it appears that he shall win me magic."

Andrew leveled his mashie-niblick at the fairy. "The day that any Graham gets the better o' me is the day I leave this fair life behind. Now stand—or hoover—aside and give a man some room to swing!"

After two aborted attempts, Andrew managed to muscle a shot in the general direction of the hole. In the gloom it was impossible to tell whether the ball had fallen short, landed safely or sailed over the plateau and off the cliffs that bordered the far side of the green. The fairy flew off to reconnoiter as the two men struggled up the steep slope.

Gorm was waiting for them at the summit. Christy's ball could be clearly seen lying less than a foot from the pin, topped with the eerily glowing cap. Andrew's ball was nowhere in sight.

"Have ye found me ball?" he asked Gorm.

"Aye," the fairy replied. He turned to Christy. "Congratulations, what is your wish, then?"

"Hold!" shouted Andrew, placing himself between Christy and the fairy. "Where is me ball, ye beasty?"

"It lies o'er the edge, about a man's length below the top o' the cliff," answered Gorm. "*I* might be able to play it from there but ye would never manage it."

"I'll be the judge o' that," Andrew said between clenched teeth. "Show me."

Gorm flew to the cliff face and pointed down to a tiny outcrop of rock that formed a ledge, about three feet long and just wide enough for a man to place both his feet. The ball lay in the middle of the ledge and Christy hooted when he saw it.

"Nae a thin' to it, Drummond, jus' grow your arms about six feet longer and swing away!" he cajoled. "Let's see now, what shall I wish fer...?

"Nae so fast," Andrew said. He turned and began to lower himself gingerly over the edge of the cliff. "Ye may, indeed, win the hole but nae until I've done all I can to prevent it."

Christy gaped at him and then at the waves crashing against the rocks far below. "Are ye mad? Ye'll fall as sure as me putt will!"

"Then I'll fall."

"But ye'll be killed, man!"

Only Andrew's head was visible, and his eyes glowed with hatred and grim determination. "I'd rather die than be bested by the likes o' ye."

Christy turned to the fairy. "Are ye nae going to stop him?" The creature shrugged. "I have nae power over mortal men. Besides, what business is it o' yours what happens to him?"

Christy dropped to his knees and peered over the edge. Andrew had managed to find a handhold, and with the iron clenched in his teeth was stretching out his legs in a blind attempt to find the ledge.

"A wee bit to the right," directed Christy.

Andrew looked up with a malevolent glare. "I'll nae be needing help from ye, Graham."

"Fine!" Christy cursed back at him. "Go kill yourself, then, and good riddance to ye!"

The big Scot reached the foothold and pressed his body against the almost vertical wall of rock. Below him the cliff fell away into the sea in a sheer façade, broken only by an even smaller ledge below and slightly to the left of the one where Andrew perched precariously. Taking the iron from his teeth, Andrew attempted to address his ball. But try as he would he could not find a position that afforded him a decent swing.

"It's nae use, Drummond," sneered Christy from above. "Stop being a fool and climb back up 'ere."

Gorm fluttered down to the ledge. "He's right. I can nae help ye if ye fall."

"I do nae recall asking fer your help," Andrew shouted, almost losing his balance as he did so. "Now off with ye before I swat ye from the air like the pest that ye are." And with that he spread his legs, addressed the ball in a hopelessly awkward manner and swung wildly with all his might.

Christy ducked to avoid being struck by the ball, which ricocheted off the cliff and disappeared into the foaming sea. When he peered over the edge Andrew was gone.

"Good God!" he cried, shaking his head. "The damn fool's murdered himself." Christy looked around him but the fairy had flown off. He was just about to rise and demand his wish when he heard a faint sound drift up from the cliff below. "Is that ye, Nimble Man?" he called, but he could see no blue glow, only the weak reflection of the Aurora dancing on the slick rock face.

He heard the sound again, first a soft scuffling and then an unmistakable grunt of someone making a great effort. "Andrew?" Christy whispered.

"Aye," came the labored reply.

Now Christy could make him out. The momentum of Andrew's swing had propelled him sideways off his perch. What had saved him was a narrow crack in the rock wall. As he lost his balance and began to fall, the quick-thinking Scot had been able to wedge the head of his mashie into the crack and then swing one foot to the tiny ledge below. He lay against the cliff spread-eagled, clinging desperately to the grip with only the toe of his left boot to relieve the tremendous strain on his right arm.

He would not last long.

Christy glanced around again but there was still no sign of the fairy. It was up to him—he could either let Drummond die or do his best to try and save him. Without knowing why he was doing it, Christy retreated from the cliff top and went in search of his golf bag. He quickly removed the leather carrying strap, then did the same with his opponent's bag and returned to the precipice. A glance over the edge revealed that Drummond was still holding on. Hoping to find a safer way down, Christy searched the edge of the drop-off to his left. Finding no access, he retraced his steps and came across a fissure in the cliff—nothing more than a wrinkle, really—that cut into the damp rock and was just wide enough to accommodate his slight body.

Linking the two straps together, Christy lowered himself into the fissure and began to work his way downward. The surface was cold and slippery. It narrowed as he progressed, and twice he had to struggle to free himself after becoming wedged in the rock.

When he could descend no farther he carefully peered around the opening in the cliff face. Andrew was ten feet away and slightly below him. He was trying in vain to get the rest of his body over to the ledge, but with each attempt it became more obvious that he was hopelessly marooned. Christy could see the sweat running down the man's forehead and dripping off his red beard.

"Hang on, Drummond," Christy said.

Startled, Andrew looked up to see Christy smiling at him. A look of relief crossed his features, to be rapidly replaced by one of suspicion.

"What are ye doing down 'ere?" he asked breathlessly. "Come to watch me plunge onto the rocks? The view up there nae good enough?"

"I've come to rescue ye, ye damn fool."

"Aye," spat the bigger man, "and maybe I'll be sprouting wings and joining the Nimble Men."

Christy chuckled. "Ye are truly a dark soul, Andrew Drummond, but we Grahams'll save even the blackest o' sheep if jus' fer the pleasure o' watching him be sheared when the time comes." As he spoke Christy lowered his makeshift lifeline from out of the gap in the cliff.

"What's that fer?" Andrew asked.

"I'm going to reach out and swing this over to ye. Grab it and I'll pull ye onto the ledge."

Andrew eyed the leather straps. "How do I know ye won't just let loose the moment I let go o' me mashie?"

Christy grinned. "Ye don't, but what choice have ye got? Ye can nae stay like that forever."

"I can hang on 'til me clan arrives," Andrew said stubbornly.

"And who's going to tell them where ye are?" Christy said. "Besides, they will nae be missing ye fer hours yet. Ye'll be long washed out to sea by then."

Andrew glanced down between his spread legs. The waves that broke against the rocks seemed to reach for him in hunger. "All right," he said, "but if ye try any tricks I swear I'll take ye down with me."

Christy had to lean most of his body out of the crevice to have any chance of reaching Andrew. He began to swing the lifeline back and forth until it was within a foot or two of the other man's outstretched fingertips.

"It's now or never, man!" Christy cried.

Andrew let go of the mashie and lunged for the end of the strap. He timed it perfectly and was rewarded with a fistful of leather, but immediately began to slip sideways, away from the ledge. "Pull, man!" he shouted.

Christy tugged hard on the lifeline and slowly pivoted Andrew up and onto the safety of the ledge. He was just about to slither back into the fissure when the stones beneath his feet gave way. With much of his weight already out over the edge, there was little he could do to save himself.

Christy screamed as he shot out of the crevice and into open air. It was only Andrew's strength that saved them both. Somehow he managed to keep his balance and hang onto the lifeline as it took Christy's full weight and swung him below the ledge, like a living pendulum. It was a full minute before Christy stopped swinging and came to rest against the cliff.

Now it was Andrew who held the power of life or death in his hands. For an instant—just an instant—he considered letting go and saving himself. But at that moment the Northern Lights burst into a display of unearthly beauty. The whole sky, from horizon to horizon, was alive with vibrant color and light. Even the ocean appeared to be a part of it, the waves a kaleidoscope of motion. Andrew had never seen the likes of it. Even Christy ceased his feeble cries for help and gazed in wonder.

* * *

Neither man was sure how long the two of them had stared at the Aurora before Andrew finally shook himself and, with his back pressed against the rock, began hauling the terrified Christy up onto the ledge beside him.

When he was safe Christy turned to Andrew. "Fer a moment I felt sure ye were going to let go o' the line."

"Fer a moment I felt the same thin'," Andrew replied grimly. He turned his gaze back to the blazing sky and sighed. "But such wonders tend to pale our petty hatreds."

Christy looked at him. He seemed both smaller and larger at the same time.

Andrew smiled and clapped Christy on the shoulder. "Come, ye can use me as a ladder if ye like."

Christy scrambled up onto Andrew's shoulders and pulled himself to the higher ledge. Using the leather straps he was able to assist Andrew up, as well. They repeated the maneuver until both were safely standing on the top of the cliff, watching the borealis reach its apex as the short northern night began to wane.

"Well," Andrew said finally, "I say it's high time ye earned your wish."

"Aye," nodded Christy wearily.

They returned to the green, and Andrew watched as Christy tapped in for his par. Gorm was still absent, but the hat was where he had left it on the tip of the flagstick. Christy reached up and removed it. He turned the cap over and stared at the light that filled its crown.

"What are ye going to wish fer, then?" Andrew asked.

"I…I don't know," stammered Christy. "After our adventure it would be criminal to be completely selfish about it."

Andrew grinned.

"I think I'll wish fer something both of us can benefit from," Christy said. Then he stood solemnly erect and droned officially: "I hereby wish that the Drummonds and Grahams will cease their feuding and act like brother clans."

"Well spoken…friend," Andrew said. "Time we put an end to the nonsense."

"Why *do* our families hate each other anyway?" Christy asked as they shouldered their clubs and headed back for town.

Andrew shrugged. "I don't know. Perhaps me da can tell us."

"Bah," scoffed Christy, "I asked mine and he had nae clue."

"There's bound to be some record o' it," Andrew reasoned.

"Got to be," agreed Christy. "I'll ask me Great Aunt Lorna; she's been hating Drummonds for over a hundred years."

Andrew laughed loudly. "Looking forward to making her acquaintance…"

The Nimble Man smiled from behind a tangle of gorse and watched the two men vanish into the early morning mist. He flapped his wings twice, winked at no one in particular and shot off into the atmosphere, leaving behind a long streak of blue that melted into the Aurora just as the sun rose to chase it from the sky.

*   *   *

When the shopkeeper had finished with his tale, the woman reached over and gently took the tweed hat from his hands.

"How much?" she asked.

"Oh, I could never charge you for it," the man replied. "I don't for a moment think it was an accident that brought you into my shop this day. Perhaps there's a trace of the magic left in it," he added, looking down at the hat in her hands.

She placed the cap on her head and stood to examine her reflection in a nearby mirror. A smile touched the corners of her mouth and turned into a firm line as she reached an inner decision. *Maybe it was too late to salvage what little they had left,* she thought, *but magic or no magic, she was resolved to keep trying.*

Thanking the shopkeeper, she left to search for her husband. The weather had cleared, and it was dark by the time she found him sitting on a bench staring out at Lake Michigan.

"Hi," She said.

He turned and frowned at the hat. "What's that on your head?"

She sighed...*Here we go again!* "Just something I picked up in a shop downtown."

She was surprised when he smiled, something he hadn't done in her presence for months.

"I like it," he said.

"You do?"

"Yeah, it suits you, somehow."

At that moment the sky lit up in a glowing palette of wavering color, and both of them turned to watch the rare display of the Northern Lights dance over the waters of the great lake.

"It's so beautiful," he whispered in awe. She slipped her hand into his and looked up at her husband's profile. The lights gleamed in his hair and painted the side of his face in colorful streaks, reminding her of the night she had first seen him, standing in the neon glow of a carnival outside of Ann Arbor.

"So are you," she said softly. "Come on, let's go get something to eat," Christine added, leading Andy by the hand back toward town. "We have a lot to talk about."

Neither of them saw the tiny blue creature smiling at them from behind a nearby tree.

The Girl With The Swing

by G. Guilford Barton

Continuing the Series
GOLF IS NO ORDINARY GAME

Being a son of the Midwest I am a big fan of the American farmer and his farm. For me there is nothing quite like strolling through a field of corn—a vast cloud-speckled sky overhead and fresh-turned earth between my toes. I found the concept of a golf course weaving its way through cropland irresistible, regardless of how ridiculous the idea. *The Girl with the Swing* is a tale chock full of old-fashioned ideas and old-fashioned values from days gone by. Days, I for one, wish were still around.

The Girl with the Swing

The shimmering curtain of late summer heat maintained an uncertain distance as I raced along the narrow ribbon of pavement. I had long since tired of the mirage and its equally illusive accomplice, the maddeningly flat terrain that stretched on forever in all directions. Together they poked and prodded at my imagination until I began to wonder whether I was really moving at all or simply frozen to the spot as the unchanging world rushed past.

So when the billboard loomed out of the haze inviting me to *Grab a cold one at Walt's General Store and Feed Emporium (just five easy miles east of the highway),* I took the exit without the slightest regret for the detour. There was nowhere I needed to be, no one waiting anxiously for my return, just the end of another long and mildly fruitful sales trip through the Farm Belt.

The wind swept through the open window as I sped past fields of corn and soy and sunflower, leaving a long trail of dust to slowly settle back to earth. In one of these fields I noticed a young man driving golf balls into a plot of cut cane. What caught my eye was the intensity the youth displayed toward the practice session, and the odd fact that he seemed to be hitting an entire bushel of balls instead of a mere bucket.

Welcome to Morely, Population 89 another sign announced as I entered the tiny town almost hidden beyond it. Beneath this, someone had scrawled: *The smack-dab middle of Nebraska.* The entire town consisted of a single block and the eight buildings that graced its parallel walks. Locating the general store was not difficult, especially since the proprietor had painted one whole side of its rusting tin roof with: *Walt's, Where You Can Get Just About Anything You're Lookin' For.*

"Yeah, right," I muttered as I left my car and climbed onto the weathered porch. The first thing I saw when I stepped through the screen door was a wide assortment of computer hardware fresh from the fertile valley of Silicon. Surrounding this high-tech display, Walt had carefully arranged an ensemble of stuffed prairie dogs posed with various musical instruments. Their bright beady eyes glittered with mockery.

My interest piqued, I began to wander down the aisles. Most of the shelves seemed devoted to the ordinary staples found in any backwater store, yet sprinkled here and there among the everyday were other, less-pedestrian wares. An Italian espresso machine tucked innocently between the Coffee-mate and the Folgers Crystals caused me to linger for a moment, as did the vintage World War II US Army Air Corps parachute trying very hard to blend in with the rest of the sporting goods. I strolled past a saxophone, a spear gun, a jackhammer, a telescope, a fax machine and a lobster trap that reeked of brine and seaweed. A hijacked New York City parking meter, its red violation flag waving impotently, lured me down an aisle to gawk at a rather shocking array of women's lingerie modeled on, of all things, old milk cans with faces painted on their battered skins.

But by far the most interesting item on display was the huge polar bear rug tacked across the back wall. Dangling from a shiny claw was a small tag claiming that the rug was once the property of Errol Flynn and the site of many a risqué romp with an assortment of Hollywood starlets. I stepped back and pitied the once-majestic brute, finding it hard to imagine wicked old Errol writhing on the snow-white fur with Monroe, or Mansfield, or whomever clutched in a drunken embrace.

I suppose the idea was for someone to purchase the rug and carry on the tradition, but the bear's hazy glass eyes had an odd glint to them, as if to suggest that they had witnessed enough fornicating, thank you very much, and would like to be left to hang in peace. Even the carnivorous mouth managed to express its contempt for the rug's sordid past, frozen not in a snarl but rather in a grimace of distaste.

Eventually I happened on a wall cooler with a beat-up surfboard listing casually against its side. I pulled out a root beer and made my way back to the counter, which was manned by an acne-ravaged teen-ager who had watched my progress through the store with interest.

"That *all*, mister?" the kid asked, clearly implying that only a fool would leave the place with nothing but a soda pop, especially with Errol's rug of iniquity just waiting to be snatched up for a song.

"Yeah. How much?"

"A dollar."

I handed a buck across the counter and stepped back onto the porch. As I surveyed the street I noticed a woman approaching from the far end of town. She was both very tall and very young, no more than nineteen or twenty, and even from a block away I could tell that she was striking. Her auburn hair shone in the bright sun as she strode toward me, clad in nothing more than a pair of denim cut-offs and a men's gray T-shirt with NEBRASKA FOOTBALL stretched across her chest in faded red letters.

She had the greenest eyes I had ever seen. Not the dull pigment found in so many, but vivid, like the bright green of a summer leaf when held up to the sunlight. Maybe I had met more beautiful girls in my twenty-nine years, but at that moment I couldn't recall a single one. The spark of confidence I caught in her amazing eyes and the way she seemed to glide over the gravel drew me to her like a moth to flame. It wasn't until she was almost past that I noticed the old hickory-shaft driver dangling loosely from her right hand.

There is only one thing that I love as much as women, and that's golf. I stepped off the porch and began to follow her without giving it a second thought. When she turned a corner at the end of town, I edged one eye around the local coffee shop and waited for her to get well down the road before continuing. I noticed that she was not quite as tall as she seemed from the porch, falling an inch or two shorter than my own height of six foot three. Her long hair, tied with a rawhide cord at the nape of her neck, swung hypnotically in rhythm to her pace, luring me onward as the insects droned in the hot fields.

About a half mile out of town she stepped off the road and dis-appeared into an abandoned apple orchard. By the time I entered the trees there was no trace of her. I searched the grove thoroughly, stopping to look both ways down the crisscrossing rows. Just as I was about to give up and head back to town I heard the faint, yet unmistakable, sound of a wooden golf club slicing through the air and striking something hard. I followed the intermittent sound until I came up against a high overgrown hedgerow planted at the edge of the orchard. The *whoosh-crack* of the club came again, and I realized that the source lay just beyond the leafy barrier.

Moving to my left, I found a small break in the hedge that, if I crouched on my knees, offered a filtered view of a huge walnut tree standing hard on the banks of an irrigation pond. The girl stood in the shade of a sweeping limb, poking at something on the ground with the end of her driver. It took me a few moments to realize that she was bumping a fallen walnut onto a better lie. When she was satisfied with its position, she casually addressed the hardened fruit, glanced down the length of the pond, coiled in a perfect take-back... and unfurled the most beautiful swing I had ever seen. The nut sailed far out over the water and landed with a silent splash.

*   *   *

I wasn't sure how long I knelt there in the dirt and watched, or whether it was after the first swing or the next, that I fell helplessly in love with her. I was wondering what to do about it when she leaned on the club and turned in my direction.

"Are you gonna hide in the bushes all day or are you gonna come out where I can see ya?"

Stifling an urge to flee, I sheepishly fought my way through the hole in the hedge and joined her beneath the tree. "How did you know I was there?"

"I got ears, don't I?"

Her hearing must have been as extraordinary as the rest of her, for I could've sworn that I hadn't made a sound. "I'm sorry," I offered lamely, "I saw you back in town and..."

"I know. I ain't blind, either."

Her challenging tone momentarily set me off balance and I groped for something to say. I nodded at the ground around her bare feet. "Do you always practice on walnuts?"

She softened some at this and gave me a hint of a smile. "'Course not, silly, just when they're in season."

I laughed and held out my hand. "My name's Adam Nye."

"I'm Mary Ellen Parker." She gave my hand a firm squeeze.

"You have a lovely swing, Mary Ellen. Who taught you how to play?"

"My ma."

"She must be one hell of a golfer."

"She died when I was twelve," she replied in a clipped tone.

"Oh…I'm sorry."

"No need to be; ain't no fault of yours."

Relieved that I hadn't offended her, I sat down and leaned against the bole of the tree. "Mind if I watch while you hit more walnuts?"

She gave an elegant shrug of her shoulders. "Suit yourself."

A cool breeze floated off the glittering surface of the pond as I studied, with rapt attention, one breathtaking shot after another. I noted carefully every graceful move of her lithe body: the way her hair hung straight down her back as she moved through the swing; the way she cocked her head to one side like Arnold Palmer as she watched the flight of the ball; the way her toes curled into the grass just before she took back the club. Each time she made a minor adjustment to her stance or grip I cringed, sure that she would ruin my vision of perfection. But each shot rocketed over the aquatic fairway, tailing slightly left or right to her will. I would have loved to see what she could do with a real ball.

I could've sat and watched her all day long, but Mary Ellen abruptly shouldered her club and began to walk away.

"Wait." I bolted to my feet. "Where are you going?"

"I've got to get home and fix lunch."

Stepping into her path I gently took hold of her arms, shut my eyes and took a deep breath. "Look, I know this is going to sound nuts, but…I think I'm in love with you."

"You're crazy." She giggled. "You don't even know me."

I opened my eyes and saw her lovely features close to mine. "I've never had a saner moment in my life. I love you and I want you to marry me."

The girl chewed on her lower lip and studied my face for a moment. "OK, but you'll have to speak to my pa about it."

I wasn't sure what response I had expected. Certainly rejection topped the list, followed closely by hysterical laughter. Ridicule, outrage, consternation and even minor displays of physical violence were not out of the question. But acceptance was the last thing I was prepared to deal with, and what shocked me most was the casual way she treated my outrageous proposal like an everyday occurrence.

As I stood gaping at her she took my hand and gave it a tug. "Well, are you comin' or not?"

I trailed after the girl in stunned silence. Eventually we emerged from the orchard into a tidy yard between a bright yellow farmhouse and a weathered barn. She paused for a moment to listen, then headed for the gaping barn door. As my eyes adjusted to the gloom I could make out barrels and crates and rusting farm tools scattered about the dirt floor. Sunlight seeped through cracks in the walls and roof to expose row upon row of old leather bridles and yokes, which hung like rotting laundry from the rafters. Against one wall stood a long wooden bench littered with an assortment of golf clubs in various stages of assembly. The rest of the barn was dominated by a late-model tractor and a huge man leaning into the engine compartment. He rose when we entered and gave Mary Ellen a wide grin.

"Hey, Pumpkin, lunch ready yet?" The smile quickly turned to a frown when he saw me standing behind her. "Who's he?"

"This is Adam, Pa," Mary Ellen said, running a hand along a gleaming fender. "Says he wants to marry me."

The farmer raised an eyebrow and stared at his daughter, who calmly returned his gaze. He wiped his hands with a filthy rag and began to circle me slowly.

"Where you from, son?"

"San Francisco originally, but I live in Omaha now."

"And what makes you think you want to marry my daughter, all of a sudden?"

"Well, I saw her practicing just now, you see…over at the pond… and…" I trailed off weakly, realizing how absurd it sounded. But the explanation must have satisfied the farmer, for he nodded and stopped directly in front of me.

"You play the game much?"

"Game?" I frowned and glanced at the girl. "I don't understand. What game?"

"Golf!" the big man answered, as if it were the most obvious thing in the world.

"Well…yeah," I stammered. "Whenever I get the chance."

"Good, 'cause if you want my daughter's hand you'll have to play for it."

"Play?" I eyed the man's big hands with dismay. "Play who?"

"Me," Mary Ellen said with a wry smile.

"You?"

"That's right." Mr. Parker gave a curt nod of his head. "If you can whip her, you can marry her."

Her father grabbed a set of clubs off the barn wall and tossed them over one side of his broad shoulders. "This sittin' all right with you, Mary Ellen?" he asked, as we walked toward a mud-spattered pickup. I gave the girl an anxious look and her green eyes smiled into mine.

She opened the passenger-side door and slid onto the bench seat. "I brought him to you, didn't I?"

He nodded and tossed the clubs into the truck bed. "You got your clubs with you?"

"Yeah, they're in my car," I answered, climbing in beside the girl. "How far is it to the nearest course, anyway?"

Mr. Parker eased himself behind the wheel and fired up the engine. "Just outside of town."

I looked from one to the other in astonishment. "You mean a little place like this has its own golf course?"

A smile played along the corner of Mary Ellen's lovely mouth. "Yeah…you might say we got ourselves a course."

We drove into town and I hopped out to open the trunk of my car. As I pulled out my bag and shoes, two men came out of the general store. One of them nodded at the farmer. "Afternoon, Roy, what's up?"

"This here fella's gonna play Mary Ellen for her hand."

The locals eyed me with interest. "A stranger?" the other man asked.

"Reckon so," Roy answered. The two men looked at each other and scampered off in opposite directions. For some reason this seemed to please the girl. She motioned me back into the truck. "Come on, let's get this show on the road."

We motored out of town and turned down a dusty gravel road until it ended abruptly at a wall of cornstalks. Farmer Parker got out of the truck and the girl looked at me expectantly.

"This is it?" I asked, looking out over the fields of surrounding cropland.

"Yep." Mary Ellen clambered down behind me and grabbed her bag from the truck bed. "Follow me."

She vanished down a narrow beaten path that led through the corn. I squeezed my way along it, knocking stalks aside, when it suddenly ended and I found myself blinking in the bright sunlight, not quite believing what met my eyes. A lush green fairway spread out from my feet, cutting a wide swath through the corn and ending at a large green nestled between a pair of bunkers some 400 yards away. A narrow ribbon of rough separated the freshly-cut grass from the surrounding cropland.

"This is incredible," I said in wonder, crouching to feel the grass. "Who maintains it all?"

"We do," replied Mary Ellen.

"Just the two of you?"

"No, silly, the whole town."

"If we can't grow and care for a few acres of grass then we have no business being farmers," her father added sensibly.

I sat down on a bale of hay and began to change into my golf shoes. By the time I had tied the last lace a small crowd had already gathered by the tee. I could see more people coming up through the corn.

Mr. Parker walked to the midline of the tee and removed his oil-stained hat. He raised a hand for silence. "As y'all know it's the custom of me and my kin to test the mettle of any man who would marry a Parker. Today, a Mr.—" He paused to shoot me a questioning glance.

"Nye."

"Today, Mr. Nye will compete with my daughter, Mary Ellen, for her hand in marriage. The format is match play and strict USGA rules apply. No gimmes unless your opponent concedes the hole. And son," he said, placing the hat back on his head, "all you have to do is split the match. Understood?"

I nodded. "I have one problem, though. Your daughter has the huge advantage of knowing the course, while I don't have so much as a scorecard to help me along."

"Nothin' we can do about that, son."

I glanced at the gathering crowd. "Can you lend me a caddie?"

The farmer thought for a moment and turned to the gallery. "Fair enough. How about it? Anyone care to carry the challenger's bag?"

A tall farm boy stepped forward. "I'm willin', Mr. Parker."

"Sorry, Lonnie," Parker replied with a shake of his head. "You know I can't allow that." He scanned the gallery again. "What about one of the women folk?"

A clear voice rose from the back of the crowd. "I'll caddie for him, Pa." The locals parted and a beautiful young woman emerged from their midst. She was a year or two older than Mary Ellen and shorter by at least a head, but there was no doubt they were closely related — face and hair, and startling green eyes. "It'll give me a chance to get to know my future brother-in-law; that is, if he wins, of course." She walked up to me and held out her hand. "Name's Maggie."

"Adam." I shook her cool hand. "Think you can get me around safely?"

"Oh, I'll get you 'round all right. But the safe part will be up to you."

"What can you tell me about the 1st hole?"

"Par-four, 382-yard, slight dogleg right," she said, pointing down the fairway. "There's an irrigation ditch out about 210 from the tee. Once you clear that it's a straight shot to a tiered green guarded by bunkers on both sides."

Mary Ellen's father had placed both beefy hands on his daughter's shoulders and was giving her some final words of advice. The girl nodded sharply at each point, and I wished that I could hear what the man was saying. When Parker finished he walked across the tee. "Whenever you're ready, son. The challenger plays first."

Not used to playing before a crowd, I nervously shifted my weight between my feet and had to step back from the ball twice before finally settling down. I swung and managed a nice shot down the left side of the fairway that came to rest 270 yards away. A smattering of polite applause rippled through the gallery as I stepped back to let the girl play.

I glanced at Mary Ellen, hoping to catch a look of admiration, but she was already staring down the fairway, her face a mask of fierce concentration. The crowd stood completely still as she addressed the ball. She waggled the club, dug in her bare toes and swung, sending the ball soaring high over the center of the fairway. It tailed slightly left before falling and rolling to a stop a yard or two short of my ball. The locals whooped and cheered for their heroine.

"Atta girl!" someone yelled.

"Go get 'im, Mary!" called another.

"Very pretty shot, Adam." Maggie shouldered my bag. "What do you normally play to?"

"On a good day I'm about a 6."

She chuckled. "Well then, you'll need to have a *great* day if you're gonna beat my sis. She's been playin' scratch since she was fifteen." Maggie reached up to brush aside a strand of hair from her face, and I noticed her wedding band.

"Did your husband have to beat you before you married him?"

"Yep."

"Don't you find this tradition of yours a little archaic?" I asked. "I mean, it sorta smacks of the Dark Ages."

"Maybe," she said and shrugged, "but that's just the way of things in my family. It was Momma that started it all. She loved the game; taught us how to play when we were still in diapers." Maggie sighed and looked down as she walked. "About ten years ago, after she took bad sick, she called us all into her room late one night.

"'Pa,' she said, taking my father's hand, '*remember the day you proposed to me?*'

'*Sure do, honey. That was the day I beat you on the lake course.*'

"She looked into my father's eyes and said, '*I never told you this, dear, but that's the reason I said yes. I made up my mind long ago that the only man who deserved my devotion was one that was my equal on the links. And seeing that you were the only one who ever came close, I figured I'd better get while the gettin' was good.*'

"'*Heck, Sally,*'" Pa said, gently stroking her hand, "'*I knew that. Why else would a fine woman like you take a second look at the likes of me?*'

"Momma smiled weakly and said, '*Promise me you'll do the same for our girls. Don't let them walk down the aisle with any man that's not worthy. It won't do.*'

"Pa looked at us doubtfully and turned back to the bed. '*Do you think that's wise, Ma?*'

"'*Promise me, Roy!*' she pleaded.

"And so he did; we all did. She died three days later. Ever since that day, whenever a Parker girl comes of age and a boy takes a shine to her, he has to prove his merit with ball and club."

"How many of you are there?" I asked.

"Seven."

"Seven!"

"Uh huh. Mary Ellen's the last of us to go."

"I take it she's the baby of the family."

"Nope, just the best golfer."

I looked over at the taller girl as she approached her ball. "How many men has she played?"

"Oh, just about every boy in town, maybe the whole county—and most of them more than once. That's why Pa wouldn't let Lonnie Matthews carry your clubs. Didn't you notice how they all looked at you?"

I had noticed, everything from disapproving frowns to outright glares of hatred. Now I understood why Mary Ellen had accepted my rash proposal—she was growing desperate. Having exhausted the stable of local talent, she was now taking offers from any quarter to avoid the prospect of becoming an old maid.

Maggie tugged at the shoulder strap. "To tell you the truth, Adam, I was kinda taken aback when I heard that she was playin' an outsider."

"Why's that?"

"Hush, now." Maggie raised a finger to her lips. "She's about to play."

Mary Ellen had taken a pitching wedge from her father and paused to consider the wind, which had kicked up slightly. I glanced at the green, its front-left quadrant protected by a gaping bunker while a smaller strip of sand outlined the right edge. The flag had been placed on the lower tier directly behind the larger trap. The girl lofted a high shot that started out slightly right of the heart of the green. It arched toward the hole, landed on the top tier, spun backwards and rolled down the slope to within five feet of the pin. The crowd went wild and Mary Ellen gave me a big grin as if to say: *You want me, big guy? Then beat that!*

I swallowed hard and muttered to myself. "Well, you were the one dying to see what she could do with a real ball."

Maggie watched my reaction with obvious humor. "Steady, Adam. You've got about 96 yards to the pin. Can you spin the ball?"

"Sometimes, but I wouldn't count on it."

"Well, the wind isn't bad." She studied the gently waving cornstalks. "Just hit it high and into the slope and it ought to feed back to the hole."

"Just a walk in the park, right?"

Maggie laughed. "I like you, Adam Nye. I kinda hope you win this here match."

"Thanks, I can use all the help I can get." I pulled out my wedge. "Well, here goes nothing." My shot came in too hot and rolled onto the upper tier. Not a bad play, but when I met Mary Ellen's eyes I thought I spotted a look of disapproval hidden behind her polite smile.

The green was as meticulous as the rest of the hole, its blades cut at just the right height. "It's gonna move about eighteen inches right," Maggie whispered into my ear as we surveyed the twenty-foot putt. "The surface is kinda slow, so put enough pace on it to get it to the downslope—but not too much or you'll roll all the way to the trap. Don't miss it, Adam, because she surely won't."

"OK, OK," I hissed.

I bent over the ball, settled my weight until I felt comfortable and stroked it toward the hole. It zipped promisingly over the short grass, but ran out of gas just short of the ridge and curved offline. As the ball started down the slope it moved even farther to the right and slid well past the hole, earning me a couple of rude snickers from the gallery.

Mary Ellen crouched on the edge of the green, laying the putter along her line. She rose and repeated the maneuver just behind the ball, this time with her eyes shut tight. Then she stunned me by quickly standing and striking the ball in almost a single motion. It fell into the center of the cup as a chorus of hoots erupted from the locals.

"Does she always do that?" I asked Maggie as we followed Mary Ellen and their father to the 2nd tee.

"Do what?"

"Putt like that."

Maggie grinned. "It *is* rather unnerving if you're not used to it— so get used to it." Her laughing eyes slid to my face. "OK, one down with seventeen to play, not the end of the world."

"No, just the beginning of the end," I said, making her laugh again. We were trudging down a muddy track between fields and

I marveled at where I was and what I was doing. "So, what's the next hole?"

Maggie paused to scratch her leg as her sister and Pa took a left around a rolled-up bale of hay. "It's a 165-yard, three-par to an island green."

"How can you have an island green in the middle of a farm?" We stepped around the hay bale and onto a slightly elevated tee. From the raised vantage point I could see how. A vast field of sugar cane spread around us and the green stood out like an oasis in its midst, completely engulfed by a sea of red-topped, shoulder-high stalks.

"It's not as bad as it looks from here." Maggie lowered my bag to the grass. "There's a big putting surface with a wide collar of rough. But whatever you do, don't hit it in the cane or you're dead."

The tall plants obscured the lower half of the green, and Mary Ellen had to stand on her tiptoes to get a look at the pin placement. The crowd had nearly doubled since the 1st hole, and one of the younger lads let out a low whistle as she stretched out her tanned legs. Those around the boy immediately hushed him up, but the catcall seemed to have no effect on the girl. Once again she uncoiled her magnificent swing, hitting a lazy shot to the middle of the green. I laid a hand on my seven-iron and glanced at Maggie, who gave an almost imperceptible shake of her head and held up six fingers.

From the sound of the impact and the almost liquid jolt I felt through the grip, I knew that I had caught it perfectly. The ball sailed high into the hazy sky and straight at the flag. It bounced once and struck the pin squarely, then rolled a couple of feet to the left and uphill of the hole.

The gallery murmured in shocked disbelief while Maggie, who had climbed the hay bale for a better view, leapt to the ground and let out a loud whoop. "Wow, what a shot!"

The rest of the townsfolk took the cue and grudgingly surrendered a mild round of applause. We marched single file along the narrow path cut through the cane from tee to green, and Mary Ellen kept turning her head to stare at me as if sizing me up for the first time.

"You've got her thinkin'," Maggie whispered.

Once on the green I marked my lie and stood back to watch Mary Ellen putt. Her ball lay some thirty feet from the hole, on the far side of a gentle mound that dominated the center of the putting surface.

She would have to putt up and across this rise and stop the ball near the middle of the downslope, all of it with the grain. I didn't see how she could hope to keep it close. Twice she stalked from one end of the green to the other, stopping to confer with her father each time she passed his hulking frame. Then, just as she had done on the 1st hole, she closed her eyes for a moment, opened them, stood and abruptly struck the ball. The white sphere cut a wide arc up the slope. It almost stopped as it crossed the ridge, then slid slowly down the opposite side snaking toward the hole. Farmer Parker pulled the pin just before the ball dropped into the cup for a birdie.

The gallery exploded in riotous glee, but Mary Ellen held up a hand to quiet them in respect for her competitor.

What have I gotten myself into? I thought as I nervously placed my ball next to the coin I had left on the grass. My putt, although short, was certainly no gimme. It was going to take a nasty slide to the right, and required just the right amount of touch to get the ball to the cup. It was the kind of shot my buddies called a "character builder." I aimed a foot above the target and tapped the ball just enough to get it moving. It bent sharply toward the hole as it lost speed, caught the left edge and ran a hundred eighty degrees around the rim before heading back in my direction. The gallery moaned sympathetically as I dropped my putter in disgust.

Number three was a long par-five that Mary Ellen easily reached in three and two-putted. Following a poor second shot, I was lucky to get up and down from 10 yards off the green to stay two back. Mary Ellen won the 4th hole with another birdie and we halved five and six. But my errant approach to the 7th green cost me another stroke. After tying again at number eight, I was in good position to win the 9th, but Mary Ellen saved par by blasting out of the bunker to within a foot of the cup. I conceded the putt and made the turn down four.

As her sister teed up on the 10th tee, Maggie leaned closer to me. "You better start thinking about winning some holes, my friend, or you can cancel those honeymoon plans."

"Doesn't she ever falter?" I hissed in frustration. "Has she no weakness?"

"Momma didn't hold with weakness." Maggie sighed and stared out over the fields of corn. A bank of low clouds sailed across the plain on a breeze that stiffened noticeably as we waited to play. A sudden strong gust pulled the hat off a farmer's head and sent it cartwheeling down the fairway. Maggie tilted back her head and sniffed at the air. "How's your wind game?"

"Are you kidding?" I laughed. "I grew up on the Monterey Peninsula. Wind, rain, fog, earthquakes—you name it, I can play in it."

"Good, then pray for more of it. Sometimes it can give her fits."

We started for home by splitting the 10th. On the 11th I finally managed to break through with a chip-in from off the fringe, only to give it back again on the 12th with an appalling drive into a field of soybeans.

The wind continued to freshen as we played, breaking loose husks of corn that danced across the fairways. Sticking with my one-iron, I kept the ball low, sacrificing distance for accuracy, but Mary Ellen began to struggle as the clouds slipped overhead and dropped the first fat drops of rain on the upturned faces of the gallery.

On thirteen the wind grabbed Mary Ellen's ball and deposited it into the left-hand trap, resulting in her first bogey of the match. She fought the weather valiantly on the next hole, saving par with a long putt in the driving rain, but she couldn't keep pace with the low rockets I kept sending into the teeth of the gale. She found herself lagging behind and forcing her shots, giving away both fifteen and sixteen.

"Pour it on, Adam!" Maggie yelled over a harsh gust. "You've got her on the run."

I won the 17th with another par, and the gallery hummed with excitement as we stepped up to the last tee with the match all square. I didn't know what a crowd of eighty-nine people looked like, but I was pretty sure that the whole town stood huddled around us in the rain, offering a temporary barrier from the wind. Those who couldn't find a place on the grass spilled over into the fields and peered through the cornstalks.

"OK, this is it," Maggie said. "Eighteen's a par-four, sharp dogleg left. See that copse of trees? They're out about 180. That's where the knee in the dogleg breaks. Just keep it in play and it's an easy par."

I nodded my understanding, realizing that the hole would play particularly tough for the girl, with the wind howling in from the right. I took my stance and waited for a lull. When it came I crushed a screaming one-iron down the right side that rose no higher than the corn. The ball bounced in the fairway and rolled just past the trees on the opposite side. My effort was greeted with appreciative applause from a few scattered spectators.

"Looks like some of the townsfolk have decided that you might be worthy of our Mary Ellen after all," Maggie said as I handed her my club.

I glanced over at her sister. "We'll see."

The rain had tapered off to a drizzle and Mary Ellen stood on the tee with her beloved driver in hand, scowling at the leaking sky and the furiously whipping cornstalks as she waited for a break in the wind.

"Five-minute rule, Pumpkin," her father gently warned.

"Give 'im what for, Mary Ellen!" someone yelled from the corn.

She waited a few seconds more and then swung. The ball started out right but began to move left almost at once. The farther it went, the faster it tailed away. I could hear her muttering to herself, "Get down, get down!" But the ball ignored her pleas and sailed on, striking a limb on one of the trees and caroming off into the wet cornstalks. The gallery moaned in dismay and Mary Ellen waded into the muddy field with her father in tow.

"Welcome to the family, bro," Maggie crowed as she struggled to keep pace with me. "She's got no shot. None. I oughta know, I've been in there enough. She'll have to take a drop or punch it out to the fairway."

The green came into view as I neared my ball. I could clearly see the pin sitting on the top tier, close to the right edge. Mary Ellen emerged from the corn and watched, hands on hips, as I lofted a high shot, trusting that the wind would carry it to the green. The ball hit on the upper level, took a big hop and rolled to the back left edge.

I looked back across the fairway. Mary Ellen stood in the mud, arms at her side, her head hung in defeat. It was the first sign of vulnerability she had displayed all day and I had a sudden urge to rush over and embrace her, to apologize for my shot. But she turned away and vanished into the field before I could move.

As I strode up the fairway I caught a momentary glimpse of the top of her head through the waving stalks. I guessed that she had about 140 yards of corn to negotiate in order to reach the green. Her red hair reappeared next to her towering father, and a moment later her clubhead flashed as it sliced through the air.

A clod of dirt shot straight into the sky and the ball floated toward the green with astonishing accuracy. It landed on the lower tier, bounced twice and began its agonizing journey up the slope. The gallery urged it on, some of them falling to their knees and imploring the ball up the hill. Mary Ellen exploded from the corn just in time to see her shot reach the ridge. It paused there for a brief instant and then, like a hound that has lost the scent, faltered to the right and wandered back to the bottom of the green.

A grim atmosphere hung over the gallery as Farmer Parker paced off the two balls and determined I was away. I had about a thirty-foot level putt, which I cautiously lagged about a foot short of the cup. I quickly marked it and stood back to await Mary Ellen. Any doubts I might have had about the girl evaporated as I watched her line up the putt. The determination on her face was almost as beautiful as her swing. She was as rare and wonderful as the course we were playing.

This girl has heart, I thought, *as big and wide as the summer sky.*

She crouched in front of her father, who whispered some advice into her ear, then stood and unleashed her uncannily abrupt putting stroke. The ball tore up the soggy slope, sporting a rooster tail of water as it rapidly ate up the distance to the cup. It slowed as it crested the ridge, veered to the right and headed straight for the hole.

"She's made it," Maggie said, and the gallery voiced the same conclusion with a rising crescendo. The ball slowed further, took a peek at the bottom of the cup and slipped past to stop an inch away.

The cheer from the crowd died, as if cut off with a scythe and whisked away over the fields by the wind. The only sound that greeted me as I stepped to my ball was the rustling of the corn—a vast, collective sigh.

Mary Ellen tapped in, and I glanced up to see her searching the gallery, her shoulders slumped in final surrender. I was shocked by the immense sorrow in those green eyes. Pretending to double-check my line, I knelt on the opposite side of the hole and tried to spot who she was looking at. The rain had stopped and the sun broke through the clouds to shine on the faces in the crowd, one of which I recognized.

I bent down to remove a small obstacle from the green, stepped back to my ball, glanced at the hole, pulled back the putter slightly and gave it a gentle tap. The ball skirted the left edge of the cup and rolled by.

Pandemonium broke out around me as people raced onto the green from all directions. Hats flew up and littered the sky. One farmer who didn't have a hat removed a rather bad toupee he had purchased from Walt's (where you can get just about anything you're lookin' for) and tossed that into the air instead. A group of young men grabbed Mary Ellen and hoisted her up on their shoulders. As they carried her off I could see her shouting in my direction, but I couldn't make it out over the din.

*   *   *

Taking advantage of the mayhem, I picked up my bag from the grass and melted into the corn. I was able to get my bearings on the nearby town when the field abruptly changed to a narrow plot of tall grass. I had just crossed a dirt track when I heard rapid footfalls approaching from behind. I turned to see Mary Ellen racing toward me across the field. She stopped in front of me, panting heavily and glaring into my face.

"You missed that putt on purpose!" she shouted, once she had caught her breath.

"Who says I did?"

The girl took another step toward me and jammed a finger between the B and R on her chest. "I do. I saw you deliberately twist the putter and pull it. What's the matter, ain't I good enough for you?"

I gave her a half smile. "How long has he been trying to beat you, Mary Ellen?"

Confusion replaced her anger and she furrowed her brow. "Who?"

"The young man you locked eyes with back on the green. The same one I saw practicing so diligently this morning as I drove into town."

She blushed. "Goin' on five years now."

I nodded, watching her eyes. "Do you love him?"

"Yes."

"Then why did you agree to play me?"

For the first time that day she refused to look me in the eye.

"Let me guess," I said gently. "Since nobody in town can beat you, you thought that a little outside competition might stir the pot a bit, maybe light a fire under him?"

A dented pickup pulled to a stop on the road and we turned to see the boy peering at us from behind the wheel.

"Why don't you just let him win?" I asked.

"Because it wouldn't be right," she said. "Besides, Pa and my sisters would know…and Ma, too."

The boyfriend honked once and leaned out the window. "Hey, Mary Ellen, come on!"

She turned back to me. "I've got to go."

"Just tell me one thing before you do. Would you really have married me?"

She chewed on her lower lip for a moment, then quickly shook her head. "Before that last putt? No, probably not. But now I'm not so sure."

She cocked her head and considered me the way she would one of her finer shots. A smile elevated one corner of her mouth. "Maybe we'll play again someday, you and I." She turned and glanced back at the boy drumming his fingers on the wheel. "After all, a girl can't wait forever."

"I don't think you'll have long to wait, Mary Ellen," I said. "You see, you're beatable now. You know it, and more important, *he* knows it."

Another honk. "Mary Ellen!…"

The girl with the swing laughed and kissed me gently on the cheek. "Good-bye, Adam. And thanks." Whatever heaviness I felt in my heart lifted away as I watched her run barefoot across the wet grass and hop into the passenger seat. The boy gunned the engine and the pickup swerved away from the shoulder, sending a shower of gravel flying down the road.

People started to filter through the fields around me as I continued on my way. The younger ones ignored me but the more seasoned cast me knowing looks. Some even patted me on the back or squeezed my shoulder as they passed. Just outside of town I came upon Maggie, waiting for me against a barbed wire fence.

"Most folks around here take the trouble to thank their caddie after a match," she said.

I shrugged. "I felt a quick exit was in order."

"Heck of a thing you did back there." She jerked her head toward the course.

"You noticed too, huh?"

"Have to be a fool not to."

I shrugged again. "Seemed like the thing to do at the time."

"You're a heck of a guy, Adam Nye," she said, taking my hand. "It's been a pleasure just knowin' ya."

"Same here, Maggie. Your husband's a lucky man."

A shadow passed over her beautiful face and she shook her head. "I lost him years ago in the Gulf."

"Oh...I'm sorry."

Her eyes quickly cleared and smiled into mine. "No need to be; ain't no fault of yours."

I draped an arm over her shoulder and we walked back to town.

"I don't suppose there's any chance I could interest you in a round of golf?"

THE FLYING SCOTSMAN
BY G. GUILFORD BARTON
Continuing the Series
GOLF IS NO ORDINARY GAME

G ood versus evil. There is nothing I find quite as compelling as a tale pitting good against evil. For isn't that the common thread of all history? *The Flying Scotsman* is the story of one man's journey into the heart of darkness, lured there by the trappings of an unrighteous world. There he must make a choice. To fight or surrender. Win or lose. Do or die. Fear, apathy, courage, faith. All can be found here, with golf providing the path leading to freedom… or destruction. And the nattily-dressed antagonist? Well, surely the Bible warns us that the devil often comes clothed as an angel of light.

THE  FLYING SCOTSMAN

Miles Crumpacker noticed the well-tailored man as soon as he entered the station. He wore a black suit and vest, a striped silk tie, a bowler hat, polished shoes and spotless white spats. An umbrella hung from his arm, and he eyed Miles with obvious interest. But Crumpacker was in too much of a rush to pay him a second glance.

Cavernous Victoria Station bustled with its typical Friday night crowds. Miles adjusted the golf bag slung over his shoulder and set off at a quick pace across the terminal. He paused for a moment to study the destination board as knots of travelers brushed past. Someone rudely bumped his elbow and Miles turned to see a minister herding his wife and two young children toward the platforms. The clergyman looked in Miles' direction and offered an apologetic smile, which Crumpacker did not return.

It had been years since he left the seminary, yet the grief slammed into Miles like an express train, leaving him breathless and momentarily stricken. He had spent those years trying to forget that his beloved wife and little girl were dead, whisked from his life by something as senseless as an inebriated lorry driver, and that the God to whom he had devoted his life could let such a thing happen. Miles could no longer imagine looking down from a pulpit at the upturned faces of his parishioners and telling them that God was good, and that He had a plan.

Miles was no longer sure there was a God.

He shook himself and walked up to the ticket booth just as the agent placed a NEXT WINDOW PLEASE sign on the counter and pulled down the shade. He turned to the window indicated and saw a line of Londoners fifteen deep. All the windows had long lines. Miles frowned at his watch. He would have to hurry.

He re-shouldered his clubs and dashed toward the platforms, thinking he could always purchase a ticket on the train. As he sped around a corner a woman with a pram and an armload of packages appeared from behind a kiosk and Miles plowed directly into her, overturning the carriage and sending the parcels skittering across the concrete floor.

The woman screamed. "Why don't you watch where you're going?"

"I'm terribly sorry." Miles bent over to right the pram and make sure that its tiny occupant was unharmed. He looked up to see the conductor giving the last call for his train, then down at the packages strewn about his feet. The mother cooed to her infant, trying to still its crying. Miles could have easily melted into the mob and made his train but he chose instead to linger and collect the woman's belongings before they were crushed by the stampede. She didn't even bother to say thank you when he handed them to her; she simply turned her nose skyward and continued on her way.

Lifting his suitcase and clubs, Miles jogged to the platform, arriving in time to see the rear lights of his train receding into the distance.

"Blast!"

Shoulders sagged in defeat, he turned back toward the terminal and almost bumped into the well-tailored man.

"Off for a golfing holiday, sir?" the stranger asked in a cultured voice that carried an elusive accent.

"I was," replied Miles sourly, "but that was the last train to Edinburgh for the night."

"Not necessarily," corrected the well-tailored man. "There is another."

"Another what?" Miles eyed him suspiciously. "A train to Scotland?"

"Precisely."

Miles peered up at the departure board. "I don't see it."

"It's not listed."

"You mean it's a special?"

The well-tailored man allowed himself a crisp smile. "You might say that. How does an exclusive rail excursion to some of golf's finest courses sound? Deluxe accommodations, first class food, unlimited stay…"

Miles smirked. "Too good to be true, that's how it sounds."

"And yet, that is what I offer."

Miles narrowed his eyes. "How much will this cost me?"

"Nothing you cannot afford to live without," the well-tailored man assured him.

"Hmmmm…Miles glanced at the clock. "When does it leave?"

"Whenever you'd like, sir."

Miles gave him a puzzled frown. "I don't quite follow."

"In that case, follow me." The well-tailored man hung his brolly on his elbow and set off at a brisk pace.

The two of them passed track upon track of waiting trains until the last one left in line was a sleek, high-speed express that idled on its rails like a purring cat. Miles grinned in delight, but the well-tailored man walked right past the gleaming bullet train and proceeded down a dimly lit platform, where a row of tarnished coaches lay hitched to a grimy black engine. Miles did a double take: It was a steam locomotive!

"You're joking," he said, eyeing the train with distaste.

"I never joke, sir," the well-tailored man replied primly.

Miles peered up into the stranger's face. The stranger gazed placidly back at him with eyes so dark they were almost black.

"You know…I don't believe you ever do." Miles turned to regard the train. "You call this deluxe?"

"Never judge a book by its cover—or a train by its engine."

Miles shrugged and walked up to the nearest coach. When he tried to climb aboard he noticed there were no steps leading up to it. He took a closer look in the gloom of the platform and saw that the coach had no visible doors.

"Odd," he muttered to himself. He stepped back and surveyed the length of the strange little train. He counted eleven coaches in all, none of which had a point of entry or egress that he could identify, save for the last one in line. He looked around for the well-tailored man, but the platform was empty. "Now where the devil did he get to?"

A conductor climbed down the steps of the trailing coach and consulted his pocket watch.

"A'board!"

Miles stepped up to the man. "Where is this train going?"

"What is your destination, sir?" the conductor asked.

"Edinburgh."

The conductor nodded, his face hidden in shadow. "Do you have a ticket?"

Miles shook his head. "No, I was hoping to purchase one on the train."

The conductor nodded again and stepped aside to let Miles board.

Miles hesitated on the platform. He glanced in both directions; the lack of fellow passengers gave him a moment of doubt. Then the engine loosed an impatient hoot of its whistle that sent him scurrying up the steps with his bags.

The train began to move and the conductor swung himself onto the bottom step. He climbed up to join Miles on the open rear of the coach, and the light from inside the car touched his face.

It was the well-tailored man.

"What is the meaning of this?" Miles demanded.

"Meaning, sir?" the conductor said politely. "Meaning is an esoteric concept understood by few. Better to ask, 'Why am I here?'"

Miles frowned. "OK…why are you here?"

"Why are YOU here, sir?" the conductor replied patiently. He leaned forward and pushed open the door to the coach. "Enter and find your answer." He indicated with his hand for Miles to proceed.

Miles' qualms were somewhat quieted upon entering the car. A plush interior greeted his eyes. It was lavishly appointed with cushioned leather armchairs and thick Oriental rugs. The walls of the coach were paneled in dark oak, the ceiling ornately coffered and tastefully lit with an elegant chandelier. A fireplace, of all things, occupied the center of one long wall. A stack of logs burned briskly in the open hearth and an ancient driver hung from a pair of brass hooks above its carved stone mantel.

Three men shared the car with Miles. One was a tall, thin severe-looking man who sported a razor-thin mustache and a sour expression. He was dressed nattily in dove-gray tweed and stood with an arm draped across the mantelpiece as he idly poked at the fire with what appeared to be an eight-iron. The thin man looked up as Miles entered the coach, then resumed gazing at the glowing embers.

Seated next to him was an entirely different sort. Rotund, mostly bald, with a warm, engaging face, the man almost completely filled the huge armchair he occupied. He struggled to his feet and made a vain attempt at buttoning his wrinkled club jacket, the sides of which had no hope of meeting in the middle. Eventually he gave up, offered Miles an awkward bow and stood grinning and wringing his beefy hands.

The third gent was by far the most impressive. He was a full head taller than Miles, with a barrel chest and shoulders that seemed too large for the small confines of the coach. His hair was cropped short in a military style, and his mannerisms were those of one accustomed to giving orders. Miles had no sooner dropped his clubs to the floor when the fellow addressed him in a loud voice, "What do you play to?"

Miles stared at him in confusion, and the big man took three precise steps forward until his large face was just inches away.

"What do you play to?" he repeated, his blue eyes bulging.

Flustered, Miles looked over his shoulder to question the conductor but found he was no longer in the car. He turned back to the man. "I'm afraid I don't follow you."

"He wants to know what your bloody handicap is, mate," the thin man said, still toying with the coals.

"Oh…it's 24, I believe," Miles replied, then added sheepishly. "I'm rather new to the game."

The big man glared at him in fury, and for a few anxious moments Miles wondered if he was about to be struck. But the fellow just turned away in disgust and stalked off a few paces to fume in private.

The thin chap gave a bitter chuckle. "Did you hear that, Whitney?" he remarked to his heavy-set companion. "Fellow plays to a 24. Bloody hell!" He bent over and angrily smote one of the logs with his iron. A shower of sparks erupted from the hearth, and the fat man instinctively avoided them with a clumsy hop.

"Now, now," he said in a jovial voice. "No need to make such a fuss." He turned toward Miles. "I believe that introductions are in order. My name is Luther Whitney." He offered a hand.

Miles shook it firmly. "Crumpacker, Miles Crumpacker."

"Jolly good to have you aboard, Crumpacker," Whitney said, vigorously pumping Miles' hand. "This here is Mr. Henry Bates." The thin man gave Miles a curt nod.

"Don't be fooled by his surly manners," Whitney said. "He's really a capital fellow and always dependable in a pinch."

Bates scowled and returned his attention to the fireplace.

"And sulking in the corner is Major Reginald Hathaway," continued Whitney, "formerly of The Queen's Guard."

"I am not sulking," boomed the Major. "I am simply lamenting the continuing dire state of our predicament!" He marched up in his sharply-creased khakis and pointed at Miles. "What the devil does Lucian mean by bringing us a 24!" he roared. Then, as if embarrassed by his outburst, the Major ran both hands through his thinning hairline and retreated to the rear end of the car.

Puzzled, Miles asked, "What does he mean by predicament?"

"Nothing," Whitney replied quickly, rebuking Hathaway with a stern look. "The Major simply has a flair for the dramatic."

A door opened at the far end of the coach and the steward appeared carrying a tray of drinks. Miles was not surprised to see the face of the well-tailored man smiling at him over the crystal glasses.

"Cocktail hour, gentlemen."

"It's about bloody time, Lucian," Bates said, grabbing a Scotch off the silver tray.

"Mr. Bates surely knows that I am always prompt," replied the steward with good humor.

"Prompt my arse," the Major said, attacking from the flank. He pulled back his sleeve to look at his watch. "I've got 10:05. Take a peek for yourself."

The steward—Lucian—glanced at the Major's wrist. "May I respectfully suggest that your timepiece is inaccurate, sir?"

"It's army issue and hasn't lost a second in twenty years." The Major stood eye to eye with Lucian, his chin jutting out in challenge. Miles watched in fascination as Reginald Hathaway's defiant stare wavered, cracked and then completely crumbled beneath the steward's calm and steady gaze. The Major sank into a nearby chair and Lucian handed him a whiskey.

"I see you've all met our newcomer." Lucian placed a pint of amber-colored ale on the armrest of Whitney's chair. He walked up to Miles and held out the tray. "Vodka and soda with a twist, if I'm not mistaken." The gleam in his eye suggested that he never was.

Miles ignored the drink. "Look here, I've had just about enough of this. Who the blazes are you? First you're promising me a top-notch golf excursion and the next thing I know you're a conductor… and now you're the bloomin' steward! I don't like being kept in the dark, my good man. There's something fishy about this whole thing and I'd appreciate some answers."

The other three passengers fidgeted uncomfortably, and Whitney shot Miles a warning glance. But Lucian merely widened his smile in response—a smile that came nowhere close to touching his eyes.

"Now, now, it's only your first day with us, sir. Let's not start things off on the wrong tee," he soothed. "You were promised a golf excursion and a golf excursion you shall have. A thoroughly peculiar one, I might add." He put Miles' drink down on the sideboard and walked back to the door between cars. "A busy day tomorrow, gentlemen. I suggest you get a good night's rest."

"Odd fellow," Miles said after the door slid closed. "What does he mean by peculiar?"

Bates downed his Scotch in a single gulp. "This isn't what you would call a normal train."

"So I've gathered." Miles waited for further explanation.

The Major stepped forward. "He simply means that tomorrow will be a singular experience for you."

"How so?"

"Tomorrow you play a round of golf with us," Whitney said brightly.

"So I've been led to believe," Miles said. "I assume we'll be playing in Scotland?"

"Not exactly," replied Bates.

Miles frowned. "Then where *exactly* will we be playing?"

"We're not quite sure." Whitney wrung his hands. "That will be up to Lucian."

A smile lifted one corner of Miles' mouth. "Ah, I begin to get the picture. This Lucian chap likes to surprise his clientele."

"You might say that," the Major said with a glance out the window.

The smile reached the other side of Miles' face as he looked around his plush surroundings. "This might prove to be a pleasant holiday, after all."

"Holiday…" Bates snorted. He began to laugh quietly and went back to poking at the waning fire.

Miles took a nip of his drink. "I say, this Lucian concocts a splendid vodka and soda. He makes a rather odd first impression, but I'm sure he's a capital fellow once you get to know him."

"Yes…capital fellow," Whitney echoed in a quiet voice.

"Once you get to know him," finished Bates as he stirred the dying coals.

An awkward silence filled the coach until the Major cleared his throat. "Finish your nightcap, Crumpacker, and Whitney here will show you to your berth."

"A Pullman car?" exclaimed Miles.

Whitney nodded. "Lucian does everything first class."

"Excellent. Bottoms up." Miles drained his glass and followed Whitney through the connecting doors and into the adjoining car. The brightly-lit passageway was lined on one side by a series of windows and on the other by four compartments. As they proceeded down the hall, Miles noted that each door had a brass number, along with a nameplate holder.

The nameplate on the first door read:
BATES – 9

On the second door was:
HATHAWAY – 13

Next in line was:
WHITNEY – 17

And on the last door the white nameplate read:
CRUMPACKER – 24

"Now, how the devil did he know that?" Miles asked.

"It's Lucian's business to know such things."

"An efficient chap, then?" Miles asked, clearly impressed.

Whitney swallowed. "Brutally efficient."

He opened the door and escorted Miles into a spacious, oak-paneled compartment with a single sleeping berth, flanked on either side by a built-in wardrobe. Nestled into the opposite wall was a porcelain washbasin. A stack of clean white towels lay piled on one side of the basin, while a silver tray of fresh fruit occupied the other.

"Marvelous." Miles sat on the immaculately made-up bed. "Absolutely marvelous."

He noticed that his luggage and golf clubs had been neatly arranged beneath the window, although he could not recall having seen anyone take them away.

Whitney followed his gaze. "As I said, Lucian is extremely efficient."

"I believe the term you used was *brutally*," Miles remarked dryly. "Surely the man has help."

"Yes," Whitney replied with something akin to fear in his eyes, "he has plenty of help."

Another awkward moment passed as Whitney stared off at nothing. Finally he shook himself back to the present and offered a little bow. "You'll find the loo at the end of the passageway. But whatever you do, do not enter the next car."

"Why in the world not?"

Whitney averted his eyes. "Because Lucian wouldn't like it."

Miles laughed. "I say, you're being rather cryptic."

"Breakfast is in the trailing car at seven sharp," Whitney said, changing the subject and turning to leave. "Don't be late," he added as the door latch snicked shut.

Miles stared after him and shook his head. "What an odd fellow." He set about arranging his things for the morning, then changed into his nightclothes, brushed his teeth and scrubbed his face until it was bright red.

*   *   *

Before retiring, Miles padded down the passageway in his slippers and used the bathroom. As he left he noticed the door leading to the next car. Feeling adventurous, he turned the lever and stepped into the intervening connector between the two cars. It was loud and drafty, and lit with a garish red light. Miles tried the door to the next coach and found it locked. He shrugged and pressed down on the lever of the door leading back into the sleeper car. It, too, was locked.

Mildly claustrophobic, Miles' sense of adventure rapidly turned into a rush of anxiety. The tight confines of the connector, along with the noise and the cold and the fact that he was in his pajamas, eased him toward the brink of panic. The sudden, shrill wail of the train whistle pushed him over the edge and he began to beat on the door with his fists. "Let me in! Let me in this bloody instant!"

And then fear—real fear—filled Miles' mind. It was unbidden and blind and reckless as only irrational fear can be. The kind of fear one suddenly gets on a moonless night deep in the woods, when you know that nothing is out there yet you can feel it right behind you—stretching out a hideous limb to—

Miles felt a hand on his shoulder. He yelped and flung himself around to see Lucian standing behind him in the connector, his ever-present smile looking ghastly in the red glare.

"Is there a problem, sir?"

"I—I seem to be locked out," Miles said breathlessly. He noticed that Lucian was clad entirely in black.

"What are you doing here?"

Miles smiled weakly. "I went to find the loo; must've taken a wrong turn."

Lucian reached around him and tried the lever. It turned easily and the door slid open. "Straight across the passageway, sir."

"And Mr. Crumpacker," he added as Miles stepped into the passage, "may I strongly suggest that you remain in your berth for the remainder of the night."

Shaken, Miles returned to his compartment and lay awake in his bed, listening to the sounds of the speeding train and wondering what it was about Lucian that he found so disquieting. When he finally fell asleep it was a slumber haunted by fitful dreams.

...It is dusk, and Miles is on a golf course. Whitney is with him. So are Bates and the Major. It is a strange course, with an eerie sky and vistas that almost seem painted on. Somewhere nearby he can hear a train.

A green stands in the distance, the pin set close to the back edge. The four of them are arguing the choice of club while each in turn looks back down the fairway they have just traversed. Miles looks over his shoulder and sees Lucian walking over the grass toward them. His hands are held out at his sides and behind him flows what appears to be water—black water—flooding the fairway as he passes.

Bates is over the ball and he hurries his swing, sending the shot skipping along the grass. Lucian and his black tide come even with him, and Bates is suddenly gone with a muffled scream.

Now it is Hathaway's turn. Quickly, he sets himself and plays his shot. Lucian reaches the Major's position and the inky flow roils about the golfer, sweeping him away in a dark current. The ball sails feebly out of the blackness and lands halfway to the green. Whitney scrambles toward it as Lucian closes in on him. He swings just as the water reaches his feet.

"Whitney!" Miles shouts. But Whitney is gone, swallowed whole by the rushing flow.

The ball sits alone on the green. Miles knows that it must reach the hole before Lucian's or all is lost. He dashes for the green and pulls out his putter. A glance behind, and Lucian is only yards away on the fringe. The white ball glows between Miles' feet with a light of its own. He takes back the club but, before he can finish the stroke the black liquid is upon him. He watches it part and flow around his legs. It is cold, frigid, and it closes about his calves like an icy tourniquet.

Miles begins to sink in the black river, sink like a stone dropped from a great height. And as he goes under he realizes that it is not water he drowns in…but shadow, a shadow cast from above.…

* * *

Miles awoke to a dark shape silhouetted against the window of his compartment. The shadow shifted slightly, and Lucian's features caught the morning light. He was dressed in his steward's uniform, with a towel slung over his forearm.

Miles tugged the sheet up to his neck. "I believe that a knock is customary."

"You'll pardon the intrusion, sir," Lucian replied, "but I feared you might be late for breakfast. Promptness is mandatory."

Miles sat up. "What time is it?"

"Six thirty, sir."

He eyed the steward curiously. "You certainly keep busy, Lucian."

"You know what they say about idle hands, sir."

"You mean that rot about the devil's workshop?" chuckled Miles. "At the moment I'm looking forward to getting my hands around my driver. So if you'll be good enough to leave I'll get ready and join the others."

"Very good, sir," Lucian said and turned to go.

"Wait a moment."

Lucian turned in the doorway. "Yes, sir?"

"What about my fare?"

An odd, hungry look crossed the steward's features. "That will be collected in due time, sir."

* * *

Miles entered the trailing coach at six fifty-eight. A long table had been placed in the center of the car and on it lay an extravagant breakfast spread. Whitney, Bates and the Major were already seated, each dressed in golfing attire and occupying a side of the table, leaving one end open for Miles. There was an air of excitement in the car that was at odds with the somber mood of the previous night, an energy in the postures and conversation of his companions that Miles sensed the moment he sat down.

"Tally-ho, Crumpacker!" Hathaway said. "I trust you're ready for the challenge?"

"Always ready to hit the links." Miles grinned as he helped himself to eggs and bacon.

"Slept well?" inquired Whitney.

"Yes…except for a rather odd nightmare."

Bates gave a dry chuckle. "You mean the black water dream?"

Miles paused in the middle of buttering his toast. "How in blazes did you know?"

"We've all had the dream," Hathaway said matter-of-factly. "It won't be the last time you have it, either."

"I don't follow," Miles said. "How can we all have the same dream?"

"I told you last night: you're not on a normal train." Bates bit into a mouthful of scone. "You're about to find out just how far from normal it is, mate."

Miles laughed and dismissed him with a wave. "You chaps are a most mysterious bunch. Everything's a riddle."

He picked up his coffee and walked over to peer out one of the windows. A dense mist met his eyes. "Looks rather thick out there;

can't see a blooming thing." He turned back to the table. "When do we reach Edinburgh? I'm anxious to tee off."

Whitney glanced around the table. "That's rather irrelevant."

"Irrelevant?" Miles laughed. "Oh, I see. More riddles?"

The Major consulted the clock on the mantelpiece and stood. "It's time, gentlemen."

"Time for what?" asked Miles, confused but trying to play along.

The others stood and the Major held up his glass.

"To par or better," he toasted solemnly.

Bates and Whitney raised whatever they were drinking and repeated, "To par or better."

Miles watched in amusement. He raised his coffee cup. "To bogey golf!"

He had simply desired to elicit a smile or two. Instead, Miles earned himself a scathing glare from all three of his companions.

"Just being realistic," he offered weakly.

The Major was about to say something but stifled it as Lucian entered from the Pullman car.

"Time to tee off, gentlemen," he announced.

"Are we arriving at the station, then?" Miles asked.

Lucian looked at the other three and his smile widened. "I see that your playing partners have yet to inform you of the circumstances."

Whitney gave Miles a sympathetic glance. "We wanted to surprise him."

"Come," Lucian said, "it is time."

Miles brought up the rear as they headed down the Pullman car's passageway, where their clubs had been stacked beside the door leading to the next car forward. Each man shouldered his bag, and one-by-one they proceeded into the connector where Miles had been trapped the previous night. He was completely at a loss as they stood waiting for Lucian to open the door. The train showed no sign of slowing and yet here they all were, lugging around their clubs like the game was afoot. Lucian slid open the door and stepped through, trailed by Bates, Hathaway and Whitney. Miles hesitated before following.

What met his eyes was the most incredible sight Miles Crumpacker had ever seen. Instead of the ordinary passenger coach that he had expected, Miles found himself standing on a golf tee. Where the aisle should've been, a wide, lush fairway stretched away from his feet. In place of seats, neat rows of pine trees flanked the fairway and marched off on either side into shadowy gloom. In lieu of a ceiling, a vivid vault of blue sky hung overhead, with fluffy white clouds floating on a gentle breeze toward a tiny green wedged between a pair of tear-shaped bunkers some 400 yards away. A line of dust-colored hills piled up beyond it and gradually faded into hazy blue mountains in the far, far distance. The experience was not merely the illusion of realism, but a kind of reality in itself, replicated right down to the drone of insects and birdsong in the trees.

Miles stood gaping in wonder.

"Not exactly British Rail, is it?" cracked Bates.

"This is..." Miles began and trailed off.

"This can't..."

"It's not..."

"Possible?" Lucian finished for him. "And yet here you are."

Miles bent to feel the grass. He pulled out a blade and smelled it. He dug his fingers into the soft turf and stared at the dirt under his nails.

An idea occurred to him and he spun around to look in the direction they had come. There, set in the midst of a vista of rolling countryside, was the silver-gray end wall of the coach with the door centered in it. The perspective was mind-boggling, the panorama boundless and yet there was the door just feet away. It was as if someone were trying to prove that the world was not real and in doing so had chipped away a piece of it to expose a different existence—one that belonged to another time and place, and perhaps even dimension.

Miles suddenly recalled reading C.S. Lewis' Narnia tales as a child.

"It's just like the wardrobe," he gasped, and the realization almost overwhelmed him. He looked up at the faces around him and saw an array of emotions painted there: amusement, concern, pity and—oddly enough—hope.

Lucian intruded into his thoughts with a businesslike tone. "You gentlemen know the match rules: Alternate shot format, R&A rules apply. No mulligans. No improving lies. No conceded putts. Everything must be holed out."

He looked at Miles. "Understood?"

Miles nodded.

"Splendid," Lucian said. "Best of luck, gentlemen," he added, and Miles watched him step through the door leading out of this impossible world.

Miles stood as the other three readied themselves to play. Their earlier jovial mood had evaporated, to be replaced by a sober efficiency. Miles tugged on Whitney's sleeve.

"Excuse me," he said, "but who exactly are we playing against?"

"We're playing the course," Whitney replied, fitting on his glove. "The goal is par or better."

"A rather odd arrangement, I must say," complained Miles.

"It's Lucian's train and therefore Lucian's rules."

Miles stood up his bag. "Well, it certainly won't be much fun."

Bates wheeled on him. "We're not here to have fun!"

"Not have fun?" Miles said with a puzzled frown. "What utter nonsense. Frankly, I think this Lucian fellow's grown a bit too big for his britches. Who does he think he is, making all the rules and ordering us about like sheep?"

"Hush!" the Major ordered sternly. "That'll be enough of that. Limber up, Crumpacker, and be ready to play when it's your turn."

"Who hits first?" Miles asked.

"We play in order, according to our compartments," Whitney informed him. "Bates first, followed by the Major, with myself third and you batting cleanup, as the Yanks so crassly put it."

Bates teed up a ball and took a few practice swings. Miles could tell his quality by his confident stance. He swung, and the ball rocketed off his club to land well down the uncanny fairway.

"Off to a good start." Whitney picked up his bag and set off.

Miles shrugged and followed him. "There's something I don't quite understand," he said, looking about him in amazement. "Are we still on the train or are we actually someplace else?"

Whitney held up his hand. "Listen."

Miles paused to listen but noticed nothing at first. Then he heard it, the rhythmic clack of train wheels on iron rail. He knew at once that it had been there all along but for some reason his subconscious mind had suppressed it—probably to guard his sanity.

"Extraordinary," he said. "But how does it all fit?"

The Major laughed and shook his head. "If we knew the answer to that we wouldn't..."

Miles furrowed his brow. "Wouldn't what?"

Whitney quickly jumped into the breach. "What he means is that we wouldn't need to worry about anything. We'd all make a fortune."

Miles eyed the Major doubtfully, sensing that he was going to say something else entirely.

They reached the ball and estimated the distance to the green to be close to 175 yards. Hathaway pulled out a three-iron and waggled it over the ball. His shot was a fair one but not nearly as crisp as Bates' effort. The ball landed short of the green and slightly offline.

Next came Whitney and things began to get dicey. Whitney's middle was so large that it interfered with his arms when he gripped the club. Still, he managed to bring his wedge around and scoop the ball off the grass. It landed shy of the hole and scooted past, leaving Miles with a five-footer for par.

"'Bout time," Miles muttered and dropped his clubs beside the green. He grabbed his putter and knelt behind the ball to survey the line. The putt was slightly downhill and looked likely to break left. Miles stood up and bumped into Whitney, who was standing directly behind him…with Bates behind *him,* and the Major behind *HIM,* all of them gauging his line in unison!

"Give a chap some room," Miles said impatiently. "You'd think we were playing for the bleedin' Ryder cup."

Both Whitney and the Major stepped back and stared at their feet. Bates pulled the pin gruffly. "Just play, Crumpacker, and spare us the editorials."

Miles lined up and steadied himself over the ball. He could feel the tension around him but didn't understand it. Aiming for a spot a foot before the hole, he gave the ball a firm tap. It rolled true—right over the spot he had picked—and into the cup.

"Well done, Miles!" boomed the Major, delivering a bone-jarring slap on the back along with his adulation.

"Marvelous," beamed Whitney. "Always good to start with a par."

"Or better," Bates added sternly.

Now that they were at the end of the hole Miles noticed the door leading to the next car. Not visible from the tee, it had grown in size as they approached the green while the mountain range that surrounded it remained impossibly far away. Miles' head swam and he had to close his eyes in order to recover his balance.

"Steady on, lad," the Major said. "You'll soon get used to it."

Hathaway slid open the door and the foursome passed through the connector and into the eighth car in line, where a new and much different hole awaited them.

Unlike the warm and sunny day of the 1st hole, a biting wind and gray skies greeted them as they stepped onto the 2nd tee. The fairway was wide open and devoid of trees. An old, angled, stone wall poked out of the ground off to the left along a parallel fairway. Right of the wall stood a fairway bunker, and beyond that a huge double green. Miles noted that the air was tangy with salt and, after staring down the fairway for a few moments, he turned to his companions.

"Now hang on a few, I know this hole," he said excitedly. "This is St. Andrews! Saw it on the telly last summer."

"Righto, Crumpacker," nodded the Major. "Top marks."

"It's the 2nd on the Old Course, actually," Whitney said.

"Par-four, 411 yards," added Bates.

"You see, my dear chap," continued Whitney, "all of the holes on this train are replicas from famous courses around the world."

"Replicas!" snorted the Major. "As far as we know this *is* number two at St. Andrews."

Bates pulled out his driver. "Or perhaps the hole you saw from the comfort of your sitting room is merely a replica of the one we're standing on now."

"Is it the same layout every time?" inquired Miles.

"No," the Major replied, "each day Lucian offers up a different set of holes for us to tackle." He glanced down at his card. "Bates drives off again."

The low handicapper hit another fine ball but Hathaway followed with a mishit, and the best Whitney could do was reach the front edge of the green with their third. Miles therefore faced a long putt for par that he left a foot short of the cup. Bates tapped it in for bogey and marched off the green in tight-lipped fury.

"Par or better," he hissed as they progressed into the next coach.

Another car, another venue. This hole a par-three that played downhill to a narrow green with bunkers on both sides. Off in the distance was an eye-popping view of the Golden Gate Bridge.

"Third hole at the Olympic Club in San Francisco," Hathaway informed Miles as he teed up a ball. He then stroked a brilliant three-wood to the middle of the green, and Whitney and Miles were able to get down easily in two from there.

The sixth car in line featured the 4th hole at Royal Dornoch, a par-four with a fairway that sloped left to right. They bogeyed the hole after Whitney's approach sailed long and into the deep grass behind the green. The next car held a straight fairway that gradually built up to an elevated green guarded by two bunkers on the front edge.

Miles stood, scratching his head. "I don't recognize this hole."

"It's the 5th at Turnberry," Bates said.

"But that's a dogleg," protested Miles.

The Major, who was up next, took a practice swing. "Wait 'til we hit the curve."

"The what?" Miles asked and then he felt it—a slight momentum shift that caused him to lean toward the right. The train had reached a long bend in the tracks and to Miles' utter astonishment the hole in front of him miraculously transformed itself into a dogleg left.

"Good Lord..." he breathed.

The group managed a par but double-bogeyed the 6th at Troon. Pars on number seven at Oakland Hills and eight at Carnoustie recharged their sagging spirits. And even the dour Bates was grinning after Major Hathaway had followed his handsome approach by snaking in a twenty-foot putt for birdie on the 9th at Spyglass.

As the foursome walked off the green, Miles realized that they were now in the car directly behind the locomotive. He was wondering what would happen next when Whitney tapped him on the shoulder. "Time to make the turn."

"How's that?"

Whitney pointed back down the fairway, and Miles saw that the hole had changed: it was now the 10th at Muirfield.

"Extraordinary!" he said with a wide smile. "So we just play back the way we came—nine holes out and nine holes in. A true links course!"

"Right," said the Major, "except that in this case the holes are *literally* linked together."

They made the turn plus 3 with hopes of challenging par, a hope that quickly fizzled away when they entered the next car in line and came face to face with Amen Corner.

"It's become a bit of a joke with Lucian," explained Whitney glumly, as he stood surveying the par-four 11th at Augusta National. "He thinks it's quite amusing to make us play this treacherous string of holes."

By the time the foursome limped off the 13th green they had dropped two more strokes to par and had virtually no chance of making it up, with only 5 to play. Miles noted that the closer they got to eighteen the more cross his playing partners became. On the 16th at Prestwick the sniping began.

"We wouldn't be in this mess if you'd learn some touch around the green, Whitney," the Major harped, following another bogey.

"Easy for you to say after hitting your wedge fat on the last hole," Whitney shot back. "We should've been on in regulation!"

"You both mucked it up," Bates chimed in. "I'm getting more than a bit tired of carrying you blokes around the track."

"Gentlemen," Miles soothed, trying to diffuse the tension. "Let's try and enjoy these magnificent holes instead of indulging in petty backbiting."

"Why don't you stifle it, Crumpacker." Bates pointed his club at him. "You're the worst one of the lot. You've easily cost us three bloody strokes all by yourself."

On and on it went until they finally sank the last putt on eighteen and stormed off the green at Royal Birkdale. Each went sulking into their separate compartments and did not emerge until dinner was served in the trailing car at seven sharp. There they were served a supper of roast duck and potatoes, which the four men ate in tense silence. When Lucian returned to clear the plates, Miles stood and addressed him.

"Look here, Lucian, you run a crackerjack rail line but I'm afraid these chaps just aren't my cup of tea. A bit too high strung, if you know what I mean. Therefore I'd like to know when we'll be arriving in Edinburgh so I can get on with my holiday."

Lucian ignored him and removed his plate. "Dessert, sir?"

"I don't want dessert!" exploded Miles, finally losing his temper. "I want to get off this bloody train!"

"Very good, sir," Lucian said, unruffled by the outburst. "Coffee will be up shortly." He was gone before a befuddled Miles could think of a reply. He glared at the stoic faces around the table. "What the blazes is going on? When does this train reach its destination?"

"You don't seem to understand," Whitney replied sadly, "this train has no destination."

"I don't follow. Every train has a terminus."

"Not this one," Bates said. "This is a railway without a beginning or an end. It has no past, no present, no future. It's a train arriving from no place bound for nowhere."

"That's not possible." Miles leveled a finger at Bates. "It was at Victoria!"

"Only because it suited Lucian's purposes at the time," Hathaway said.

Miles strode to the nearest window. The thick curtain of fog still enveloped the train. He couldn't even see the ground rushing past just feet away.

"It's like booking passage on a lost ship," the Major said. "Lucian calls it 'The Flying Scotsman.'"

Bates grimaced. "Thinks it's some sort of clever joke."

"Where are we now?" Miles asked still gazing out at the mist.

"We're in limbo," Whitney said.

Miles wheeled around. "But I need to get off!"

The Major fidgeted in his chair. "There is only one way off this train."

"How?"

"Par or better," Bates said.

"What?"

"If we can master Lucian's course," Whitney explained, "he'll let us go."

"Let us go?" Miles looked around the table. "Who the devil does he think he is?"

Whitney sighed. "My, but you have a tiresome way of phrasing things."

"He can't keep us hostage," continued Miles. "It's kidnapping! We'll inform the authorities."

"And just how do you propose to do that?" Bates asked. "Besides, do you actually believe that someone with Lucian's...abilities... would give a hill of beans about the authorities?"

Panic started to grip Miles. "So you're saying that I'm trapped here?"

Whitney rose and laid a hand on his shoulder. "We all are, old chap."

Miles shrugged off the offer of comfort and spun around. He dashed to the rear of the car and yanked aside the plush curtain that had been draped across it. Where the door had once been, now there was only a blank wall of metal.

"Blast!" Miles cried and dropped the curtain. He hurried over to the fireplace and picked up the eight-iron that Bates used as a stoker. Hesitating for only an instant, he slammed it against a window. The club recoiled off the glass and fell from his stinging hands.

"Don't you think we tried that?" Bates asked tiredly.

Miles rubbed his hands and thought furiously, then he bolted for the Pullman car.

"Don't!" Whitney shouted, but Miles was already through the door. He raced down the passageway directly at Lucian, who approached with a tray of coffee held high above his head.

"Trouble, sir?"

"Bugger off!" Miles said as he brushed past. He reached the connector and, disregarding his experience of the night before, plunged into it and tried to open the door to the next car. This time it opened and Miles found himself in a common passenger coach lined with vacant seats. He sprinted through it to find the same thing in the next car…and the next…and the one after that, until he eventually reached the end of the forwardmost coach.

A tiny window glowed red in the far wall and Miles pressed his face against the dirty glass. At first he could make little out, then he saw the stark outline of the fireman shoveling coal into the boiler's firebox. An insidious fire raged inside, and as Miles stared at it he thought he could see faces in the hellish flames—terrified visages trapped in unimaginable torment.

Miles pounded on the glass and the fireman stopped shoveling to turn toward him—a mask of black soot. He stepped closer to the window, and with a sleeve, wiped his grimy face.

Lucian leered at Miles through the filthy pane.

Miles recoiled from the window in horror and fled back down the length of the train. And as he ran he began to notice that the seats he passed were no longer empty—most were occupied by a wavering phantom or a rotting corpse.

He re-entered the trailing car ashen-faced and out of breath. The others had finished their coffee and were gathered around the hearth. Without a word Miles slumped into an empty chair.

Bates smoked a cigarette. He crushed out the butt on the arm of his chair. "So…now you understand."

"I need to know one thing," Miles said weakly. "What happened to your fourth? What became of the man I replaced?"

A long silence followed, filled only by the sound of the train racing through the night. Finally, Whitney spoke up.

"There *is* another way off," he said softly.

Miles gripped the arm of his chair. "Tell me."

"You can choose to play Lucian yourself—three holes, match play."

"And if I win?"

"He lets you off."

"And if I lose?"

"You saw who the real passengers of this train are," Bates said, his face gray with remembered fear. "Lose and Lucian punches your ticket for you—a one-way express to hell with no return."

Miles lowered his head into his hands.

"We'll do better tomorrow," Whitney said encouragingly.

"Bah!" scoffed the Major. "What did we fire today…nine over? Do you actually believe that we can improve nine strokes?"

"I can certainly play better," argued Whitney. "And you've been known to heat up on occasion. And Crumpacker, here," he patted Miles' arm, "he's just taken up the game. Think of how much improvement he'll show, given time."

Miles squirmed in his seat and looked up. "That's not exactly the truth."

Hathaway looked at him sharply. "What's not?"

"You see," Miles said, "I've been playing for almost ten years now. I love golf but never seem to get much better at it. I've taken scores of lessons, play twice a week, and practice religiously." He gave a meek shrug of his shoulders. "I'm afraid that I just don't possess the necessary set of skills."

The Major gaped at him in disbelief, and Whitney bowed his head.

"It's bloody hopeless," Bates moaned and ran his hands through his hair in frustration. "Maybe we'd stand a chance playing four-ball, but alternate shot…? Not in a million years."

Miles sat up. "Look here, why don't we all challenge Lucian to a match?"

"What are you getting at?" asked Bates.

"I mean take him on as a team."

"That's what we're doing now," Whitney said.

"No." Miles balled his fists. "I mean challenge him to a three-hole match."

"I'm afraid you don't have your tee all the way in the ground, Crumpacker," the Major said. "Didn't you hear what Bates said? It's a lost cause."

"But that's over a full eighteen holes," pressed Miles. "If we play things right, the four of us can surely string together three good holes."

Whitney shook his head. "Lucian selects which holes we play, and he'd choose the toughest the world has to offer."

"What difference does that make? Lucian will have to play the same holes we do."

"You don't follow," Bates said in anger. "The fellow is Nicklaus, Hogan and Bobby Jones rolled into one." He pointed toward the front of the train. "You saw what was in those coaches. Lucian doesn't lose!"

"How do you know?" Miles challenged. "Maybe he's lost dozens of times. Maybe he counts on his victims being too afraid to challenge him." He pounded his fists on the arms of the chair. "I say it's our only hope!"

"And I say you're mad as a hatter," Bates shot back. "Don't forget the dream, Crumpacker. We can't escape the black tide and I, for one, don't plan on ending up like one of those wretched sots."

Miles rose and stood by the fire. "Then what's your plan?"

"To live and fight another day."

"You call this living?" Miles looked at them in scorn. "Riding this damned train day after day for what? Weeks, months, years, a lifetime? How did Lucian put it, an *unlimited* stay? I happened to notice that none of you are too keen on the prospect of staying."

When all three refused to meet his accusing gaze, Miles walked to the door. "I'm going to bed and pray that when I wake up it'll all turn out to be a silly dream."

*   *   *

Miles did not pray, but he did dream. He bolted awake as the black water closed over him again, his eyes searching the darkness around him for a deeper shadow. But as he sat there amid his entangled bedclothes, Miles realized that the shadowy tides had already overtaken him, that they had in fact engulfed him years ago at the death of his wife and child and the subsequent lingering demise of his faith.

He stood in the dim light of dawn and looked at himself in the mirror. Miles had not said a prayer since the day of the accident. He had prayed then, fervently and hard, and the shock he felt upon learning that his wife had died on the operating table—at the *very time* Miles was deep in prayerful petition—had caused him to seal that part of his heart and soul away.

Miles closed his eyes and tried to pray, but the words refused to come. He looked at himself again, eyes wet with grief, both old and new. A middle-aged man with a slight build and a high handicap. *Was this how David felt before he went off to face Goliath?* he wondered. *No,* Miles concluded, *David had a bottomless well of faith—David believed.*

Miles slowly began to dress, his decision made.

*   *   *

Breakfast passed in silence, the only sound the dull ring of silver against bone china. When Lucian returned with the tea, Miles stood and faced him. "My colleagues have been kind enough to inform me of the conditions on your little railway. I've decided to challenge you to a match."

They all looked up in surprise, Lucian perhaps the most astonished of the lot. "Very well, sir," he said. "We'll meet on the 1st tee in, let's say, fifteen minutes?"

Miles, who was so terrified that his hands were rattling his cup on the saucer, could only swallow and nod his agreement.

"Don't be a fool, Crumpacker," the Major said after Lucian had cleared the plates and left the car. "You're a 24 handicap. He'll squash you like a bug."

"I'll take my chances."

"Please, Miles," pleaded Whitney, "don't throw yourself away like this."

"I threw myself away many years ago."

"You'll lose, man," Bates said.

"Perhaps," replied Miles with a courage he didn't feel. "Or maybe I'll find a part of me I thought lost. You see…I *know* why I'm here. I know why Lucian singled me out from all the others. What private hell the three of you have stumbled into, I can only guess. You're welcome to remain here and suffer it as prisoners—or worse, as slaves. I'm not asking you to come along. Besides, with me out of the way perhaps Lucian will select a replacement who's longer off the tee."

The other three looked away in disgust, or perhaps shame, and Miles savored the dregs of his tea in silence. He dabbed his chin with the linen napkin, then went to his compartment and sadly laced on his spikes, sure that it would be the last time he would ever do so. *I do hope you know what you're doing, old man,* he sighed as he shouldered his clubs and made his way slowly to the end of the passage.

Whitney was there, waiting for him. "I've seen three others take on Lucian head to head and my conscience won't allow me to stand by and let another one face him alone."

Miles almost swooned with relief and the two men clasped hands.

The Major emerged from his compartment and ambled down the passage dressed in the scarlet uniform of Her Majesty's Guard. He puffed out his chest. "I am reminded of something an American Indian once said before going into battle: *Today is a good day to die.*"

"Or at least as good as the next," Bates cracked, joining the threesome. He pulled a club from out of his bag and held it high in the air. "All for one and one for all!"

Hathaway laid his three-iron across Bates' driver. Whitney did the same with his sand wedge and Miles added his putter to complete the alliance. They stood with crossed clubs, grinning foolishly at each other until Miles said, "I imagine we look rather silly."

"Perhaps," conceded Whitney, "but, by George, I feel like we just might pull this off!"

"Then by all means let's have at it." The Major slid open the door and they proceeded into the next car, where Lucian stood waiting on the tee. He did not seem surprised to see the four of them together. The only sign that he noticed at all was a quick lick of his lips—a furtive gesture of hunger.

"Welcome, gentlemen," he greeted them, clad in a black golf shirt and slacks. His black spikes gleamed on his feet. "I trust you are all ready for the day's challenge. Three holes, match play…winner take all."

All four men easily recognized the hole that spread out behind Lucian. A dazzling sea churned off to their right, its surface littered with broad fields of kelp that bobbed in the rolling swells. To the front rose a wide-open fairway bordered on either side by wild clumps of sawgrass. There was no green in sight, just a large rock that seemed to grow out of the grass 100 yards out.

"Pebble Beach number eight," the Major announced unnecessarily. "Treacherous."

"But not unmanageable," Bates said. He scowled and turned to Lucian. "We have one condition," he said firmly.

"Yes?" Lucian asked.

"We want to set our own order of play."

Lucian smiled. "You know the rules—play is according to your handicap."

"That fine," said Bates, "but we determine who leads off."

Lucian shook his head. "Sorry, but that won't do."

"Very well," Bates said tersely. He walked back to the door and pulled it open. "Come, gentlemen. It would appear that our host has no stomach for a real challenge."

The others turned to leave, but the door suddenly slammed shut of its own accord. "As you wish," Lucian said, his black eyes smoldering. "But there is never any giving without a measure of taking. I, too, have a condition to add."

"And that is?"

"You must win outright. To halve the match is to lose it along with everything else you have to give. Agreed?" His smile bordered on a sneer.

"Agreed," Bates nodded, "provided that we can choose who leads on each hole."

"As you wish!" Lucian hissed angrily. "Now, enough toying with the rules; choose your player and drive off."

"That was nip and tuck," Whitney whispered as the foursome huddled together. "Never seen him so put out."

"It was risky," Bates agreed, "but I saw an opportunity to negotiate a concession or two in our favor. Lucian wants this match and wants it badly."

"It was brilliant, old man," Miles said, grinning from ear to ear. "Who drives first?"

"You do."

Miles' face fell. "What? No, I can't possibly—"

"Don't turn to jelly on us now, Crumpacker," scolded Bates. "You got us into this by showing some much-needed backbone. Now is no time to lay up because you haven't the guts to shoot for the flag. You have to drive off and get us far enough along to give me a decent chance at going for the green. Whitney and the Major can do the short work."

Miles looked up the blind fairway. "How far do I need to hit it?"

"Two thirty ought to be enough," Bates said. He pointed to the boulder in the fairway. "Just aim over the rock and get it up on the plateau. I'll take it from there."

"Time, gentlemen," Lucian said.

Miles pulled out his driver. *Two hundred and thirty yards,* he thought. *Even on a good day I have trouble hitting a ball that far. What if I top it? Or hook it? Or, God forbid, slice it into the ocean? I'll need to hit the shot of my life.* Then it occurred to Miles that *every* ball he would play that day would be the shot of his life. He broke out in a sudden sweat and his hands began to tremble. Twice he tried to tee up a ball; twice it toppled off its perch.

"Easy, Miles," Whitney soothed from his side. "Just a nice easy swing. Let the club do the work."

Miles nodded and thought of his seminary days, recalling a relaxation technique taught to him by a crusty old abbot. He closed his eyes and focused on quieting his breathing while at the same time trying to count the beats of his heart. A sense of calm washed over him, and when Miles opened his eyes again the fairway looked as wide as the ocean.

He swung easily and hit a towering drive that sailed straight over the aiming rock before tailing away slightly to the left and disappearing over the rise.

"Well struck!" Hathaway cried in admiration. "A capital shot!"

Whitney appeared close to tears of joy while Bates simply nodded his approval and turned to watch their opponent.

Lucian took a fluid practice swing, then stepped to his ball and unleashed a frighteningly long drive that flew well past Miles' effort.

"See what I mean?" Bates said as they trudged up the fairway. "He's unbeatable."

"Unnatural perhaps," argued Miles, "but not unbeatable."

Whitney sighed. "We'll find out soon enough."

They reached the plateau and both balls could be seen lying safe on the lush grass. Here the ocean took a huge bite out of the headland, giving the players a choice of following the fairway as it swept around the yawning chasm, or hitting straight across the gulf to the tiny green on the opposite side. Miles regarded it as one of the most spectacular shots in golf, and not one for the faint of heart.

Lucian's ball lay in perfect position, just a few club lengths from the edge of the precipice, a mere 150 yards from the green. Miles' shot, although quite good, was well back from the cliff edge, which meant that Bates would need a proficient iron to clear the ocean safely. He tossed a few blades of grass into the air to test the breeze, then selected a four-iron and lined up on the distant pin. The ball was hit squarely, and as it soared over the canyon Miles found that he could not contain his excitement.

"Go ball…fly!"

Whitney stood beside him with his fists clenched as he waited for the tiny orb to clear the hazard. When it landed safely on the green, all four men gave a cry of triumph, which was tempered somewhat as they watched the ball roll slowly down the slope and off the front edge.

"Not the best position," Bates said, "but it could be worse."

Lucian hit a gorgeous eight-iron to the center of the upper tier and the five players hiked the circuitous route around the fairway to the waiting green. Hathaway had forty feet of sloping green to negotiate. A difficult putt, but to his credit he revealed no sign of stress. Whitney was a good short-and-middle-distance putter, so the Major knew that all he needed to do was get within a few feet for a decent shot at par. He pulled back the putter and gave the ball a solid whack. It tracked nicely up the slope and rolled to a stop just three feet short.

"Well done," Miles remarked as the Major joined him on the fringe.

Bates nodded confidently. "Whitney should be able to hole out."

Lucian plumb-bobbed his line and the challengers watched anxiously as his sixteen-footer barely missed on the low side. He tapped in for par and stood aside to let Whitney have a go. The heavy set fellow was clearly nervous. He paced from one corner of the green to the next, circled the hole three times and even lay down behind the ball to study the break.

Finally, he stood and aligned his putter. Miles couldn't watch. He closed his eyes, held his breath...and was rewarded with the sound of the ball falling to the bottom of the cup.

Miles took a peek. "He made it?"

"Yes," the Major replied with relief, "but it was a close thing. He almost missed it high—rolled completely around the rim before dropping."

Spirits were high as they passed through the connector and onto the next tee. Miles looked around him and saw another rugged coastline, this one with a bone-white lighthouse anchored on a narrow point of land thrust out into a cold-looking sea. Iron-gray skies loomed overhead to blanket a fairway that rose gently to an undulating green in the distance.

"I don't know this hole," Miles said with a puzzled frown.

"I do," Bates said. "Turnberry again, the 9th. It's named Bruce's Castle."

"As in Robert the Bruce?" Miles asked.

Bates nodded. "You'll see the remains of the place when we reach the green."

Hathaway studied the layout. "Looks innocuous enough."

"Not too difficult," agreed Bates. "Just keep the ball in play and the putts short." He thought for a moment and turned to the Major. "I'll drive off and try to leave you with a mid-iron into the green."

The Major nodded. "Carry on."

Bates stepped to the tee and delivered a smashing blow that carried far down the middle of the fairway. Lucian's drive ended up roughly even with Bates', but on the ocean side of the hole.

"We're away," Bates said as they neared the ball. Looks like the pin's in back. Try and get it to the upper tier."

"Righto!" Hathaway said enthusiastically. He had 150 yards to the front of the green and went with a seven-iron. His high, lofting shot fell near the ridge that bisected the putting surface, hopped once and rolled a few feet closer to the hole.

"Perfect!" Miles cried in delight. "We might even make birdie from there!"

"Don't go counting your chickens just yet," Bates said sensibly. "Let's see what he does first."

Lucian seemed troubled over his ball. He kept looking at the green and then at the club in his hand.

"I think he planned on playing it safe but now he knows he's going to have to gamble," Bates whispered.

Reaching into his bag, their opponent pulled out another club—a longer iron—and addressed his ball. His play came in high like Hathaway's, but slightly hotter. It bounced near the flag and scooted off the green into the thick rough that bordered the back fringe. Lucian's jaw hardened in response, and he slammed his club back into the bag.

The ruins of the old castle were clearly visible from the green, low rings of ancient stonework looking like rotted teeth waiting to be pulled from the ground. Lucian's ball could barely be seen in the deep grass.

"He has some work to do to get up and down from there," Bates said excitedly. "He'll never get it close with that lie."

When it came to golf Bates knew his stuff. Unable to get any backspin on the ball, Lucian's shot popped out of the rough and rolled twenty feet past the hole, coming within a breath of descending to the lower tier.

Bates turned to Whitney. "Just get it close."

Whitney obeyed by lagging to within inches and a relieved Miles tapped it home for par.

They half-expected Lucian to concede the hole, but he clearly had other ideas. He studied the line from every angle possible before finally settling over his ball. His confident stroke sent it on a long and gently curving journey right into the heart of the cup, leaving the four men in stunned silence.

"Damn and blast!" said the Major in frustration as they moved to the next car in line. "We can't play any better than that."

"Yes we can," Bates replied, but Miles saw his shoulders slump the moment he stepped through the door.

"It's the bloody Road Hole," moaned Bates.

St. Andrews again, thought Miles. He glanced over at Lucian to see a gloating smile on their host's face.

"You didn't think I was going to make it easy for you gentlemen, did you?" He laughed, an earthen clattering sound like two rocks being struck together. "I believe I'll play first," he said and stooped to tee up his ball.

Miles looked past him at the infamous hole, perhaps the most difficult par-four in golf. On the right loomed a series of railway sheds and the bulk of the hotel, along with the old stone wall that zigzagged the length of the hole and seemed to jut across their path. The fairway was an extremely narrow finger of safety between the wall and the heavy rough that lined the left side. The green, on the other hand, was large and relatively trouble free. It was the getting there that was the challenge.

Lucian hit a low, sizzling drive into the stiff breeze blowing off the firth. It looked like a fine shot to Miles but Whitney leaned close. "He's too far left!"

The ball landed just left of center and Lucian displayed his displeasure by staring at it coldly.

"OK," Bates said to his teammates, "let's see if I can better that."

As he readied his shot Whitney whispered, "See the Old Course Hotel sign on the wall? He'll aim for the 'o' in 'Course' and try to cut off as much of the corner as he can."

Bates swung and the ball flew straight over the rail sheds and sign just to the left of the hotel. It bounced twice in the fairway and rolled to a halt about 180 from the green.

Miles kept looking toward the hotel and the town beyond as he followed the others up the fairway. "Tell me something," he asked Whitney, "what's to prevent us from just strolling into town and making good our escape?"

"Have you seen anyone?" Whitney said.

Miles looked again. "Now that you mention it...no."

"And you won't, either. It's probably inhabited by the same poor blokes you saw riding this train."

When they reached Lucian's ball Miles understood why the left side of the fairway was not a desirable place to make one's approach. Such a position placed the menacing Road Bunker close to the path to the green.

"He'll aim right and try to play a hook around the bunker," theorized Whitney.

Which is exactly what happened. Lucian hit a two-iron that started out right and curved beautifully toward the green. The wind held it up nicely until an odd thing happened.

It suddenly stopped blowing.

One moment saw it steadily slicing left to right at a handful of knots, and the next there was dead calm. Without the breeze to counter the draw, Lucian's ball tailed sharply at the end of its flight, landed on the left side of the green, then rolled off to vanish into the Road Bunker.

"He's in the stew, for sure." Bates cackled with glee as he stood back to study their approach. He had put them in an ideal position with a clear shot to the length of the green. But the pin was set well back, very close to the path and road that lay just beyond the putting surface.

"Don't make it any harder than it is, Hathaway," he coolly instructed. "Just hit it hard and low, and it'll feed right onto the green."

"Right," the Major said, looking both absurd and heroic, standing in the middle of the fairway in his red uniform. His swing was a smooth one, the shot low and straight at the flag.

"Get down," Miles urged when he saw that it was too long. The ball impacted past the hole and bounded off the back of the green. They all watched in dismay as it skipped across the road and struck the wall on the other side.

"Bugger it!" cursed the Major.

"Never mind," Bates replied calmly. "We're not cooked yet." He grabbed Miles by the arm and said, "You and Whitney follow Lucian and check out his lie. And keep a sharp eye on him to make sure he doesn't improve it."

Miles gaped at him. "Do you really think Lucian would cheat?"

"In a heartbeat," Bates called over his shoulder as he headed for the road. "The fellow invented cheating."

Whitney and Miles hurried across the green while Bates and the Major searched for their ball. Moments later Whitney ran up to them, slightly winded and flushed with excitement.

"Lucian's done for," he said. "He's up hard against the embankment with no play but back toward the fairway."

"That gives us some breathing room," Bates said. "Where's Crumpacker?"

Whitney jerked a thumb back toward the bunker. "Watching Lucian."

"Good." Bates laid a hand on Whitney's shoulder. "Think you can get on from here?" The ball lay far up the roadway past the end of the green and just feet from the base of the wall.

Whitney looked at his lie. "Blimey, I don't know."

"Don't worry about getting it up in the air," Bates said, trying to be positive. "You've got the whole length of the green to work with. Just blade it with a four-iron and let it roll on."

Whitney swallowed and took a few practice hacks on the road. He lined up the shot, took another peek at the target and whacked clumsily at the ball. It shot off his clubface with wicked speed, hitting the green and picking up pace as it traversed the slick putting surface. Miles watched it shoot past, in horror. Lucian was also watching with a hungry gleam in his eyes. As the ball rolled off the front edge of the green he grinned and descended back into the cavernous bunker.

"I'm terribly sorry," Whitney moaned in anguish as the rest of the foursome joined Miles on the green. "I'm afraid I've doomed us all."

"This is a joint hanging and the executioner has yet to tighten the noose," the Major said, nodding to where Lucian stood below them considering his options. His ball lay very close to the almost vertical wall that cut into the putting surface above. It would take a miracle shot to get it up and anywhere near the cup. But all Lucian needed was to halve the hole. It was obvious that he did not relish the idea of playing back toward the fairway and risk making 6, so he chose instead to aim well right of the hole, where the wall of the pot bunker was not nearly as high. If successful, Lucian's ball would lay at the heart of the green, leaving him a manageable two-putt for bogey.

Lucian swung and a shower of sand erupted from the bunker. The ball hit the rim of the wall and fell back into the sand, this time farther from the wall. Whitney and Miles could not contain themselves and hooted with glee from the green. Lucian dug his feet back into the sand and tried again with identical results. This time all four men celebrated the mishap with raised fists and joyous hugs.

Lucian watched them dance on the fringe with unconcealed hatred, all pretense of politeness gone from his now-distorted features. Without taking his eyes off the rejoicing foursome he took a careless one-handed swing at the ball. It floated out of the bunker, landed on the green and arrowed straight into the cup, rattling the pin like the bones of a skeleton.

"He's been toying with us," Whitney said into the stunned silence. "Simply toying with us this whole bloody time."

"Fools!" Lucian said as he climbed out of the bunker. "Did you *really* think you could beat me?…your master?" He laughed. The clattering sound again. Inhuman. And as he approached he seemed to grow in size, or maybe it was just his shadow that grew.

Miles looked back down the fairway and saw the blackness filling up the tee and spreading along the ground toward them.

"Dear God in heaven," Whitney whispered. "It's the dream!"

"Dream?" Lucian sneered. "Your dreams are but reality and your reality merely dreams. The Flying Scotsman rolls on, my pitiful friends, and it will continue to roll over the likes of you until time itself ceases to be." The shadows were halfway up the fairway. Lucian laughed and spread his hands out to beckon them onward.

And suddenly Miles was angry—angry like he had never been before. It was hot and sharp and bright, like edged steel in his mind. Without thinking he strode to the ball and, with the green an oasis in the shadows, blindly struck at it with his putter.

It tore across the short grass, rising and falling and bending with each undulation. Bates and the others watched its arduous journey in mute fascination until it became obvious to everyone that the ball was going to defy all odds and reach the hole.

"Yes!" Bates shouted, and began running for the flag with Whitney and the Major close behind. They arrived just in time to see it slow and come to rest on the very brink, teetering on the lip of the cup.

"No!" Whitney cried and dropped to his knees. But the ball refused to move farther.

"I'm sorry, gentlemen," Lucian said, "but it's time to settle our little wager." He lifted his hands higher and the shadows advanced.

Miles fell to his knees beside Whitney. He raised his eyes to the heavens and this time the words came simply and easily, *Please, God. If it be your will…help us now.*

As Miles looked up at the dwindling patch of light in the sky, a single ray escaped the aperture of shadow and lanced downward to illuminate the town's jumble of rooftops and highlight the loftiest feature of the humble skyline: the Cross perched atop the ancient steeple of St. Andrew's Cathedral.

Lucian recoiled as if physically struck, while Miles and the others leapt to their feet in expectation. A slight breath of wind ruffled their hair. It quickly freshened to a breeze, then a strong gust. Miles Crumpacker grinned as the wind once again began to howl in off the North Sea.

The ball shivered once and fell into the hole.

At the exact instant it hit the bottom of the cup the course around them disappeared and they were standing in the aisle of a passenger coach. Far up ahead the engine's whistle loosed a forlorn wail.

"Hang on!" Miles shouted to the others and braced himself between two rows of seats.

They heard the wreck long before they felt it—a terrible, piercing scream of tormented metal—as the engine derailed and the lead cars jumped the tracks to overturn, domino-like. Their own coach seemed to give way in slow motion. First came a series of jarring bumps as the wheels left the rails, then a hideous grinding sound as it was dragged forward by the destructive momentum, and finally a gradual capsizing as the car heeled over and violently slid down the embankment.

It came to rest on its side at the edge of a broad fen. Miles quickly took stock of his injuries, thankful that all he found were bruises. Bates had the wind knocked out of him when a seven-iron flew across the coach and hit him in the stomach. Whitney sat on a bench seat with a hanky pressed against a nasty gash on his forehead.

The Major got the worst of it. He had been thrown clear across the aisle and suffered a badly broken arm. Bates trussed up the limb in a makeshift sling, and his three companions helped push Hathaway out a shattered window and onto the top of the coach. They lowered him gently to the ground, then scrambled up the bank and turned to look down at the ruins of their former prison.

*   *   *

"Extraordinary," Whitney said as they stood surveying the damage. The train lay scattered on the boggy ground in a mass of twisted and crumpled metal. Steam rose from the ruptured boiler, and a low moan like that of a dying animal issued from somewhere along its length.

Miles turned and gazed down the gleaming rails. In the near distance nestled a small country town and beyond that, high on a hill, rose the towers of Edinburgh Castle.

"Ah…I see we've arrived in Scotland after all," the Major said as they started down the tracks in a column of twos.

Bates helped him along by his good arm. "So it would seem."

"What will you do now?" Whitney asked Miles.

"Go back to seminary, finish what I started a long time ago. And you?"

"Return the money I embezzled from the firm," Whitney replied. "Most likely go to prison, I suppose."

"Doesn't that frighten you?"

"Yes," nodded Whitney, "but not nearly as much as what I saw on the train." He turned to look uneasily back down the tracks. "I wonder what became of Lucian?"

"I would like to believe he perished with his train," Miles said, following Whitney's gaze, "but I doubt that his kind is that easily disposed of."

Far down the line behind them, a very well-tailored man made his way smartly in the opposite direction.

LOCAL KNOWLEDGE

BY

G. GUILFORD BARTON

Continuing the Series

Golf is No Ordinary Game

I have always had a certain amount of admiration (or is it envy) for caddies, those constant companions of golfers at the highest of levels. Maybe it's their access to golf's most hallowed grounds, or their effortless displays of etiquette, or those spotless overalls they wear branded by the pro whose bag they carry. But I think what impresses me the most is their seemingly omniscient knowledge of whatever course they're on. This story takes that "local knowledge" to the next whimsical level as the reader meets a young lass by the name of Rachel—a clairvoyant caddie.

LOCAL KNOWLEDGE

She appeared at the starter's hut as if by magic—one moment Donald MacGregor was alone with his pipe and racing form, the next he was staring over the counter at the top of a wild tangle of unkempt reddish hair. He leaned over the edge and took in the rest of the child whose diminutive height and slight build lent her a waifish appearance. MacGregor guessed that she couldn't have been more than seven or eight, perhaps even less.

"What do ye want, lass?" the starter asked.

The girl's gray eyes were round with anxiety. "I've come to caddie."

The old Scot smiled gently and puffed away on his pipe. "Now lass, ye know very well that ye have to be at least twelve summers to carry another's bag."

"But I am twelve. Had me birthday last week."

MacGregor eyed her suspiciously. "Ye're a might wee for twelve. What's your name?"

"Rachel Armstrong."

"Ah, ye must be William's lass, then." He took another long pull on the pipe as he considered her. "Do ye think ye can lift a set o' clubs?"

"Aye, sure," she answered hopefully. "I can carry the barley bales for me da in the fall and they weigh more than I."

"I'm short a lad or two today," MacGregor muttered to himself, staring up at the clear blue sky, "and the fine weather will bring the golfers." He nodded toward a group of caddies huddled under an old oak. "Very well then, if ye think ye can manage it take a place with the others."

Rachel skipped excitedly toward the boys lounging in the coolness of the shade. She cherished the game and took great pride in her considerable knowledge of golf's intricacies and the exploits of the era's noted luminaries. As she approached the tree a tall, dark-haired youth called out, "Do me eyes deceive me, lads, or is that young Rachel Armstrong come to loop?"

"Ye know very well it's me, Bobby O'Maley." Rachel spread her feet and crossed her arms. "I told ye I was coming as soon as I turned o' age."

"Why aren't ye out working the farm?" the tall boy asked.

Rachel shrugged her small shoulders. "Shearing isn't for a day or two so me da said I could come if I wished."

Another boy pulled a long blade of grass from his mouth. "Ye'll wish ye were back there soon enough. Looping ain't worth the trouble the way these buggers tip."

The other lads laughed knowingly from where they lay beneath the gently swaying canopy of leaves. The shifting patches of sunlight momentarily brightened their drab, rural attire but did nothing to improve their dour outlook.

"This is nae a place for a wee lass like ye, Rachel," warned a third. "Go on home before ye fall into a bunker and hurt yourself."

Rachel glared defiantly at the group and made to sit in their midst but was roughly kicked from behind by the tall boy.

"The queue ends over that way." He jerked his thumb to the end of the line farthest from the clubhouse. "If you're gonna stay ye'll wait your turn like the rest o' us."

Rachel sat in the unusually hot sun until the line began to move, as the caddies were snatched up by players on their way to the 1st tee. MacGregor was correct in his prediction: the fair skies produced a steady stream of golfers and soon young Rachel sat alone under the big tree. She kept her eyes fixed on the door of the clubhouse in anticipation of her first loop. Would it be someone she knew, a friend of her father's perhaps? Maybe old Doc Gilmore would step through the door, or even Mayor Hoolihan out for his daily round. But the man who eventually emerged was a complete stranger to Rachel. Tall and thin with a deeply tanned face and smiling eyes. He scanned his surroundings briefly before spotting her beside the trunk of the oak.

He looked at Rachel doubtfully as he approached. "Are ye caddying today?"

"Aye, sir."

"What do they call ye?"

"Rachel Armstrong."

The man cast a dubious glance at the girl's bony arms. "Armstrong, ye say. Strong enough to carry me bag for eighteen?"

"That and more, sir."

The man smiled. He liked the lass' spirit and decided in advance to tip her generously if she indeed lasted the entire round. "My name's Mr. Leslie." He handed over his heavy bag and Rachel shouldered it with surprising ease as they made their way toward the tee. "I'm on a fortnight's holiday and this is my first time in Oban. Have ye played the course often?"

"I've never played it, Mr. Leslie."

"Never played it?" Leslie asked, wondering what good was a caddie who had no knowledge of the course.

"Nae, sir." Rachel glanced up at him. "But I've carried me grandda's clubs 'round many a time. And I paid close attention."

"Hmmm," Leslie mused, "we'll just see how close."

On the first tee he called for his driver. "Where should I be laying me drive, young Rachel?"

The girl thought for a moment. "Grandda likes to play down the right side and come in from there, but I think ye'd be wiser to stay toward the middle."

Leslie gave her a humorous look. "And why's that?"

"Because you're sure to hit it in the ravine if ye aim right."

Leslie felt a hot flash of anger and he briefly wondered if he had unwittingly allied himself with a young scamp. "You're still young, Rachel," he said firmly, "so I'm willing to let the offense pass. But in the future try and remember that a caddie never offers impertinent comments."

She looked down at her feet. "Sorry, sir."

Leslie nodded at this show of genuine repentance and took his stance, aiming squarely down the right side of the wide fairway. When he swung, the ball sailed off his club, curving sharply off line and into the yawning ravine. The calamity shook Leslie to his very roots. Quite the accomplished golfer, he never *ever* sliced. After years of diligent practice spent developing a right to left game, Leslie was so confident of his pronounced draw that he would routinely aim directly at right-side hazards without the slightest apprehension.

Leslie stood and stared at the place where the ball had vanished, then turned his gaze toward the girl standing behind the tee. He detected no smugness in the lass's expression, only a certain sadness at the loss. He decided to shrug off the experience as the result of a poorly timed suggestion.

On the next hole he stroked a beautiful drive and found himself left with a long approach shot to a green lying safely behind the narrow arm of a small loch.

He stroked his chin as he gauged the distance. "What say ye, Rachel, the four-iron or the five?"

Rachel's eyes seemed to follow the flight of an invisible ball as she considered her response. "Play the five. The four will nae clear the loch."

Leslie chuckled and tousled the girl's red hair. "Don't ye mean the other way around? The four is the longer iron, lassie."

"I know the clubs, Mr. Leslie," Rachel said with a child's soft indignation, "and it's the five ye should swing with."

The golfer furrowed his bushy brows and called for his four-iron. His swing caught too much turf and the ball struck the opposite bank before rolling back into the loch. Leslie cursed quietly and prepared to hit a provisional, but at the last second he held out his hand toward the girl. "Give me the five."

This time he hit the sweet spot. The ball sailed high over the water and fell to the center of the green.

Leslie stared across the water in bewilderment. "How did ye know that would happen, Rachel?"

"I canna really say, sir. I'm just able to...*see* things on the links. My grandda can, too. He says it runs in the family."

Excitement grabbed hold of Leslie and over the course of the next few holes he put Rachel to the test. Each time she knew the right club to play, where the ball would go and even how a sudden gust of wind might influence its flight. Standing on the 7th green with a grand view of Oban Bay in the distance, Leslie had her analyze the line of a snaking thirty-foot putt.

"Well," she said, her gaze slowly moving toward the hole, "it's going to break right about eight inches on the uphill slope, then turn a foot left on the way down. Just before it reaches the cup it will kick off a spike mark and miss on the high side."

Leslie aimed four inches to the right of the hole and stroked the putt. The ball broke right eight inches on the uphill slope, then turned a foot left on the way down. Just before it reached the cup it kicked off a spike mark and missed on the high side. Stunned, Leslie knelt before the girl and gently took hold of her slim shoulders. "Can ye do that every time, Rachel?"

She blinked at him anxiously. "Aye, I believe so."

Picking up his bag from the grass, Leslie leapt to his feet and marched briskly back toward the clubhouse with the lass in tow.

"What about the rest o' the round, sir?" Rachel asked as she was dragged along in his wake.

"No time for that," Leslie said, "we've got to catch the next train to Edinburgh."

*　*　*

Mr. Leslie strode into the clubhouse and right up to the clerk posted at the front desk.

"Please send someone to fetch Rachel's father straightaway," he demanded. "And call the hotel. Have them gather up me things and send them on to the train station." The alarmed clerk retreated into the rear office and emerged a moment later with the manager.

"What seems to be the trouble, Mr. Leslie?" The agitated manager wrung his hands and shot Rachel a hostile glare. "Ye only just arrived this morning. Has the lass offended ye in some way?"

"On the contrary," Leslie responded, his face still flushed with excitement, "young Rachel here has given me new hope. Now, I have a few calls to make. Please see that the lass is made comfortable 'til I return."

The manager raised his eyebrows at the clerk and sent him to collect the girl's father. Then he led a bewildered Rachel to the room's plushest armchair and treated her to a smashing ham sandwich and root beer as she awaited her father's arrival. The sheep farmer stormed into the lobby just as Leslie hung up the phone.

"What's this all about then, Gunn?" he roared at the manager. "Is Rachel all right?"

"She's just fine, William, and it was nae me who sent for ye." He pointed at Leslie. "It was him."

The farmer, who matched his daughter in slightness of build, wheeled on Leslie. "Shearing's only a day away and I've got plenty to do beforehand, sir, so kindly state your business."

"In that case, I'll keep it short, Mr. Armstrong," Leslie said calmly. "I wish to borrow your daughter for a week."

Armstrong gaped at him. He turned to Gunn (who shrugged) and then back to Leslie. "Borrow her…what for?

"Are ye familiar with the Ryder Cup competition, Mr. Armstrong?"

"'Course I am," snapped the little man. "Only a fool wouldn't be."

"Then you know that the British team has nae beaten the Americans going on ten years."

"What's that got to do with my Rachel?"

Leslie grinned. "I think the lass can help swing the match in our favor."

Armstrong looked at him as if he were a mad sheep. "How can a wee lass o' twelve help win the cup from the Yanks?"

"Because she's a clairvoyant, man!" cried Leslie. "She can foresee what will happen on the course."

The farmer turned to Rachel, who had been observing the exchange with great interest from her nearby chair. "Is it true, lass, do ye have your grandda's gift, then?"

"Aye."

Her father, shaken by this revelation, drifted into deep thought and Leslie took the opportunity to jump on the offensive. "We have to get her to Troon at once," he urged. "The match begins on the morrow."

"Troon," the girl whispered in awe.

"Troon," the manager said in envy.

"Troon!" the farmer shouted in consternation.

"Troon," Mr. Leslie confirmed, "and there's nae time to lose."

"It's impossible," Armstrong said, shaking his head as his daughter sagged in disappointment. "I need all me kin for the shearing; I can nae spare a hand."

Leslie stepped closer and loomed over the farmer. "Listen to me. This may be our best chance to take the Yanks, and on Scottish soil, to boot." He sensed Armstrong beginning to waver at the thought and pressed on. "Think o' your country, man, think o' Britain!"

Armstrong wrestled with the idea for a moment but his resolve hardened as he considered the work ahead of him. "Blast Britain. I will nae let her go, especially with some bloke I don' know."

The phone began to ring in the background as Gunn jumped into the fray. "That'll be enough o' that, Armstrong. Don't ye nae know who this is? Mr. Leslie happens to be the president o' the Royal & Ancient."

"I don' care if he's Bonny Prince Charley himself, he's not taking me lass to Troon or anywhere else!"

"Mr. Armstrong," the clerk called unsteadily from the desk, "it's for you."

"Tell whoever it is that I'm busy," the farmer said, squarely facing Leslie, who smiled down at him in a peculiar manner.

The clerk held out the phone. "But sir, it's the Queen on the line."

Armstrong swung his head around. "The Queen?"

"Aye," replied the deathly pale clerk.

Armstrong hesitated for an instant, then slowly made his way to the waiting receiver. "Hello?"

"Aye, Your Majesty." (He nodded into the phone.)

"Nae, Your Majesty." (He shook his head.)

"Nae, Your Majesty." (Another shake.)

"Aye, Your Majesty." (A nod.)

"Aye…I mean nae, Your Majesty." (A nod and a shake.)

"Thank ye, Your Majesty. Good-bye." He placed the receiver quietly into the cradle and stared at it blankly.

"What did she say, man?" asked the awestruck manager.

"She said that the pride o' the nation depended on my cooperation."

Leslie lifted an eyebrow. "And what else?"

"And that she would dispatch a full company o' the Black Watch from the garrison at Glencoe to help me with the shearing."

Rachel looked up innocently at her puzzled father. "What does it all mean, Da?"

Armstrong laid a hand on his daughter's head. "It means you're going to Troon, lass."

*   *   *

Royal Troon rested like a jewel on the Firth of Clyde. Even from the train Rachel could sense its storied past, feel the timeless struggles that had been waged there by the greatest of golf's warriors. She turned from the window and leaned closer to her temporary guardian. "Do ye think it's fair, Mr. Leslie?"

Leslie peeked over the top of his paper. "Do I think what's fair, lass?"

"Me caddyin' for the British team, seeing that I've got the gift."

Leslie put down his reading. "It's the Yanks that are coming, Rachel. Ye may have the gift but they bring with them their own formidable powers and we'll need all o' our resources if we hope to prevail."

At the station they were met by a short, rotund chap who paced up and down the platform like a pigeon, then appeared to fly alongside the coach as it slowed to a stop, flapping his arms in agitation.

"Ye were nae supposed to arrive 'til this evening, Leslie. And what's the meaning o' this telegram?" the man demanded, clutching the pink message in a beefy hand. "A savior, ye claim? Ye've got the whole clubhouse in an uproar."

"And here she is," Leslie said, stepping off the coach and helping Rachel down to the platform. "Alister Graham, meet Rachel Armstrong."

Rachel offered a little bow. "A pleasure, Mr. Graham."

Graham looked at the lass with incomprehension that quickly turned to horror. "Are ye completely daft, Leslie? Brown's called off the early practice rounds in anticipation o' your arrival. He'll be furious!"

"I'll take the responsibility, Alister," Leslie replied calmly, "ye just get us to the course in one piece."

They raced along the waterfront in an open top Rolls and arrived at the clubhouse just after the breakfast hour. Eric Brown, the British team captain, waited for them in the foyer. He had great faith in Leslie and took in the sight of young Rachel a bit more stoically than Graham, patiently awaiting an explanation. When Leslie revealed the lass's abilities Graham sighed and dropped into a nearby chair, but Brown gazed hard at the taller man.

"We'll see," he said and grabbing hold of Rachel's arm, led her off to the 1st tee.

"What will the ball do?" Brown asked as he teed up a white sphere.

Rachel stared down the middle of the fairway, then she shifted her gaze to the left-hand rough and turned to peer with narrow disapproval at the Englishman.

"I don' think it's very nice to try and trick me by playing a deliberate hook, Mr. Brown," she said. "See that bit o' dune peeking through the heather?" She pointed well down the track. "If ye play the shot ye intended that's where ye'll end up."

Brown's face reddened and he gripped the club for an obvious right to left swing. The ball sailed in a vivid arc across the gray skies and landed with a shower of sand on the tiny patch of dune. The British captain stared long and hard at the ball, while Mr. Leslie chuckled and gave Rachel's shoulder a kind squeeze.

After three holes of Brown quizzing the girl on every shot, Leslie pulled him aside. "Satisfied then, are ye, Eric?"

"Right," the Englishman said and took hold of Rachel's arm again. "Time to meet the others."

He marched the lass straight into the locker room, where the rest of the team was deep into planning its first day's strategy. Tony Jacklin had the floor and was busily shoring up the confidence of his comrades.

"It'll be a cakewalk, lads," he encouraged. "Hogan's long over the hill and Snead failed to make the cut in his last match!"

"What about Palmer?" reminded an unconvinced Neil Coles.

"Arnie will be on enemy soil," Jacklin soothed, "without his vaunted army to reinforce him."

"He won't be needing an army, not with the likes of his teammates," lamented Bernard Gallacher. "I feel like London facing the bloody Blitz!"

"And what about that young buck they're bringing with them?" inquired Alex Caygill. "What's his name…Nicker something?"

"Nicklaus," corrected Peter Alliss.

"Are they so arrogant they can afford to bring a wee lad along for the ride?" continued Caygill.

"There's nothing wee about him," Gallacher said. "He must tip the scales at 20 stones."

Maurice Bembridge cut off the ensuing chuckles with his booming voice. "Underestimating the lad would be a mistake. He's a coming force to be reckoned with."

"Gentlemen," interrupted Brown from the doorway, "before we embark on our quest today I want you to meet someone." He placed both hands on the girl's shoulders and gently pushed her into the room. "This is Rachel Armstrong, from Oban. Young Rachel here has the unique ability to predict events on the links. She won't be able to make the shots for you but she can offer key words of advice that may be of use against the Americans."

The room digested this unusual news with typical British aplomb. Finally Christy O'Connor chuckled. "Blimey, talk about your local knowledge."

A boy ran shouting past the open window. "The Yanks are coming! The Yanks are coming!"

The team quickly filed out onto the cobbled lane and immediately saw that the lad was mistaken—the Yanks were already there. They stood gathered on the sandy shore of the cold sea: Ben Hogan, Arnold Palmer, Sam Snead, Billy Casper, Tony Lema, Ray Floyd, Gene Littler, Dave Hill, Miller Barber, Tommy Aaron, Lee Trevino and the young Jack Nicklaus—the flower of American golf, looking as if they had just waded ashore in a small-scale invasion.

The great names rattled inside Rachel's head and she felt like bolting for the nearest available cover. Tony Jacklin noticed her distress and reached over to pat her arm. "Don't worry now lass, they may play like gods but they're mortal just like you and me."

"What are the morning pairings?" Leslie asked.

Everyone turned to look at Graham, who couldn't take his eyes off the menacing Yankee horde.

"Alister," Brown said impatiently, "the pairings?"

"Righto!" Graham reached into his pocket and pulled out a wrinkled sheet of paper. "Jacklin and Townsend to face Hill and Aaron. Alliss/O'Connor vs. Snead/Littler, Brown/Caygill vs. Floyd/Lema and Bembridge/Gallacher opposing Palmer/Trevino."

The British captain considered for a moment. "Rachel, you'll carry Mr. Bembridge's bag and offer Mr. Gallacher any aid you can."

"Whatever ye think is best, sir."

"Let's have at it then, lads," Brown encouraged. "The matches won't win themselves."

There followed a brief crisis when it became obvious that Rachel would not be able to manage Bembridge's massive bag. A smaller one was brought out, and the kindly Maurice agreed to carry less than the maximum number of clubs in exchange for the girl's special insight. Rachel then proceeded to earn the golfers' confidence on the practice range by accurately predicting the location and distance of each shot.

Nine o'clock chimed from the town square and they made their way to the 1st tee, where the happy-go-lucky Lee Trevino and the ever-intense Palmer were already waiting. As it turned out Arnie needn't have troubled about his beloved army, for a whole new host of followers had gathered at the tee, attracted by curiosity and the gratitude they felt for the man who had almost single-handedly put the British Open on the American map.

Trevino took one look at Rachel and cackled. "What's the matter Maurice, were they all out of full-size caddies?" He winked at the girl to let her know that it was all in jest.

"Never you mind, Lee," Bembridge retorted, "you'd be better served to worry about me rather than my caddie."

"You hear that Arnie?" Trevino said to his partner. "Maurice says that we ought to be worried."

But Palmer said nothing. He had a premonition that the day would go against them and was anxious to prove it wrong. The format was match play, with the morning foursomes playing two-man alternate shots. Gallacher, playing the tee shots on the odd-numbered holes, drove off, followed by Palmer. Both shots were well played but Gallacher got the better distance. After Trevino stroked a beauty of a nine-iron to the center of the green it was Bembridge's turn to answer. His ball lay just shy of the right-hand rough and a mere 80 yards from the flag. With the wind slicing in off the firth, the moment called for a right to left approach.

"I'm thinking of playing a wedge and coming in over the bunkers on the right," Maurice said.

Rachel silently tracked the proposed flight and shook her head. "Nae, Mr. Bembridge. The wedge is the correct choice but play to the center o' the green."

"But that will likely roll all the way to the left and well down the slope," protested the Englishman.

"Nae, it will land safely."

Bembridge shrugged and aimed for the heart of the putting surface. When he swung, the ball immediately began to move to the left, just as he had feared. Then a fierce gust blasted in from the sea, pushing the shot even more off line. The ball sailed over the rear bunker, struck a wooden rail on a temporary grandstand, bounced back onto the green and rolled across the slope to within six feet of the hole. Trevino's constant stream of running jokes trickled to a halt and Arnold Palmer hung his head in disgust.

Gallacher smiled. "I was wonderin' what ye were up to, Maurice. Ye'll have to teach me that approach sometime."

After Palmer missed his twenty-footer on the high side Gallacher sank the short putt to put them up one. They remained that way until the 10th where Gallacher, warned by young Rachel of an impending hook, was able to adjust his shot and set up Bembridge for an easy birdie that pushed the resident team up two. Rachel saved the day again on twelve, helping Maurice negotiate a slippery downhill putt to save par and halve the hole. Things appeared rosy for the Brits until a poor showing on seventeen, combined with the brilliance of Palmer, gave back the one-stroke cushion, and they staggered into the final hole with the momentum squarely in the American camp.

Trevino started things out with a mammoth clout into the teeth of the wind on the par-four 18th, and when Bembridge responded by hooking his ball into the rough the gallery began chattering and shifting their feet nervously. The morning mist was just beginning to clear as the British twosome pondered their options.

"Can you reach it with your spoon, Bernard?" Bembridge asked anxiously, staring at the distant green.

Gallacher glanced at Rachel, who shook her head.

"How about the driver, then?"

"It'll fall in the rough," she answered.

"What will he do?" Maurice nodded in Palmer's direction.

Rachel's eyes grew wide as she traced the soon-to-follow shot. "He'll make the green easily."

"Then so must we," Gallacher insisted.

Rachel's head was bouncing all over the fairway as she discerned the possibilities. Finally, she said, "No ye don', lay up with a two-iron."

"A two," exclaimed Gallacher. "But that will put us well short!"

"Layup with your two, Bernard," Bembridge commanded. "The lass has yet to steer us wrong."

Gallacher scowled and lined up for the shot, sending the ball straight at the pin but far short of the green. Palmer scratched his head at the odd choice and then promptly played his own shot, a

stunning five-iron that swept onto the left edge of the putting surface and rolled to a stop thirty feet from the waiting cup. The gallery
simultaneously applauded the effort and moaned its displeasure as
Gallacher stomped off in anger.

"Grand, that's just grand!" he stormed. "We might as well just
concede the hole."

"We're not conceding anything 'til the lass says so," Bembridge
said with an inquiring eye toward Rachel, who said nothing.

When they got to the ball Gallacher quickly sized up their
dilemma. "Now what do we do?"

The green was tiered, with the upper level on the fairway side
and the hole hidden on the back.

"I think the moment calls for a lofted mashie," Maurice mused.

"Nae," countered Rachel, "bump it with your five."

Now it was Bembridge's turn to doubt. "If I do that it'll surely
roll off the backside."

The lass simply smiled at him in silence until the Englishman
turned back to the ball.

"You're not going to do it, are ye, Bembridge?" Gallacher asked
in alarm.

"We've come this far Bernard, there's no turning back now." He
took his five and sent the ball bounding toward the green. It reached
the upper tier in three hops, settled to a roll and raced down the
slick slope.

"I don't believe it," Gallacher managed to utter just before the ball
struck the base of the pin and bounced a few inches backward. A
shaken Trevino missed the long putt, and the Americans conceded the
match. Captain Hogan, his hawk-like profile recognizable on the over-
looking verandah, turned and marched in fury back into the clubhouse.

Gallacher and Bembridge kept silent as they left the green to the
wild cheers from the gallery. "The girl's a wonder," Maurice said
finally, patting the beaming youngster's head.

"Aye," Gallacher agreed casually, "she's a Scot, after all."

*　*　*

The afternoon foursomes went much the same way, as Coles and
Hugget teamed up with the diminutive caddie to beat Floyd and

Snead in the deciding match, five and four. As the sun slipped behind the bank of rolling fog over the firth, the British found themselves ahead 7-6 at the end of the first day's action.

That night the American team held a meeting in Hogan's room.

"Where's Lema?" the captain inquired.

"He's still at the pub," replied Littler.

Hogan's eyes narrowed. "All right, gentlemen, what seems to be the difficulty?"

Palmer sat with his head in his hands. "I don't know, Ben. Lee and I should've won that match, but Gallacher and Bembridge kept coming up with just the right shot. It was uncanny!"

"It was frustrating as all hell, that's what it was," added Trevino. "Even when you thought they'd blown the hole they'd pull something impossible from their bag and club us over the head with it."

Grim laughter rippled across the room and Billy Casper, who had sat out the morning round, held up his hand for silence. "I followed the two of you around and it seemed to me that the Brits were depending quite heavily on that red-headed caddie for advice."

"You're right," agreed Miller Barber, who had also been present in the gallery. "They even seemed to argue with the girl on occasion. I could see her shaking or nodding her head firmly to their questions, almost as if she were overruling them."

Hogan raised his brows in the direction of Sam Snead. "Wasn't she one of the caddies for Coles and Hugget?"

"Yep," answered Snead, "and she was the only one they sought advice from. The other caddie, who had to have at least twenty years more experience, always stood off to one side and well out of the huddle."

"So what do you think is going on?" Hogan asked the group.

Nicklaus shrugged his wide shoulders. "Maybe she's got some special course knowledge."

"Or maybe she's psychic." It was Tony Lema speaking from the doorway. "I've just had a very interesting conversation with Gallacher's caddie. He was by no means happy about being left out of today's strategy and was busy drowning his indignation with a few pints of ale. Turns out the girl comes from some hick town in the Highlands and she has the ability to prognosticate every shot the Brits—and we—take. Leslie found her yesterday and whisked her halfway across the country."

No one doubted the truth of what he said. They had been to Scotland enough to know that odd things happened on these shores.

"Well, gentlemen," Hogan said, "what do we do about it?"

"There must be something in the rules preventing it," insisted Palmer.

The Americans spent a long time poring over the rule book without success. They were about to give up when Tommy Aaron raised his head. "Isn't there a club rule about females not being allowed on the course?"

Hogan slapped his knee and grinned fiercely. "You're right, Tommy boy, there certainly is!" He marched out of the room and returned a few minutes later with a copy of the club charter. Hogan flipped quickly through the first few pages, running a tanned finger down the thick text, and stopped to read a passage. "Says right here that…*Troon is a gentlemen's club only. Ladies shall not be allowed in the locker room or on the course under any circumstance.*"

"Then we've got 'em!" exclaimed Lema.

Ben Hogan shut the book and stood. "Let's go have a talk with the cup committee."

*   *   *

Rachel awoke the next morning to a bright blue sky shimmering behind the curtains of her open window. The British team had given her the best room in the hotel, and Rachel had never slept in such a bed. The casual observer would have had a difficult time noticing her tiny frame among the mounds of down comforters and pillows. She rose and dressed in her best Armstrong tartan skirt and wool pullover, then descended the stairway to find Mr. Leslie waiting for her in the sitting room.

"The others have all gone off to practice," he said warmly. "Come, we'll have breakfast at the club."

As they were taking their morning meal Eric Brown entered the room and marched toward their table at a brisk pace. He appeared extremely upset and almost bowled over a waiter carrying a tray of boiled sausages.

He placed both his big hands on the table. "There's trouble, Leslie!"

"What's happened?"

"Hogan's found some clause in the charter that prohibits females on the course. He took it to the committee and they're upholding the rule." Brown looked at the girl sadly. "I'm sorry, lass, but we'll have to manage without you."

Leslie threw down his napkin. "Blast the Yanks! We've should've known they'd come up with something clever." He picked the napkin up again and dabbed his mouth with it, thinking furiously. "Well, there's only one thing to do."

"What's that?" asked Brown.

Leslie rose. "Why, change the charter, of course."

*   *   *

They found Alister Graham lounging in his office. Both men stormed through the door so fast that the club president had insufficient time to either remove his feet from the desk or spirit away the open bottle of Scotch into the bottom drawer.

"Comfy, Alister?" Leslie asked with contempt.

"Very," replied Graham, refusing to give ground. "Don't ye gents know how to knock?"

"No time for formalities, Graham," replied Brown, "we have to get the club charter revised."

Graham's eyes looked as if they were about to pop from his head. "What?!"

"It forbids females on the course," Leslie said. "Something ye should have warned us about. Hogan's taken it to the committee, and they're siding with the Americans. We have to rewrite the charter if Rachel's going to be able to loop for the lads. Without her we can kiss the cup good-bye."

"That charter is a hundred and fifty years old," Graham warned. "Do ye have any idea what it takes to change it? We'll need to get consent o' the board and at least half o' the membership!"

"Then I suggest you put the whiskey away and get to work," said Eric Brown menacingly.

As a storm of turmoil gathered around the clubhouse, the morning matches proceeded on schedule. The second day's format called for four-ball play, in which two, two-man teams would compete against each other, with each team member playing his own ball. The best score of the four balls would win the hole for the team, and the team that won the most holes would win the match."

The Americans began the day poorly, dropping two of the four matches. Later, Trevino and Littler beat Barnes and Alliss, and Floyd/Barber evened the effort of Hugget/Gallacher for the Yanks' only points of the morning. But that afternoon the Americans charged back. Down 10-8, Casper and Floyd disposed of Butler and Townsend, and Hill/Snead stunned the team of Alliss/Caygill 2 and 1 when Dave Hill sank a dramatic eagle putt on seventeen. Play ended near eight in the evening with both teams even at 12 and the British reeling. Events were just as unstable at the clubhouse, where the dining room brimmed with irate members.

"Gentlemen, gentlemen!" Graham shouted over the din as he pounded his gavel. "Can we please have your comments one at a time or we'll never get through this. Now, Fergusson, what have ye to add to the discussion?"

A large, red-faced fellow stood and glared at the men around him. "I don' know about the rest o' ye fellows, but I will nae have any part o' allowing the womenfolk onto the links. The moment we do that we'll have surrendered our last refuge o' manhood."

"Aye, aye!" called a number of supporters in agreement.

"Think about it, man," Fergusson pleaded. "Can ye imagine ol' lady Napier out on the course with her knitting club? My God, it'll take a week just to get a round in!"

"Which ought to fit in nicely with your game, Howard," retorted Graham.

A chorus of raucous laughter rolled across the room as another man stood to be heard. "Fergie's right, the women are fine and precious creatures, to be sure, but they do nae' belong at Royal Troon. The next thing ye know we'll have tulips lining the fairways and wallpaper in the loo!"

More laughter followed, forcing Graham to wield his gavel a half-dozen times to bring things back under control.

"May I remind Mr. MacFee that this is the 1960s," Graham said, "not the dark ages, and frankly, the place could use a wee bit o' sprucing up."

"Then why not have the lot start in your office, Alister?" shouted another member. "Maybe we'll even vote for one to take your place!"

Graham reddened and raised his gavel threateningly, forcing Leslie to intercede.

"Enough o' your arguing," he bellowed over the din, "time is short and we need to come to an agreement. Need I remind ye that the real issue at stake isn't the social makeup o' your club, but the future o' British golf! Ye all saw what happened to the lads today, and without Rachel's guidance the Yanks will roll over them for sure on the morn. But with her they'll have a fighting chance to win the day and restore the cup to Scottish soil where it rightly belongs. It's up to ye all to do your duty. Did ye nae heed the telegram from the Queen herself?" He emphasized his point by waving the bright slip of paper over his head.

Grim silence filled the room, and it appeared for a moment that Leslie had won the day until someone from the back row yelled out, "Aye, and she'll probably be the first one o' them in line clamoring for a tee time!"

This time the mirth refused to be cowed by the president's gavel. It wasn't until the senior member stood to address the assembly that order could be restored.

"What ye say is all fine and good, Mr. Leslie," began the old man. "Very patriotic, very moving. But what is to become o' us after ye go back to St. Andrews and take your lovely cup with ye?"

The mob crowed its assent and demanded Leslie's reply but he simply smiled at them benevolently. "That's where you're wrong, Malcolm," he said. "I've spoken to the committee and arranged to have the cup reside here at Troon for as long as it remains in Britain."

An awed hush descended on the gathering and Leslie surveyed his captives with a catlike grin. "So ye see, gents, it's up to ye. Ye can go about your ways and let history slip through your fingers, or ye can give the world a wee nudge and then point to the fruits o' your labor with satisfaction for years to come. Now let's see a show o' hands, shall we?"

*   *   *

Rachel heard a soft rapping on her door and descended from her mountain of covers to peek through the keyhole. "Who's there?"

"It's us, lass," rumbled a deep voice, "Mr. Bembridge and Mr. Brown. We have good news."

Rachel opened the door and blinked into the brightly lit hallway and the excited faces of the two golf pros. "What's happened?"

"Mr. Leslie has been successful," Eric Brown said. "You'll be able to caddie for us after all."

Rachel beamed at him. "That's wonderful, Mr. Brown!"

"Sleep well now, child," soothed Bembridge, "tomorrow will be a big day."

"Aye, Mr. Bembridge." She yawned. "I'll dream sweetly now. Good night."

But her dreams were not sweet; they were haunted by a large bear that roamed the edges of Rachel's sleep and cast long shadows across her subconscious paths. She dodged and darted trying to escape the animal, but it kept looming up beside her, blocking the sunlight from reaching her upturned face.

*   *   *

It was a tired young lady that met the assembled British team in the morning mist, where she was promptly assigned to accompany the team captain in his singles battle with Snead. Although the Slammer played exceptionally well he was no match for Brown's deft efforts or Rachel's timely insights. By lunchtime the Brits were up 17-15 after taking five of the eight morning matches. But for the third day in a row the afternoon tide pulled in favor of the Yanks and the fate of the cup came down to the final match of the day: Tony Jacklin squaring off with the young but formidable Jack Nicklaus.

Rachel, of course, would caddie the critical match and she knew something was amiss the moment she stepped onto the 1st tee. The air seemed somehow thicker to her, difficult to see through. When the big American teed off with a monstrous drive, Rachel was shocked by her inability to anticipate it. Jacklin leaned over for some last-minute instruction, but all Rachel could manage was a frown and a bewildered shrug of her shoulders.

"What do you *mean* you can't see?" whispered the pro.

"I don' know, sir." Rachel peered up at him, close to tears. "Something's blocking me view o' things."

"All right, all right," calmed Jacklin, "don't get yourself all fogged up. Just try and concentrate, try and picture my next shot."

But try as she may, the best Rachel could do was to make out Jacklin standing over his ball preparing to swing. The rest was a blur of green and gray, with a yawning black hole right where the fairway ought to have stretched out in her mind.

Forced to play blind, Jacklin gave it a valiant effort. He halved the first two holes and won the third, but stumbled badly on the next two. Rachel trudged along beside him, struggling with her newly found handicap, delicately probing the edges of her sight in a vain attempt to discover the problem. The effort proved exhausting, forcing her to rest awhile on the 6th tee.

As she sat on the cool grass an odd thing happened. Nicklaus had just clubbed another prodigious drive and stood to one side to allow Jacklin a go at it. The sun, clawing its way through the fog, broke over the American's broad shoulder, and Rachel looked up to see his dark silhouette against the sky. Then he shifted slightly and eclipsed the sun, throwing a long shadow over her freckled face.

Rachel quickly bolted to her feet and grabbed at Jacklin's elbow, pulling him aside and over to where Bembridge, Brown and Gallacher stood watching.

"It's him!" she hissed. "It's me dream…he's the bear!"

"Slow down, child," steadied Bembridge, "what are you talking about? Who's a bear?"

"The Yank! Mr. Nicklaus." She nodded at the sandy-haired American. "He's got the gift, too and he's using it to stymie me own sight!"

"Bloody hell!" Brown exclaimed, glaring at Nicklaus. "Well, if it's a war he wants then it's a war he'll get. Fight back, Rachel. Don't let him get the better of you."

Rachel tried to concentrate but broke off almost at once. "He's terrible strong, Mr. Brown, I don' know if I can do it."

"Ye must try, lass," encouraged Gallacher. "Tony needs ye—we all need ye."

So Rachel tried her best to break the spell that the young American held over her. She tried on six to no avail: Nicklaus up 2. She failed again on number seven: Nicklaus up by 3. The 8th was halved when Jacklin sank a thirty-footer for birdie, no thanks to Rachel.

But on nine the black hole began to reveal signs of wavering. Rachel had decided to shift her focus from the game and concentrate on the source of her dilemma, boring into the back of Jack's blond head with her mind. She soon started to glimpse events around the periphery of the action: the top of a club in mid-swing or the wide arc of a ball as it swung out over the gorse and then back into play. The harder she pressed the more she could see, and on the 10th hole it was enough to help Jacklin stem his steady bleeding. Bolstered by this success, the Englishman managed to hold his own on eleven while Rachel and Nicklaus waged their private battle.

As the girl gained confidence the bear began to falter. He kept shaking his head on the 12th, trying to clear his vision, and eventually gave the hole away with a poor approach. The pair halved thirteen and again on fourteen with Nicklaus twice scrambling to save par. By this point, the mental pendulum had swung to Rachel's side and it was the American who began to suffer from "eye" trouble. He became tentative with his club selection, pondering his lies longer than usual.

Jacklin took fifteen with a well-crafted birdie: Nicklaus 2 up. A par on number sixteen left the Brit down by only 1, and on seventeen, following a complicated series of instructions from Rachel, Jacklin squared the match with a magnificent fifty-foot putt for his bird.

Nicklaus dug in his psychic heels on the deciding hole and followed Jacklin's fine effort with a tremendous drive that sailed well past his rival's ball. But he must not have had a clear view of the tail end of his shot, for it took a bad hop and trickled into one of the pothole bunkers that menaced the fairway. Rachel studied the American as Jacklin contemplated his next move.

"Shall I go for the pin or play it safe?" he asked.

Rachel gazed at the distant green. "Play to the center."

"Are you sure, Rachel?" Jacklin gave Nicklaus a nervous glance. "What will he do?"

"Oh, he's in a puzzle, he is," the lass said pulling out the three-iron. "He can nae tell for sure but he senses that nae matter what he does he'll wind up in either the gorse or the sand. Right now he's trying to decide which evil is the worse."

Jacklin took the club. "Then what happens?"

Rachel took a long look at the green, frowned and chewed her lower lip. "I canna see that far ahead."

Jacklin laid a perfect shot to the heart of the green and waited for the American to play.

"He's decided on the sand," Rachel whispered into Jacklin's lowered ear. They saw the clubhead flash in the sun over the lip of the bunker and the ball soar high into the air, landing well short of the putting surface and bounding into the trap that stood guard on its front edge. His shot from there rolled above the cup, leaving him with twelve feet for par. Jacklin lagged uphill to within 2, then he and Rachel watched in silence as Nicklaus surveyed his line.

Rachel leaned toward the pro and cupped her hand over her mouth. "He's goin' to miss it high and end up putting right over your line."

It unfolded just as the girl said it would, with Nicklaus settling for bogey and giving the Brit a perfect line to the hole. As Jacklin crouched for a final read Rachel walked up to the waiting American, grinned broadly and nodded her head in triumph. Leaning on his putter, Jack Nicklaus chuckled and shook his head before he had a chance to catch himself. He cast a quick sideways glance at his anxious teammates and seemed to hesitate. Then as the gallery watched in amazement he stepped over to Jacklin's ball, picked it up and handed it to his shocked opponent—thus conceding the hole, the match and the cup to the British.

Hogan went through the roof, tossing his cap to the ground in anger and stomping off the course. As the British team mobbed Jacklin, Nicklaus bent low and spoke briefly to Rachel before retreating to face the sour music. After things had calmed down a relieved Jacklin embraced the young caddie. "I'm grateful not to have to sink that putt, but why did he concede?"

"He did nae wish to draw any more suspicion on himself," she said. "It was either win and risk his own career or lose and play another day."

"But I don't understand, child," Bembridge said. "Surely the putt was in the hole."

"Nae, Mr. Jacklin would have missed on the low side. I could see that clear as summer and I let Mr. Nicklaus see it, too. That's when we had him."

"Had who?" asked a confused Gallacher. "Ye must excuse us, lass, but without your gift we're all a wee bit dense."

"It's the other Yanks, sir," she explained. "Did ye nae see how closely they were watchin' me and Mr. Nicklaus? While I was concentrating so hard on him during the match I picked up a feeling from his teammates following in the gallery. A doubt, a questioning o' his remarkable abilities. Was it nae Billy Casper who said that Nicklaus plays the game as if he knows what's going to happen next? They all saw him shake his head at me prediction," she continued, "and when ye would 'ave missed that putt, they would 'ave known for sure that he had the gift, too."

Leslie smiled with pleasure as he grasped the girl's amazing bluff. "A brilliant stroke, lass, but what did Jack say to ye afterwards? Was he angry?"

Rachel gave a toothy grin. "Nae, he just said that he had never met a more worthy opponent."

* * *

And so the Ryder Cup returned to British soil, where it was proudly displayed at Royal Troon until the Yanks wrested it back again two years later. If you look closely at the trophy you'll see Rachel's name engraved alongside that of the greats — the only caddie ever awarded such an honor. She can even be seen in the official team photograph, a tawny youth posed before the group, grinning awkwardly into the camera beneath her tangle of red hair. But these things are not what Rachel cherishes most from her experience. Instead it's the homage continually paid to her by the women of Troon, forever emancipated and free to walk the links in peace. Even the Queen herself, who rarely misses an opportunity to get in a round or two whenever she's in the neighborhood.

Author's Note

Obviously these events never transpired. The fictitious Ryder Cup match depicted above was rather loosely based on the one played in 1969, which was held at Royal Birkdale in Southport, England, where Jack Nicklaus did concede Jacklin's final two-footer. But the putt was only for a tie that allowed the American team to retain the Cup for another term. The British team is as I have described it, but neither Ben Hogan nor Tony Lema graced the American squad and Nicklaus was already a tour veteran of eight years, not the young greenhorn I've made him out to be. And Jack, forgive me, but there were times when you did play this wonderful game as if you knew what was going to happen next.

GLENCOE

G. GUILFORD BARTON

This story is inspired by a haunting Scottish folk song titled "Glencoe." The song tells the sad tale of brother clans caught up in treachery, betrayal and murder. Not the most shining moment in the history of Scotland. Although I've turned it into a ghost story, I must confess that I do not believe in ghosts. I do, however, acknowledge the existence of something just as grim and terrible—revenge.

GLENCOE

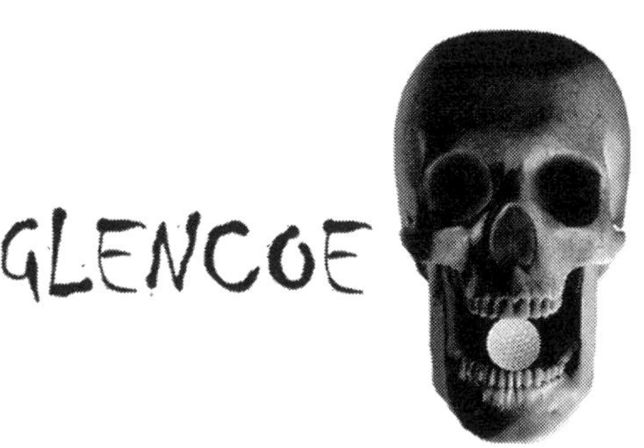

Cruel is the snow that sweeps Glencoe and covers the graves O'Donnell,
And cruel was the foe that raped Glencoe and murdered the house MacDonald.
Old Scottish folk song

T he American stepped into the clubhouse and surveyed the cluttered room with ill-disguised contempt. He stood in the doorway for a long moment as if reluctant to commit himself, then slowly began to prowl the perimeter of the room like an inspector general, lifting this, leaning over to examine that, running a manicured hand along the ancient mantelpiece—shaking his head with each arrogant step. Two men watched him from the shadows that clung stubbornly to the corners of the tiny space and refused to be banished by the late afternoon sunshine streaming through the high windows.

One of them cleared his throat. "Can I help ye?"

The startled intruder spun on his heels and the putting cleek he held clattered to the stone floor. He peered into the gloom. "Yeah, I've been up in Fort William on business and I came down here for a round of golf."

"Did ye now?" responded the other man. "Do ye have any clubs?"

"No, I was counting on renting a set," said the American, squinting to catch a glimpse of the man behind the voice.

The old starter shared a knowing look with his companion and leaned forward, exposing one side of his craggy face to the sunlight. "We don't have any for rent, but you're welcome to borrow mine." He nodded toward a battered bag leaning beside the door.

The American pulled out the driver and waggled it in the light. "Hmmm—these will have to do, I suppose," he said in a tone that suggested they wouldn't do at all. "How much for the round and clubs?"

"Five pounds for the golf, nae charge for the clubs."

"Five pounds!" laughed the colonial. "You people got a lot to learn about making a buck. No wonder this place is so run down; wouldn't be caught dead in a dump like this back in the States. But everyone said, 'Jack, you simply must play one of the old courses while you're in Scotland.' So here I am." He rudely tossed the bills onto the battered counter. "How much more for a cart?"

The other Scot removed a gnarled pipe from his mouth and pointed it at the stranger. "Nae one uses those contraptions here, Yank, but ye'll find a caddie or two out by the first tee."

The American sighed dramatically and picked up the clubs. "Might as well be stuck in the damn Stone Age," he muttered just loud enough for the two men to hear.

As the American approached the door the starter asked, "Can I have a name for our log?"

When he gave it to them both men instantly froze—the starter with his pen suspended just over the surface of his ledger and the other with his pipe halfway to his open mouth.

"My ancestors came from somewhere around here," added the stranger. "Look, I even bought a pair of these damn silly socks made with the family tartan." He pulled up a single pant leg to give them a glimpse of his garishly-clad ankle.

The two Scots stared at the foot in silence. The starter softly closed his book. "Make sure ye're off the course by sundown."

"Why's that?" the American demanded from the threshold.

"Just be off before dark."

*　*　*

The American made his way to the 1st tee. "Crazy old coots." Looking up into the barren hillsides caused him to shudder slightly.

There was something about the valley he found unsettling. Perhaps it was the still air that pressed down from a clear, yet somehow brooding, sky. Maybe it was the way the waters of the nearby loch churned and heaved without the aid of the slightest breeze. Or was it the decidedly uninviting woodlands that flanked the fairways? Even the river seemed to sing a menacing tune as it twisted and carved its stony course at the bottom of the steep ravine.

As the American approached the first hole he came upon a group of adolescent boys kicking a soccer ball back and forth between them. "Are any of you guys caddies?"

"That depends. Are ye a golfer?" cracked one of the boys to the delight of his mates.

"Very funny. If you want any sort of tip you'll watch your mouth, sonny," snapped the stranger, shoving the bag into the boy's arms. "Let's go, time's a wasting."

* * *

Guided by the caddie, the American proceeded to play the best round of his previously undistinguished golfing life. After three holes it was clear that he had found his swing. At the turn he was challenging par. While the shadows lengthened down the back nine, he held the course by the throat, and by the time he had driven yet another perfect shot into the heart of the 17th fairway he felt like the master of all he surveyed.

"This is incredible!" he shouted into the twilight. "I can do no wrong."

"Aye, you're having a grand round," admitted the boy running after the ball, "but we best be hurrying…it's getting dark."

"Hey, wait up!" the American called after him. "We've got plenty of daylight left."

"We do nae." The lad cast a nervous glance into the shadows gathering beneath the trees. "The dark comes on the glen quicker than other places, almost as if it's been there all along, just waiting to leap out at ye."

The American gazed up into the pale sky. "Bull, we'll finish with time to spare."

But the boy shook his head violently. "We can nae be caught out here when night falls."

The American lined up his next shot and effortlessly sent it soaring toward the green. It bounced twice and came to rest six feet from the pin. He grinned as they hurried toward the putting surface. "What's with everybody around here anyway? First those two geezers in the clubhouse try to spook me and now here you are jumping at your own shadow. I thought you Scots were supposed to be tough or something—turns out you're all afraid of the dark."

"It's nae the dark we be fearing," the young man said with another glance over his shoulder, "it's the banshees."

"What the hell is a banshee?"

The boy appeared to shiver. "Spirits o' the dead that prey on the souls o' mortal men."

The American's answering laughter echoed off the hillsides, only to be abruptly swallowed by the yawning ravine. "Ghosts!" he cried when he had sufficiently recovered. "A haunted golf course! Wait until they hear about this one back in New York."

"It's nae a thing to laugh about!" hissed the caddie.

"Tell me." The American chuckled as he reached for his putter. "Why do they choose to torment this particular place?"

"Do ye nae know the history o' the glen?" asked the young man in astonishment. "'Tis the site o' the great massacre."

"Massacre? What massacre?"

"The Glencoe massacre!" The boy lowered his voice searching the tree line again.

The American stepped back to survey his line. "Never heard of it."

The caddie leaned toward him to whisper. "In the winter of 1692 the local clan angered King William of Scotland by refusing to swear their allegiance, so he ordered that the entire MacDonald family be put to death. The execution party arrived in the midst o' a bitter storm and were shown nothing but warmth and hospitality by the MacDonalds, who were ignorant o' the fiendish plot. That very night the lowly cowards showed their gratitude by murdering their hosts as they slept. Only a handful escaped into the snow, and most o' them froze to death. Since that terrible day they have roamed the glen in search o' their revenge."

"Revenge on who, the living?"

"Nae on all living men, only the traitorous clan that murdered them…the Campbells."

This was spoken so softly the American was not sure he had heard it correctly. He looked up from his ball and into the frightened young face. "Did you say Campbell?"

"Aye," answered the boy with obvious dread. "Why do ye ask?"

The American hesitated for the briefest moment, then he too looked toward the woods. "My name is Campbell."

A low moan drifted out of the ravine, spread beneath the trees, rose to a piercing wail and slowly spiraled back into the chasm.

"What the hell was that?" asked Campbell. Receiving no response, he turned in time to see the clubs fall to the ground and the caddie running off into the gloom.

"Hey, come back here you little twerp! It was only the wind." But the boy topped a small rise and disappeared behind it. Campbell swore under his breath and bent over his ball. "Banshees…what a load of crap." He shrugged his shoulders and casually sank the six-footer for birdie.

"One more hole." Campbell grinned as he approached the 18th tee. "All I need is a par to break 70! My God, the boys at the club aren't going to believe this."

By the time he reached the tee it was noticeably darker, and he began to wonder if the boy had been right about the urgency of the evening overtaking this land. Even as he watched, the last of the day slipped away into night, almost as if ink were being poured to cover the valley, spreading along the horizon and slowly filling up the sky until only a patch of light remained high in the chilly air.

Campbell bent over to tee up his next shot. "I better get moving." In the middle of his backswing the ball fell off the tee. He replaced it, addressed it, pulled back the club…and off it toppled. Swearing loudly, he returned the ball to its tiny pedestal. This time he stood and watched it for a moment. Satisfied with its stability, he once again began to swing…and once again it fell off. No, he noted with a twinge of concern, it had *hopped* off. As he stared at it lying on the dark grass, Campbell became aware of a change in the sound drifting up from the river far below—it sounded like laughter.

"Fine," he muttered to no one in particular, "I'll play it from the grass." Campbell promptly drove a mammoth clout straight down the fairway. He watched as the ball rose in silhouette against the shrinking patch of pale sky and hung there for a time…too long of a time. He took a few steps sideways to gain a different perspective but no matter where he stood the result was the same: the ball was stuck fast at the apex of its flight. Then an even stranger thing happened. The ball appeared to be heading *back* toward him. Just as Campbell convinced himself that he was seeing things, it landed softly at the front edge of the tee box and rolled to a stop at his feet.

Now the American was sure that he heard laughter from the woods on his right—and more than anything else Jack Campbell hated to be laughed at.

"All right, you devils have your fun if you want, but ghosts or no ghosts, I'm going to finish this round." He clenched his jaw, preparing to strike the ball once more. But the white sphere jumped straight into the air, to be whisked away over his head and deep into the ravine.

"I'll just get another," Campbell cried defiantly. As he reached for his bag, it slid silently away from him. He chased after it but it was pulled from his reach again...and again...and again...until Campbell found himself running down the fairway as fast as he could manage. Yet still, the bag outdistanced him, vanishing into the night.

"Bring it back, you bastards!"

To Campbell's astonishment the bag materialized out of the dark and stood before him. He took a pace forward, and one by one the various clubs lifted out to surround him in a picket line of steel and wood.

"Out of my way!" demanded Campbell, taking another step toward his bag. The wedge suddenly swung on its own and struck him on the right shin. A bolt of white-hot pain shot up the American's leg and he shrieked. He tried to break out of the circle and the two-iron sliced through the still night to hit him in the shoulder. Next it was the driver's turn, then the putter's, then the five-iron's, then the nine's, beating him back up the fairway, across the tee, through the rough until finally, bruised and bloodied from the onslaught, Campbell found himself on the edge of the ravine with nowhere left to run.

Then he remembered his cell phone and frantically yanked it from his back pocket. He hit the power button and dialed for the operator. Someone answered on the third ring.

"Help me!" he screamed before the other party had a chance to speak. "Get the police, I'm being attacked!"

"Are ye now?" answered an oddly hollow voice from the other side.

"Wh…who is this?"

"I am the Laird MacDonald," answered the voice, "and ye're nae going anywhere…*Campbell*." The last word was spat at him from some lost and hateful place.

Campbell turned off the phone, but it rang in his hand almost immediately.

"Now why did ye do that, laddie, when we were having such a nice conversation? We've waited a long time for a Campbell ta dare show his face again in the glen—we're ever so glad ye came."

The American eyed the menacing clubs around him. "What do you want with me?"

"That's simple, we'll be wanting yer life's blood."

"Listen," Campbell reasoned, "I'm just an American businessman out for a round of golf. I had nothing to do with what happened here."

"Yer name *is* Campbell, is it nae? And ye are wearing the tartan."

Campbell looked down at the socks peeking out from a rip in his pant leg, and cursed. "But I'm not responsible!"

One of the clubs rose and poked him hard in the chest. He retreated a step and felt his foot slip over the edge. "It's not fair!" he wailed.

"*Fair?*" roared the voice from the handset as an icy wind howled up from the ravine to freeze Campbell's spine. "Were ye being fair when ye came out o' the snow ta slaughter yer brother clan? Were ye being fair when ye repaid our kindness with the point o' yer claymores? Were ye being fair when ye snuck up on us unarmed in our beds? Were ye being fair when ye did nae spare the lasses or the children?" the Laird MacDonald demanded. "Do ye call any o' that fair?"

"It was the 1600s for God's sake!" Campbell struggled to maintain his balance. "I wasn't even there!"

"Very well," answered the voice, "let nae man say that the MacDonalds are nae a just folk. We'll give ye a chance."

"A chance?" the American asked hopefully.

"Aye." Two balls appeared from nowhere to land on the tee. "One hole, winner takes all."

"What does that mean?"

"It means that if ye win or even halve the hole ye'll get to keep on drawing a warm breath."

"And if I lose?"

"Well, let's just call this hole sudden death—in the true spirit o' the words." The driver floated to one of the balls and waggled over it. "I'll play first ta show ye the way."

"Wait. You have the advantage since I can't see in the dark."

The phone let out a hideous screech and two green and red streaks shot out of the ravine to wrap around each ball until they glowed with their own light. Another bolt of eerie flame screamed toward the pin and engulfed the flag. Then the driver swung and sent the Laird's ball high and deep into the fairway. Faint cheers and hoots issued from around the tee as Campbell took the club offered by his invisible foe. The grip was bone-chilling cold and he had to force his hands to grasp it firmly. When he swung, the ball flew off the club and sailed down the left side, leaving a ghostly trail in its wake. The sound of mocking applause greeted him as he walked to his ball, escorted by the tiny forest of marching clubs.

The Laird hit another fine shot that landed on the green, but Campbell, feeling the deadly pressure, pulled his second badly, hooking it into the trees. As he neared the edge of the woods he could see his ball glowing near the base of an old elm. He could also see that it was raining in the forest, with fat drops of liquid falling to spatter the ground. He didn't know how he knew but he was sure that it was blood dripping from the leaves…MacDonald blood. The phone rang again in his pocket.

"What?" Campbell answered angrily.

"Nae a thing, laddie," chuckled the voice, "only that I would nae go in there if I were ye."

But what choice did he have? It was play or die. With a deep breath Campbell stepped beneath the canopy of leaves and into the evil precipitation. It stung him like acid wherever it struck his exposed skin and ate holes through his clothing, quickly reducing them to rags. When he finally reached his ball, one look toward the hole told him of the futility of his quest—it would take a miracle shot just to reach the fairway.

"Damn you, Jack Campbell," he cried in despair, *"you spent the entire day in play with not so much as a whiff of the rough and now, now with*

everything on the line you hit it in the freaking trees!" And for the first time in his adult life tears spilled over Campbell's face, mixing with the blood to fall and hiss on the flaming ball between his feet.

With no hope in his heart, he brought the club down in a mighty arc that sent the ball rocketing through the forest like a demented missile, skirting a host of trunks, avoiding scores of limbs, dodging a myriad of leaves as it accomplished its impossible mission by striking the pin and falling close to the cup.

Campbell burst from the trees in joy and strutted to the green where the Laird MacDonald was already rolling his next shot within inches of the hole. An invisible hand removed the flag in silence and the ball was tapped in for par.

Campbell stood over his putt with a mixture of glee and disdain. But just as he drew back the club, just as he was about to bury the ball into the heart of the cup, he saw them: the MacDonalds—the dead clan—still dressed in their blood-spattered bedclothes. The young and the old, the weak and the strong, the fair and the fey. Many of them dismembered, some of them headless, all of them grim and watchful as they pressed around him—a silent gallery of misery. Their ghastly patriarch stood just to Campbell's left with the pin clutched in a rotting hand. He leaned his cloven head close to the American's. "Remember now lad, there's nae gimmes."

And with this visage of horror fresh in his mind, Jack Campbell played his final shot.

*   *   *

These days, if you are fortunate enough to visit the links at Glencoe, you'll find the sky a wee bit bluer, the woods a tad less dark, the loch still as glass and the music floating up from the river, dwelling on the lighter notes. The locals say the banshees have gone, just up and disappeared one day. All save for one, that is. You can find him almost any night out on the 18th green, a truly wretched creature, wailing in anguish as he misses the same short putt over and over and over again.

ON THE FRINGE

BY G. GUILFORD BARTON

Continuing the Series
Golf Is No Ordinary Game

*O*n the *Fringe* is a story about another dimension, one visible only to those bold enough to believe in its existence. Such a place is not as farfetched as one might think since we, too, are surrounded by an unseen world and an unseen war. Ever the history buff, I use the tale to pay homage to Winston Churchill's "few" and to those blessed souls who choose to walk by faith and not by sight.

ON THE FRINGE

F light Leftenant Owen Lancaster never went anywhere without his golf clubs. Not even Hitler and the Blitz could keep the lad off the courses of South London, whose many new bunkers were the result of stray bombs courtesy of the *Luftwaffe*.

When he enlisted in the RAF during the summer of 1941 Owen took his clubs with him. He had been flying Spitfires for less than a month when they sent his squadron to Northern Scotland, on the slim chance the Germans might try to sneak a flock of bombers in the back door and hit the tank factories at Glasgow. Initially Owen was excited at being stationed in the home of his favorite pastime, but his euphoria evaporated when he learned that the nearest links were over fifty miles away in Inverness. So he spent his days by the radio with his mates, waiting anxiously for either the war to come to him or he to it. At night he did what all fliers worth their wings do: he hit the local pub.

Late one evening Owen found himself alone at the bar after his fellow pilots had staggered back to their makeshift barracks. As he slouched there on his stool the barman placed a full pint of ale in front of him.

Owen glanced up at him. "What's all this?"

The barman nodded toward a table by the wall. "*He* sent it over for ye."

Owen turned and saw a gnarled figure huddled in a chair and hoisting a pint of his own in the pilot's direction. The room was almost empty, save for a few knots of local men, so the young airman picked up his beer and went over to thank the old fellow.

"Who are you?" Owen asked.

"A patriot," replied the stranger.

"Well, thanks for the beer anyhow."

The old man motioned for Owen to take a seat. "Where are ye from?"

"London," the flier answered but remained on his feet, hesitant to get himself trapped with the old gent.

"You're a golfer, then?" the man asked with a twinkle in his eye.

"How did you know that?"

"Just something about the way ye hold yourself. I bet ye're a fair player."

Owen sat down. "Truth is, I happen to be the club champion back home. If it hadn't been for the war I might have even tried to qualify for this year's Open at Turnberry."

"Aye, that would've been grand." The old man sipped at his beer. "Bloody war's caused too much hardship."

"Yes," agreed Owen, "I'd give anything for a round about now."

"Then why don't ye?"

"Why don't I what?"

"Play a round."

Owen gazed deep into his ale. "The closest course is over toward Inverness."

The old Scot chuckled at this. "Did nae one tell ye about the one outside o' town?"

Owen looked up, startled. "What? Where?"

"Out on the north end o' the moor. Have ye nae seen it from the air, then?"

"Never noticed it. We don't fly over that part of the moor much."

"Ye must play it and tell me what ye think o' it."

Owen grinned at the thought. "I'll do that." He drained the last of his ale and stood to leave. "I should get back to the airfield. Never know when the Jerrys might try something. Thanks again for the pint."

"I live in a yellow cottage near the first tee," the old man said. "Visit anytime ye please."

* * *

On his next patrol Owen detoured his Spitfire over the northern end of the moor, and sure enough, there was a course laid out just as the old man had said there would be. He made out eighteen fairways — nine going out and nine more coming home — with ten greens, eight of them double greens. A lone golfer looked up from the 17th tee and waved at him as he zoomed overhead. Owen waggled his wing tips and made note of the little yellow house before turning back toward base. He landed his fighter on the grassy field and rolled it to a stop beside his wingman's plane.

As he climbed out of the cockpit his mechanic ran up. "The CO wants to see you, Owen."

"What for?"

"How should I know?" The mechanic lifted off the engine, cowling. "He just said for me to tell you to report to his tent the moment you landed."

Owen pulled off his life jacket and leather helmet and carried them into the CO's tent. "You wanted to see me, sir?"

"Yes, Lancaster." Squadron Leader Higgins glanced up from a stack of weather reports. "Pitlow tells me you peeled off today and went sightseeing by yourself. That true?"

"Yes, sir."

Higgins looked back down at the gloomy weather bulletins. "Why?"

Owen fidgeted for a moment, not knowing what to tell his CO. Finally he decided on the truth. "I was looking for a golf course that I'd heard rumored about in town."

"What in heaven's name for?"

"Thought I might get the chance to get a round in sometime."

"Hmmmph," grunted Higgins. "First off, you know the rules: no going solo on patrol. You either stay with your wingman or you stay on the ground. Understood?"

"Yes, sir."

The officer rose from his desk and stood looking out the door, with his hands behind his back. "Second, there are no golf courses in this vicinity."

"Sure there are," insisted Owen.

"Where?"

"On the northern moor."

"Impossible."

"But I just saw it!"

Higgins returned to his desk and picked up a reconnaissance photograph. He handed it to the young pilot. "Here, see for yourself. This was taken two days ago."

Owen studied the photo, recognizing the chalky bluffs and barren rock-strewn fields past the north end of town. But where the links should have been he saw only desolate moor and a few flocks of grazing sheep. "I...don't understand, sir, I just saw it with my own eyes."

"Well, fortunately I do understand, Lancaster. Too much beer and not enough sleep. The pub's off limits for two weeks' time...and you're grounded for five days." Higgins sat down again and went back to his weather reports. "Dismissed."

"But, sir..."

"I *said* you're dismissed."

Owen immediately went to the barracks, which was really just a converted barn, and gave his wingman an earful. "Thanks a lot, Billy, you got me banned from the *Shivering Ewe* for a whole bloody fortnight."

Bill Pitlow lowered his week-old London Times and looked up from the bunk he was stretched out on. "Don't go blaming me, Lancaster. You know you're not supposed to leave my wing and go joyriding on your own."

Owen tossed his flight jacket on a nearby chair. "You could've covered for me."

"Higgins was waiting on the field when I got back. What was I supposed to say? That you had to stop and use the loo?"

Owen plopped himself down on the bunk next to Pitlow's. "I'm grounded until Monday."

Pitlow shrugged. "Could be worse. Did you find your golf course?"

"Yes," Owen answered, "and no." He ran a hand through his sandy blond hair and described what he had seen and his subsequent encounter with his CO. "It's the damnedest thing, Billy, I could swear that I saw it down there."

"You probably saw what you wanted to see," reasoned Pitlow.

"But what about the golfer? He waved at me."

Pitlow shrugged again. "We've seen a lot of strange things up there, Owen. Maybe he just *looked* like a golfer. It was probably just a shepherd."

Owen sighed. "I guess you're right."

Pitlow sat up. "Listen, you've got five days on the ground. Why not hike out that way and take a look for yourself?"

*   *   *

While the rest of the squadron flew patrol the following afternoon, Owen strolled through town and out onto the moor that bordered it to the north. He spent two hours exploring the wild landscape, extending his search right to the edge of the cliffs that fell away into the cold sea. Nowhere did he come across anything that resembled a golf hole. As dusk approached he gave up and wandered back toward town. Spotting the old man's cottage, Owen strode through the rickety gate and knocked on the weathered door. The occupant answered so quickly that Owen wondered if he had been standing on the other side.

The old Scot stood aside to let Owen into the house. "I've been waiting for ye."

The young pilot stepped into the dim and sparsely furnished room. "You have?"

"Aye, I saw ye out on the moor this afternoon." The old man motioned him further into his humble lodging. "Have a seat, lad."

Owen chose a chair by the sputtering fire and settled into it. "I was looking for that course you mentioned the other night."

The old man's eyes glittered in the firelight as he regarded the airman with amusement. "And did ye find it, now?"

"No," Owen said, "only sheep and rocks."

The Scotsman nodded but said nothing. He took a pipe from the nearby table, lighting it with a stick from the fire.

Owen fidgeted in his chair. "But it's there, isn't it?"

"Aye," the old fellow said, releasing a cloud of smoke that twirled its way up to the low ceiling, where it spread along the dark beams.

"How come I could see it from the air yesterday but not from the ground today?"

"Ah, if I knew the answer to that I'd surely tell ye." The Scot leaned back in his chair. "Sometimes it's there and sometimes it's nae there.

Ye can nae always see it and nae everyone has the ability in the first place. Some folk have lived their entire lives around here and have never seen it once."

"Then how come you were so sure that I'd be able to?"

"I told ye it's the way ye hold yourself, the way ye look out at the world, that tells me ye can see things that others can nae."

The two fell silent for a time and studied the fire burning in the ancient hearth. Finally Owen stirred. "Will I see it again?"

"Who can say?" The old man shrugged his bony shoulders. "Do ye wish to?"

Owen leaned forward in the firelight. "Yes."

"Then meet me here tomorrow at noon. And bring your clubs."

*　　*　　*

Just before noon the next day Owen grabbed his battered golf bag and left the tent. Pitlow sat outside. "Where in bloody hell are you off to?"

"Into town."

Pitlow eyed the clubs and said, "What for?"

"For a round."

"Don't tell me you're still on about the blooming course that ain't there?"

"I saw it, I tell you!"

"And I saw Heinrich Himmler doing a jig outside of the *Shivering Ewe* a week last Tuesday," retorted Pitlow. When Owen made to leave, his friend stood and grabbed him by the elbow. "Listen to me, Owen, this is serious. You can't go stooging about, chasing unicorns and fairies and hope to keep your wings. The lads are already talking about it, saying how they wouldn't want you for a wingman."

Owen looked him in the eyes. "And is that how you feel, Billy?"

"To tell you the truth, I'm beginning to wonder," Pitlow said. "Makes a chap kind of nervous to think his wingman might be seeing things. You know what it's like in a dogfight—chaotic as hell. What if you mistake my Spitfire for a ME-109, swearing you saw the German Cross on the wings?"

"That's not going to happen, Billy." Owen turned to go. "I'm not daft."

"Then stop acting like you are!" cried Pitlow at his friend's back.

Owen hiked to the yellow cottage and stood in the front yard. Looking out across the moor he saw only unkempt grass and rocks protruding up from the soil in a haphazard pattern. The old man appeared at his door but said nothing.

"Not today?" Owen asked.

"Nae."

"Tomorrow, then?"

"Aye. Good day to ye." The old Scot retreated back into his house.

They repeated the same ritual four days in a row.

*   *   *

Owen stood on the garden path and glared at the wild expanse before him. He turned and knocked curtly on the cottage door.

When the old man opened the door, Owen shoved a finger in his face. "I've been here every day just as you asked."

"Ye must be patient."

"But this is the last day I can come!"

"Fretting will nae make it show itself, lad," the Scotsman said. Then he glanced over the young man's shoulder. "Then again, perhaps it will."

Owen spun around...and there were the links. Where only moments before, gorse and rocks met his gaze, lush fairways and distant greens now spread out at his feet.

"I don't believe it," the flier said.

"Aye," chuckled the old man, "it can be a wee bit unnerving. Let me grab me clubs." He vanished into the gloomy interior and reappeared a few moments later with an ancient-looking bag of clubs slung over his shoulder. Together they walked the handful of yards to the 1st tee.

As Owen prepared to strike his first shot the Scotsman leaned close. "I must warn ye now, laddie, ye're likely to see things as ye make your way around."

Owen relaxed his stance. "What kind of things?"

"Strange things. Fey things. Wondrous things. The past and the future. Things that are nae really there."

Owen looked out onto the course. "I see."

"Nae, ye don't, but ye will."

As they played the first few holes Owen kept imagining that he heard the bleating of sheep from somewhere close by, but whenever he looked around there were none in sight. Finally he asked his playing partner about it.

"Aye, they're there," the old Scot said as his lined up a short putt.

"Where?"

"They're on another plane, lad, another dimension…but they're there, nonetheless."

As Owen lined up his approach to the 6th green he spotted a lovely young woman in a sheer white gown strolling across the neighboring fairway. She appeared headed for the cliffs. "Who's that?"

"Ahhhh, now," the old man remarked sadly, "that is Maureen MacDaniels. She was the fairest lass this town has ever known."

"What do you mean *was*?" Owen said, gazing after the alluring figure.

"She died at the tender age o' seventeen some twenty-two years ago."

Owen dropped his club. "What?"

"It's the past ye're seeing now, lad."

"How did she die?"

"She took her own life."

"A beautiful young girl like that? But why?"

"When she was but sixteen she took a lover, an older boy who was called off to fight in the Great War," recounted the old man. "He refused to marry her before going but promised to do so upon his return from the battlefield. Poor Maureen learned o' his death on the same day that she discovered she was carrying his child. She came from a strict Catholic family. Only disgrace, shame and banishment awaited her."

The girl skirted the edge of the cliff now, looking down into the waves.

"How did she do it?"

"She cast herself into the sea."

As he said this the girl suddenly spread her arms and leaned over the edge, disappearing in a billow of white fabric.

"My God!" Owen cried in horror. "Why didn't you say something sooner? I could've stopped her!"

The Scotsman shook his gray head. "Ye canna change the past, lad."

Two holes later Owen and the old man were putting on a double green when he noticed another golfer approaching. He had just made the turn and was playing from the 10th fairway. The golfer had a beautifully fluid swing, and his mid-iron shot seemed to float on the salt air before falling softly to the green. Owen watched him stride up the fairway. "I think that's Bobby Jones."

"Can't be," the old man said.

"Sure looks like him."

"Impossible…"

"Maybe, but it's still him."

The great American stepped onto the putting surface looking slightly bewildered. "I don't mean to disturb your game, gentlemen," he said in a soft Southern drawl, "but what is this place? Does it have a name?"

"Not one that's official," the old Scot answered, "but some o' the folks in these parts call it *The Fringe.*"

Jones smiled at this news, obviously pleased with the name.

"What brings you to our humble town?" Owen asked, somewhat in shock at his proximity to such greatness.

Bobby leaned on his putter. "Funny you should ask. I was on the road to Loch Ness—to see the Monster," he added with a wink and a grin, "when I saw this here course scattered against the cliffs. There was a shimmer in the air around it, like the kind you see in a mirage. And somehow I knew that I had to play it, and that so few get the chance and even fewer take advantage of it. I've been playing since early morning. Just going 'round and around. Wonderful layout, challenging greens, but not another golfer in sight. I was just beginning to wonder if I was hallucinating the whole thing when I spotted you gentlemen."

Owen chuckled. "Maybe we're all hallucinating."

"Then it's a marvelous illusion," Bobby said contentedly, gazing out across the fairway. "Well, I need to be in Inverness before supper so I best be on my way." The American walked to his ball, and following a brief lining up, stroked it into the heart of the cup. As he strode to the next tee he waved. "Farewell, and best of luck with the rest of your round."

* * *

The two played the back nine with no further visions besides the uncanny beauty of the course itself. But on the final hole they heard a sound, a deep rumble blowing in from across the sea.

Owen gazed out over the gray waves. "What's that?"

"I don' know," replied the old Scot. "Never heard the likes o' it before."

The sound increased noticeably as they listened, and the young flier suddenly went rigid. "I know that sound. I heard it back in South London dozens of times. They're bombers—German bombers."

As they watched, a line of black specks appeared low on the horizon. "I have to warn the squadron," Owen cried, and turned to run back to the airfield.

The old man grabbed him by the sleeve. "You're too late, lad." Off to their left a swarm of Spitfires and Hurricanes roared past and streaked over the cliff tops.

"Give 'em what for!" Owen shouted over the din. The British fighters closed the gap with remarkable ease and dove toward the flock of bombers. They failed to see Messerschmitts fall out of the clouds above them.

"Look out, lads!" screamed Owen as the German fighters lined up his mates in their gun sights. "On your tail, Pitlow!"

The toy-like clatter of distant machine gun fire reached Owen's ears even as his wingman's plane burst into flames and spun toward the waiting sea. The horrified pilot watched helplessly as half his squadron was shot down or crippled within seconds of the engagement. The other half turned to face the new threat, giving the bombers a clear path inland. The big planes continued on toward the coastline with only a single Spitfire in pursuit. Whoever the pilot was, he focused solely on the bombers, paying no heed to the two Messerschmitts that hounded him. The RAF airman released two quick bursts from his guns and one of the bombers spouted a column of smoke from its left engine. Another burst and the entire wing broke away, sending the bomber tumbling into the surf.

Owen let out a great whoop. "That's giving it to 'em!" Even the old man cheered. Then the lead German fighter opened up and riddled the side of the Spitfire with bullets. The British flier immediately peeled away and turned for home hoping to save his mortally wounded plane, but it was obvious he would never make it. Losing altitude fast, the most the pilot could hope for was to reach the moor and avoid crashing into the cliff face. He aimed his plane toward a spot close to where Owen and the old man stood.

"Don't be a fool," Owen whispered, "you can't land here; it's too rocky." Looking around him, all Owen saw was wide-open fairway, but he knew the rocks were there—he could feel their deadly presence. "Bail out. Ditch in the sea. Don't be a fool!"

But the fighter came on. The fragile Spitfire missed the cliffs with a bare three feet to spare and touched lightly down on the moor. And for a moment it seemed like the brave soul just might make it, just might be rewarded for his act of heroism—then the plane exploded in a ball of fire. For Owen and the old man it was an odd sight. To their eyes it appeared that the pilot had a clear field to maneuver in. They couldn't see the boulder that suddenly crumpled the fuselage and drove the 12-cylinder Rolls Royce engine back into the pilot, killing him even before the fuel had time to ignite.

Out over the sea the fighters continued to do battle. The old man looked at the burning wreck of the Spitfire. "He was a brave lad, whoever he was."

Owen, who had noted the number on the tail of the doomed British fighter, nodded, his eyes filled with fear and anger. He looked up to watch the bombers pass overhead like a flock of great dark carrion birds. "That brave lad was me."

"What's that ye say?"

"That was me at the stick; that was *my* kite."

"Then it's the future we're seeing now," the old Scot said with relief. "And the future *can* be changed. Ye must hurry!"

"Why? What makes you think it'll happen soon?"

He pointed a bony finger at the road that wound along the edge of the course. "Ye see that lorry?" Owen spotted a tank truck that had braked in the middle of the road, the driver leaning his head out the window to gape at the bombers passing overhead. "That's our petrol ration from Edinburgh. Comes the first Friday o' every month. Like clockwork, really..."

But Owen was already running for town. It was the first Friday in June.

* * *

Owen dashed into the squadron leader's tent without bothering to knock. "Germans, sir!" He bent over, trying to catch his breath. "Bombers coming in from the north!"

Higgins put down his incessant weather reports and regarded the young pilot tiredly. "What *are* you talking about, Lancaster? First it's golf courses that aren't there and now it's phantom bombing raids?"

"It's not a phantom raid. It's real—I saw it."

The officer held out his arms. "Then where the bloody hell are they? We've had no word from group control or our advance spotters along the coast."

"It hasn't happened yet," Owen said, trying to sound as rational as he could. "But it will, and soon."

"And just where were you when you *saw* these bombers?" Higgins asked with sarcasm.

"On the moor," Owen replied, knowing what his superior's next question would be.

"Playing golf, I suppose?"

"Yes, sir."

"On the course that's not there?"

"Yes, sir. I mean, no, sir—"

"Leftenant, I thought I gave you strict orders to keep away from the *Shivering Ewe*."

"Do I look drunk, sir?" Owen leaned across the desk and fixed the officer with a steady gaze.

"No, as a matter of fact, you don't."

"Then please listen to me," pleaded the pilot. "I know it sounds completely crazy but it *will* happen; they *will* come. What harm would it be to scramble the squadron north just for a look? If there's nothing there we can all come back and have a nice long laugh at my expense. You can even have me court-martialed if you wish. What harm would it do?"

The CO picked up his pen and returned his gaze back to the reports. "It would be a waste of petrol," he said primly. "That will be all, Leftenant."

"But sir—"

"THAT WILL BE ALL!"

* * *

Owen left Higgins' tent and found Pitlow napping in the shade of his Spitfire's wing.

"Wake up, Billy." He shook his wingman by the shoulder. "We've got a mission to fly."

Pitlow opened his eyes and peered sleepily up at his friend. "I thought you were grounded."

"I am, but we still have a mission."

The other flier stretched and looked around the airfield. "Then where is everybody?"

"It's just you and me, mate. We're flying north to look for German bombers."

"You're daft," Pitlow laughed. "Does the CO know about this?"

Owen gave a half smile. "Sort of."

"If you think I'm going to risk my wings, not to mention my neck, to go joyriding with you—"

"Fine," Owen snapped, pulling on his leather helmet. "I'll go alone, then."

He began to climb the ladder into his plane and Pitlow grabbed him by a boot. "You'll be court-martialed."

"Maybe, but I'm still going."

Pitlow grinned up at him. "For King and for Country?"

Owen laughed and nodded. "For King and for Country."

"Well, why didn't you just say so in the first place?" Pitlow dashed for his fighter. They donned their life vests and parachutes and strapped themselves in. Before the rest of the squadron knew what was happening the two Spitfires were lifting their wheels off the grassy runway.

Squadron Leader Higgins rushed out of his tent. "Who's that? What are they up to? I authorized no mission."

One of the other fliers shaded his eyes. "It's Lancaster and Pitlow, sir."

"Bugger it," Higgins muttered under his breath as he stalked off to the radio tent.

* * *

"Tell me what we're looking for again, Owen, me lad," Pitlow called over the radio as the two planes flew north.

"The German *Luftwaffe*."

"Righto! Shouldn't be hard to spot."

Squadron Leader Higgins' voice intruded into their headsets. "Lancaster, Pitlow…come in."

"Here, sir," replied Owen.

"Then I order you to stop being *there* at once and to return *here* with your kite…immediately!"

"Won't do, sir; we're on a mission."

"Blast your mission, Lancaster!" shouted the CO. "Pitlow, what are you doing up there?"

"I'm staying with my wingman, sir."

"Don't get smart, Pitlow. You're in enough trouble as it is. What did that maniac tell you?"

"He said the Krauts are on the way."

"He also thinks there's a golf course out on the blooming moor," retorted Higgins. "Now turn around, both of you, and get back here before I order you shot down!"

"Look down, Billy," Owen said, peering through his cockpit canopy as they passed over the moor. "Tell the squadron leader what you see."

Pitlow craned forward: "Bloody hell!" Below his wings stretched a long fairway that ended in a picture-perfect green, its red flag billowing toward the north in the stiff breeze that blew out to sea. "It's…it's a golf course, sir."

"Repeat that Pitlow; you're breaking up. Did you say golf course?"

"Yes, sir, just like Owen described."

A few moments of dead silence followed, then Higgins was in their ears again.

"You two circle the cliffs and wait for us. I'm scrambling the entire squadron!"

*　*　*

When the fighters had formed up they headed straight out to sea. They had not gone more than a few miles when Pitlow's excited voice called over the radio: "Tally-ho! Jerrys at eleven o'clock low!"

"Right, lads," Higgins calmly ordered. "Peel off in pairs and engage."

"No!" shouted Owen.

"What is it now, Lancaster?"

"Messerschmitt 109s above us. We've got to deal with them first."

 Higgins searched the sky above him "Where? I don't see anything."

"They're in the clouds, sir."

"How do you know that?"

"I just know!"

"Remember the golf course, sir," reminded Pitlow.

"Right!" the squadron leader cried. "Up we go, lads."

One by one the fighters turned their noses skyward, and as they rose the German fighters descended from their hiding place. But this time *they* were the ones taken off guard. After five minutes of fierce dogfighting the Germans were routed and the remaining British fighters turned their attention back to the bombers—all except for Owen and his Spitfire.

He had been following the descent of a wounded Messerschmitt when a banking 109 strafed a row of bullets across his fuselage. Losing altitude fast, Owen turned toward the coast. Now he knew why he hadn't bailed out or ditched in the sea: the bullets had shattered both his legs, making it impossible to escape his coffin-like cockpit. His only chance was to make for the moor.

Pitlow saw him first and realized in a moment what his friend intended. "Owen, don't be a fool, you'll never make it."

"No choice, Billy."

"Bail out. Ditch in the sea!"

"I can't move my legs; it's the moor or nothing."

He could clearly see that the course was gone; only the rock-strewn pasture awaited him. "It's there," he whispered. "I know it's there."

"Good luck, Owen," Pitlow offered sadly.

"It's there…"

"Godspeed, Lancaster," Squadron Leader Higgins radioed quietly.

"I know it's there!"

His wheels missed the cliffs with a bare three feet to spare and touched lightly down on the moor. And for a moment it seemed like he might not make it, that he might not be rewarded for his act of heroism—then the fighter rolled to a gentle stop above the windblown cliffs. For the others it was an odd sight. To their eyes it appeared that Owen and his plane had passed clear through the boulder that stood directly in his path. They couldn't see the 10th fairway that greeted Owen's watering eyes an instant before his wheels touched home.

*   *   *

Leftenant Owen Lancaster never flew his Spitfire again. Crippled for the rest of his life, he never walked again either. Not counting, of course, the many days he spent out *On the Fringe*, lovingly playing the game that had saved his life.

CONTINUING THE SERIES
GOLF IS NO ORDINARY GAME

OLD

TOM

G GUILFORD BARTON

The game of golf has many storied heroes. Jones, Hogan, Palmer and Nicklaus easily come to mind. Other greats can be found further back in the dim halls of golf's pantheon, like Harry Vardon and Francis Ouimet. But there is one man whose shadow, in my humble opinion, eclipses them all—a larger than life Scotsman by the name of Old Tom Morris.

OLD TOM

T he Senior Member of the club bolted awake as Charlie McDoon began to howl with laughter from a nearby chair. The old fellow had nodded off by the clubhouse fire and, thoroughly cross at having his peaceful interlude interrupted, roused himself and went over to see what all the fuss was about. He found the young man knee deep in Volume I of Manchester's *A History of Golf*, that massive tome loaded with glossy full-page color plates depicting 19th century golfers in the various stages of play, sporting such helpful captions as "The correct use of the putting cleek." With each turn of the page Charlie let loose another mirthful hoot, reminiscent of the time he had holed out the 525-yard 16th in 3.

"And just what do you find so amusing, Mr. McDoon," inquired the Senior Member, "that you feel you have to wail like a banshee every time I'm about to make myself comfortable?"

"Sorry, sir." Charlie stifled another laugh. "I just can't get over these portraits of ancient golfers hacking their way through prehistory."

The Senior Member frowned and peered over Charlie's shoulder. "I fail to see the humor, Charles. Those men and women are our forebears, and many are of the opinion that they played the Game in its purest form."

"Pure golf? You can't be serious!" McDoon pointed down to the book. "Just look at some of these swings. It's a miracle that they could hit the ball at all, let alone go 'round in less than 200."

"It may be true that the scores were not as low as those of the modern era," admitted the Senior Member. "But glossy full-page color plates don't always give the total picture, so to speak. Times were different back then and the game of golf was no exception, yet our founding fathers managed remarkably well while coping with conditions and circumstances that you and I would find most daunting."

"Ha! Why, I could whip any of these so called 'champions' without even bothering to keep my head still." Charlie turned to a new page. "Take this old coot (no offense, sir), here on Plate No. 36—just get a load of that follow-through."

The Senior Member pursed his pale lips. "That, Charles, is Old Tom Morris."

"Yeah, so?"

"He just happens to be one of the Fathers of the Game, the Keeper of the Golfing Grail, if you will, and you had best not poke fun at his form if you know what's good for you."

Charlie chuckled. "Why, what's he going to do? Show up on the 1st tee and crack his knuckles in the middle of my back swing?"

"Laugh if you must, my boy," said the Senior Member in a hushed voice, "but legend has it that his spirit still roams the links at St. Andrews."

"Well, this isn't Scotland and I think the breadth of the Atlantic would be a bit of a long distance haunt for any ghost—even if he did win the British Open four times." McDoon glanced at his watch. "Yikes, I'm late for my round with Simms." He smirked at his elderly companion. "Wish me luck?"

"Bah!" snorted the Senior Member with a dismissive wave of a spotted hand. He did not approve of mismatches, and Simms' 18 handicap withered in the brightness of McDoon's 6.

Charlie rose to leave. "You know something—I wish I *were* off to play that Morris fellow instead. Mind you it still wouldn't be much of a match, but at least it might prove interesting."

The Senior Member watched him go with a sigh. He was somewhat fond of Charlie, but the young man's youthful arrogance could prove to be a bit tiresome at times. He recalled Charlie's final salvo and shook his head, knowing from long experience that one needed to be very careful what one wished for on a golf course.

* * *

The autumn sun shone brightly on Charlie as he made his way to the 1ˢᵗ tee. He paused to admire the manicured fairway and smiled, beginning to warm up to the idea of giving Simms his weekly thrashing. It was while in the midst of this happy thought that he was struck by the errant drive of Arnold Remlap, the club's resident hacker. Unfortunately, Mr. Remlap's cry of "fore" arrived well after his ball and the sound of the ensuing impact with Charlie's head was not unlike that of a well-struck fairway wood played from a good lie.

When he came to, Charlie found an old gentleman looming over him.

"Are ye all right, lad?" asked the stranger in a rich Scottish burr.

"Yeah, I think so." Charlie massaged the lump on the back of his head as he scrutinized his new companion. The fellow was a big man with a great white beard, a tweed jacket and cap and an old-fashioned pair of plus-fours—the overall effect struck Charlie as oddly familiar.

"Well, how about a game, then?" said the stranger with a gleam in his eye.

Something about that gleam made Charlie—who was not one prone to self-doubt—a little uneasy. "I'd love to, really, but I'm already late for my match with Simms."

The stranger laughed. "I don't think ye'll find him here, laddie."

"What do you mean? I saw him warming up in front of the club-house just a few minutes ago." Charlie turned to point. It took only a single glance to tell him that something was very much amiss.

Towering over him was an ancient stone edifice, its stately facade chiseled and worn by centuries of wind and brine from the nearby sea. (This was his biggest clue of trouble since Charlie's clubhouse was located in the middle of Kansas.) He also noticed that suddenly the day had turned cold, with a howling wind blowing in off the iron-gray waves. The renewed impression of familiarity made him more than a little uneasy. He glanced up at the writing carved above the doorway: The Royal & Ancient Golf Club.

Charlie peered over his shoulder. "Your name wouldn't happen to be Morris, would it?"

"Aye."

"In that case, you must excuse me," sputtered Charlie as he tried to make good his escape. "I just remembered that I have a very important appointment with Arnold Remlap's driver—"

"Nae, laddie," said Old Tom Morris as he arrested McDoon's flight with a burly hand. "We've got a date on the links first."

Charlie regarded the impressive character before him and realized that the Senior Member had been right after all: glossy full-page color plates don't always give the whole picture. All of a sudden the thought of playing golf with this uncanny Scotsman had lost all of its appeal. Fortunately for Charlie it was time for his "youthful arrogance" to tap him on the shoulder and demand his full attention.

So what, if you're in Scotland? it said silkily in his ear.

Yeah, so what? thought Charlie brightly.

So what if the weather's a bit nasty? cooed his ego.

Yeah! What's a little weather? Charlie's eyes caught fire.

So what if he's a ghost? The flame in Charlie's eyes flickered, and the voice quickly added: *Never mind that! You still have your single-digit handicap, right?*

Right.

Now, get out there and kick some Highland butt!

Charlie McDoon stood up to his full height and looked the Scot in the eye. "Just let me get my clubs." But when he bent down to retrieve them, he found in their stead an old leather bag full of an assortment of oddly-shaped sticks.

Old Tom smiled wickedly.

Charlie scratched his head. "Hey, where are my clubs?"

"Those *are* yer clubs, man."

"My clubs?"

"Aye."

"My…golf clubs?"

"Aye!"

"Funny," puzzled Charlie, "but I distinctly recall purchasing a set of perimeter-weighted, stainless steel, offset-aligned, graphite-shafted irons just last month."

"Laddie," said Tom, with a shake of his tweed-covered head, "last month will nae happen for another hundred and forty years."

"So what if it's 1850?" reasoned the voice.

Charlie's knees trembled. "Yeah, so what?" He removed one of the clubs and began to waggle it, then peered closely at the club face. "Are these square grooves? I play much better with square grooves, you know."

Old Tom just glared at McDoon and handed him a small sphere that he had pulled from the pocket of his jacket.

"What's this supposed to be?" asked Charlie.

"That's a featherie," replied Tom with another sly grin.

"A what?"

"A featherie!"

"Beg your pardon?"

"A featherie!" shouted Tom. "Are ye deaf, man?"

"What's a featherie?"

"It's a golf ball!"

Charlie examined the hard leather orb, turning it over and over as if looking for something. Presently he handed it back to Morris. "Sorry, but I only play a Titleist."

Old Tom gave it right back to him. "Ye'll find nae such thin' around here."

Charlie shrugged and subjected the brine-soaked ball to closer scrutiny. "Ummm…is this a one-piece or two-piece ball?"

"I don't get yer meaning."

"Is it wound or solid?"

The Scotsman stared at him.

Charlie pointed at the ball and raised his voice. "What's inside?"

"Feathers."

The young man nearly dropped the ball in astonishment. "What?"

"Feathers! Ye know what *they* are, don't ye? Now are we gonna play or stand around 'ere yammering all day?"

McDoon sighed. "All right, all right, where's the 1st tee?"

Morris lent Charlie his nastiest smile yet. "Ye're standing on it."

"I am?" Charlie frantically searched about in all directions. "Then…where's the hole?"

"Are ye blind as well as deaf?" Old Tom pointed in the direction that Charlie was already looking. "It's out yonder!"

It was at this point that Charlie McDoon, who after all had been taking events in remarkable stride, finally began to become unhinged. For spreading out before him was the most ungodly stretch of undulating, overgrown, trampled, pitted, potted and generally unplayable hell that he had ever dared to imagine. And this was the fairway! The rough—which appeared only slightly more unkempt than the rest of the course—was an unfathomable jungle of gorse, heather, dunes and knee-high grass that looked as if it might easily conceal some quicksand, to boot. The only visible refuge in this vast sea of peril was the tiny green: impossibly distant and aloof.

Charlie reeled in horror. It was several minutes before he found that he could speak. "Now, let's make sure I'm clear on this," he said as calmly as he could. "You…you want me to drive this…this… ball, with these…these clubs, in this…this…weather, into that… that…that…" He trailed off, unable to finish the horrific thought. "I mean, don't they even mow the fairways?" he wailed in anguish.

Tom flapped a big hand at him. "Nae, the sheep take care o' that."

"Sheep?" whispered Charlie. He began to shake all over.

"Steady, lad," said the Scotsman. "Why don't ye drive off? Ye'll feel mooch better once the journey's begun."

Charlie's foundering mind—grasping at any flotsam left from the wreckage of his self-confidence—decided that it was high time for another pep talk.

So the course is a bit seedy, soothed his dog-paddling ego. *It can't be any worse than that municipal course you played last year.*

"Nothing could be as bad as that!" Reassured, McDoon began to grope through his golf bag. Unable to find what he was looking for, he turned to Morris and asked if he could borrow a tee. Tom flashed his hundred-forty-year-old smile and pointed to a square wooden box nearby. Charlie ambled over and peered inside: it was full of sand.

"Seems to be some sort of ashtray."

Rolling his eyes, the Scotsman nudged Charlie aside and scooped up a handful of sand. Then he bent down and made a small mound with it on the grass.

"Don't tell me, let me guess," said Charlie. "That's the tee, right?"

"Aye." Tom placed the featherie on the crest of the tiny hill. "Now go get yer club."

Crestfallen, Charlie returned to his bag and considered the assortment. It came as no surprise to him that none of the clubs were numbered or marked in any way to help give some clue to their identity. He finally chose the most likely candidate, but Old Tom shook his head. "Nae, use yer play club."

"My what?" asked Charlie.

"Yer play club."

"Beg your pardon?"

"Yer driver!" cried Tom.

"Well, why didn't you say so?" Charlie selected another wood (this being relatively easy since "woods" were all he had to choose from).

Tom shook his head again. "That's a spoon."

"A what?" replied Charlie.

"A spoon!"

"Beg your pardon?"

"Blast! It's what you call a…" and here he grimaced, "a number-three-wood." Morris stormed over and pulled out a club, shoving it into Charlie's hand. "*That's* yer play club!"

Charlie took a couple of practice swings and was about to address the ball when a thought occurred to him. Unfortunately it was out of his mouth before the more sensible part of his brain could round it up and send it back for further consideration.

"You don't happen to have any metal woods lying about, by any chance?"

This was simply too much for Old Tom. "Metal?" He pronounced this to rhyme with beetle. "*Meetal* woods? What in the name o' bloody Prince Charley is that supposed to be?" roared the red-faced Scot. "Are ye totally daft, man?"

Charlie thought this a likely possibility.

"Well," continued Morris, "we don't have any o' yer bloody square grooves, or yer bloody perimeter weights, or yer bloody graphite shafts, or any bloody *Titleist*—and we sure as 'ell don't have any woods made out o' bloody meetal! We just have the land beneath our feet, the sky o'er our heads, the clubs, the ball and the spirit to play the game the way 'twas meant. NOW DRIVE OFF!"

Thoroughly cowed, Charlie took his stance, looked longingly toward the green, shuddered, waggled the club twice, took a deep breath and swung…and he immediately knew why the swings he saw in the book looked so strange. The old wooden shafts were so whippy that it was almost impossible to hit the ball flush with his normal stroke; Charlie's powerful effort flexed his club so much that it missed the ball entirely. He decided to try a more controlled, sweeping type of stroke that would accelerate gradually to the point of impact. He swung again and, with a satisfying *POP*, the ball shot off the club, sailed down the fairway, bounced twice and came to rest behind a small hillock some 75 yards away.

"A grand stroke, lad!" said Tom. "A good, grand stroke." He promptly teed up his ball and propelled it 10 yards past Charlie's.

McDoon strode to his ball in a cloud of euphoria, a feeling that lasted just long enough for him to climb the miniature rise and behold his lie. The ball rested in a deep depression made by the hoof of an animal (undoubtedly one of the aforementioned sheep) on just the other side of the hillock. To make matters worse a large rock protruded from the ground within half a club length of the ball and directly between it and the green.

"Acch, a cuppie lie!" commented Morris. "That's a hard break, laddie. And after such a pretty drive, too."

McDoon took a step back. "You mean I have to play it from there?"

The Scot gave him an icy stare. "Use yer mashie."

"My wha…which one is the mashie?"

The old man handed him one of the clubs and he studied his lie. Charlie quickly found that the only stance from which he could hope to strike the ball was with one foot on the rock and the other on top of the hillock, leaving him with his feet a good ten inches above the ball, nestled cozily in its track.

Charlie took a mighty swing; the path was precisely correct to bring the club face square to the ball. Unfortunately for Charlie the top of the hillock also lay along the same arc, and he consequently buried his club into it.

"Ye hit that a wee bit fat," suggested Tom.

Charlie glared at the Scot and adjusted his stance. He swung again, this time neatly avoiding the hillock. He also, just as neatly, avoided the ball but managed to strike the rock a fine blow.

"A wee bit thin, I'd say," offered Morris.

On his next swing Charlie managed to top the ball, which hopped out of its hole, hit the rock, bounced onto the hillock, teetered on the crest and rolled back down into the hoof print.

This time the Scotsman said nothing and feigned interest in a passing seagull.

His fourth attempt finally saw the ball explode from its hiding place and fly straight and true…directly into the rock, after which it ricocheted back down the fairway into a patch of tall grass near the tee box. Charlie now lay 6 with only a dozen yards to show for it.

"Ye're still away, I believe!" yelled Tom as Charlie made his way back to the ball.

McDoon glared over his shoulder. "Oh shut up, you old goat."

On his next shot the long grass pulled open Charlie's clubface and the ball—badly sliced and pushed by the fierce wind—sailed far into the dreaded rough. With his earlier thoughts of quicksand in mind Charlie carefully made his way into the wilderness. A long search revealed his ball peeking from the midst of a large clump of gorse.

"How's she lie?" cried the Scotsman from the fairway.

Charlie cupped his hands around his mouth. "I'm in the gorse."

"Use yer niblick," yelled Tom.

"My what?" bellowed Charlie.

"Yer niblick!" screamed Morris.

"Beg your pardon?" hollered McDoon.

Morris threw down his club and raged at Charlie in Gaelic before stomping off to his ball. The younger man shrugged and chose the club he thought best suited for the task (which just happened to be his niblick) and swung as hard as he could into the center of the clump. The ball shot out, followed closely by a terrified rabbit, only to sail into a nearby shrub. Charlie swung the club into the colorful growth and produced the same results, including another rabbit. Three rabbits later and he was back on the fairway.

For those of you who've not been keeping score, Charlie now lay twelve with still another 200 yards to the pin. The sanctuary of the green seemed to shimmer, like a mirage, beckoning to him like the mythical sirens, and he could only wonder on what dreaded obstacle his ship would next run aground. But the fates had finally granted Charlie a relatively decent lie and his next three shots were uneventful, providing you don't count the time his ball caromed off a sheep grazing in the vicinity of the green. (If he had known that this just happened to be the same beast responsible for his earlier "cuppie lie," Charlie might not have minded the loss of distance.) A nice mashie from there placed him safely on the carpet in 16. In the meantime Old Tom methodically proceeded down the fairway to lie only a few yards from the pin in 5.

Charlie breathed a sigh of relief. "Finally I get to putt!"

For if there was one thing that Charlie excelled at it was putting. He loved to putt; he *lived* to putt. It was his one great gift and many an unsuspecting soul had lost his shirt to Charlie McDoon on the practice green. But as they approached the putting surface Charlie realized that it was hardly the safe haven that it appeared from a distance—it more closely resembled the North Sea during a full blow. Great waves of earth seemed to rise and fall about him in a rollicking sea of green. Here and there the treacherous waters gave way to a series of calmer ripples and even an occasional deep depression, like grass whirlpools that could swallow an unlucky shot and golfer whole. And as if this wasn't enough of a challenge, it was also time for the peculiarities of the featherie to come into play. For unlike the modern golf ball it was not perfectly round, especially after being struck repeatedly by a hard object.

Poor Charlie. Standing on the edge of the green he could just make out the top of the pin beyond a mighty swell. Two harrowing strokes later found him still ten feet from the hole and on the verge of tears—another putt and he was inside of a foot. Now it was the Scotsman's turn. He lined up and stroked to within a few inches of the hole directly between it and Charlie's ball.

"Ha! Ye're stymied!" he cried, leering at McDoon.

Charlie glared back at him and waited for Morris to mark his ball so he could putt out. When the Scot failed to make a move, Charlie bent over to do it himself.

"What are ye doing?" cried Tom. "I said ye're stymied."

Charlie straightened up. "What are you talking about?"

"Ye can nae move me ball."

Charlie goggled at him in incomprehension.

"Ye can nae move it, lad."

"You mean…I have to putt around it?"

"Aye."

Charlie threw down his putter. "What kind of stupid rule is that?"

The big Scot took a step closer and pushed a menacing finger in his face. "Hold yer tongue, laddie. It's a rule from whence the Game was invented. Now quit yer whining and play yer shot."

Charlie stormed off to his bag in a rage: a topped-drive, duck-hooked second, in the rough, two strokes in the trap, three-putt green, *all-on-the-same-hole* sort of rage. He was so worked up that he unwisely chose to play a shot *over* his rival's ball even though the green sloped sharply away just beyond the hole. It took just a few seconds for his ball to roll completely off the green. Two putts later and his ball was right back where it had started: stymied again!

This development took even Old Tom by surprise. Charlie, resigned to utter humiliation, trudged up to his ball and this time took the safer, if more circuitous, route to the cup and holed out in 2. Morris made his putt for a 7 on the hole. Charlie carded an incredible 25.

*　*　*

Since few of us enjoy dwelling on the misery of others, it will suffice to simply say that Charlie's ordeal did not end there. Seventeen hair-raising holes followed. Dazed and shaken, just when the sun went down he sat on the fringe of the 18th green and watched Old Tom tap in to finish his round with a 126. Charlie, who had managed a staggering 201, dreaded the harsh ridicule he was bound to hear from the Scotsman even though he knew he had it coming. But the old gentleman surprised him with a look of grudging respect.

"Ye showed great courage out there, laddie, long after many would nae have gone on." He gripped Charlie's hand and gave it a rough shake. Then he winked and added, "An' I hope that it *proved interesting.*"

Charlie's cheeks flushed red.

Old Tom roared with laughter and slapped the younger man on the back. "Come now, any man who can take that many strokes deserves a good drink!"

"Aye," said Charlie McDoon, laughing as they walked off toward the clubhouse, where they joined the other members in scotch and golfing tales late into the night, until Charlie finally collapsed into a chair before the fire and fell asleep.

*　*　*

The first thing Charlie saw when he woke was Old Tom Morris staring at him—from the pages of *A History of Golf* that lay open in his lap. The next thing he saw was the Senior Member eyeing him suspiciously from a nearby chair.

"You were right," said Charlie after a long silence. "The Game *was* different back then and so were those who played it. When we take up ball and club and walk the links, it is their shadows that we cast. Our heroic drives find the fairways safely only because they have prepared the way. And when our shots fall softly to the green, they are there before us—and we will always be away." He lapsed back into silence, gazing at the photo.

Suddenly he stirred and pulled out of his pocket an object that made his eyes tear up when he saw it. "Do you know what this is?" he asked in an awed whisper.

"Of course I do," replied the Senior Member. "It's a ball marker."

"Yes! Yes it is, isn't it?" Charlie leaned forward. "Tell me, have you seen my clubs around?"

The Senior Member peered at the younger man with concern. "I believe I saw you lean them against the starters' hut."

"Yahoo!" Charlie jumped up and bolted for the door.

The Senior Member followed him as far as the window to see what would happen next. Charlie took hold of a couple of his perimeter-weighted, stainless-steel, offset-aligned, graphite-shafted irons and waved them joyfully in the air, all the while yelling something about how they were made of metal, as nearby members scurried for cover. Then the young man ran to the 1st tee and scanned the course lovingly in the glow of the setting sun as if seeing it for the first time. The Senior Member last glimpsed Charlie McDoon dashing off toward the maintenance shed where, rumor has it, he tried to kiss the greenskeeper and got a black eye for his trouble.

The Senior Member shook his head at these odd goings-on and shuffled back to his chair by the fire. On his way he paused to notice a curious object in the gloom beneath Charlie's chair. When he bent to pick it up he was utterly astonished by what his old eyes found nestled in the palm of his hand: an authentic featherie! And he would never know whether it was just his imagination or a trick of the firelight but he could have sworn that Old Tom Morris winked at him from his glossy full-page color plate.

BIG BERTHA

G. GUILFORD BARTON

Continuing the Series

GOLF IS NO ORDINARY GAME!

I am often awestruck by the power of Creation, particularly the kind of power revealed in storms. Tornados both terrify and fascinate me, haunting my dreams. On the other hand, thunderstorms have always been a source of delight and wonder. As a kid, lightning once struck less than a dozen yards from where I stood, and I'll never forget the way the air around me crackled and hummed for almost a full minute. The story that follows is about what might happen if that kind of incredible power somehow channeled through a human body. It's also the tale of an underdog who suddenly finds himself on top of the world when he comes face to face with a hurricane by the name of *Big Bertha*.

BIG BERTHA

M itch pressed his face against the stone wall of the clubhouse and tried to shut out the unearthly howl of the wind. He did not understand what was happening to him, could not reconcile the impulses that raged through his body with the storm that raged around him. He opened his eyes and saw Jason huddled at the base of the wall with his arms covering his head. He knew that, close behind him, Ollie and Pete were rooted in similar states of terror. Yet Mitch had no fear of the storm, only of what it was doing to him. He shut his eyes tight and tried to lash his reeling mind to the mast of his memory, to recall the bright and sunny day the four of them had hatched this insane idea. A day that receded far into the misty past, steeped in antiquity, impossible to remember clearly—so, so, so very long ago.

Yesterday…

*   *   *

"Catch the news today?" Jason said, pouring himself another beer from the pitcher.

"Nope," Mitch said.

"There's a hurricane moving toward the coast."

"Yeah, so?"

"You know what I think would be a rush?"

"No, what?" asked Mitch.

"Playing golf in a hurricane."

Mitch laughed and shook his head. "That's crazy."

"No...really." Jason leaned closer. "Think of the stories we'll have to tell—we won't have to buy another beer for the rest of the semester."

"Only if we live to tell about it." Mitch sat back to grin at his friend. He and Jason roomed together at college and had played on the golf team since their freshman year. Mitch was a good athlete, but due to his size golf was the only sport he could come close to lettering in.

"It's crazy," Mitch repeated.

"It's not crazy."

"OK then, you're crazy."

They had been kicking around Hannigan's since leaving the course following an afternoon practice round, and Mitch had his eye on a pretty redhead in the corner. She sat with a group of coeds and he was slowly working up the nerve to go over and join the conversation.

"Well?" Jason said.

Mitch tore his eyes off the girl. "Well, what?"

"Will you do it?"

"Do what? Play in a hurricane?"

"Yes!"

"You're crazy," Mitch repeated. He smiled at the girl and she offered one back.

"So you keep saying but that's not an answer."

Two of their teammates drifted across the bar and sat down at the table. Pete Lazansky owned the low handicap on the team and Ollie Owens the highest. All three of Mitch's companions dwarfed him at the table. At only five foot five and 130 pounds sopping wet, he was used to being the smallest guy in any crowd. Even most of the girls towered over Mitch. He glanced over at the redhead to make sure she wasn't smirking at him.

"So, what are you two arguing about this time?" Pete asked, as he helped himself to the pitcher.

"Jason wants me to play a round with him in a hurricane," Mitch replied.

"Not in the hurricane itself," corrected Jason, "but in the *eye* of the hurricane. And there'd only be time for a few holes."

Ollie looked across the table at Mitch. "You gonna do it?"

"Only if I'm drunk." Mitch twirled his mug on the table.

"No problemo," said Jason. "I'm buying."

Mitch put down his mug. "Do you know how much energy is in a hurricane?" Jason rolled his eyes. "Do tell, professor."

"The bigger ones pack more punch than our entire nuclear arsenal."

Jason waved the warning away. "The one out in the Atlantic—Bertha, they're calling it—isn't supposed to be a real big one. And besides, it's losing strength."

"I'll do it," Pete said.

"You will?" Mitch asked.

"Sure. My dad was in a hurricane once. He said it was no big deal." Ollie belched. "I'm game, too."

Mitch groaned and lowered his head into his hands. "You're all nuts."

"Afraid big bad Bertha's gonna huff and puff and blow you away little buddy?" Jason teased.

Mitch glared back and Pete elbowed him in the ribs. "Come on Mitch, we need a fourth."

"And just how do you propose going about this?" Mitch asked.

"Well…the forecasters are predicting landfall sometime tomorrow morning near Myrtle Beach," Jason said. "I say we just toss the clubs in Ollie's Jeep and head for the coast."

"When?" Pete asked.

Jason shrugged. "How about now? We could be at the coast by sunup."

"Sorry, I'm busy." Mitch exchanged another smile with the redhead and made up his mind to talk to her. He stood and instantly recognized the disappointment on her face, waiting for it to progress into amusement. Sure enough, the girl put her hand to her mouth in an effort to cover a long stream of giggles.

Mitch swore under his breath and drained his mug. He slammed it down, ticked off yet again at the unjust nature of the gene pool.

"Let's go play some golf," he said.

* * *

They took turns driving and listened to the news throughout the night as they made their way toward the coast. The eastbound lanes were strangely deserted, but a steady stream of vehicles crawled in the opposite direction. The rain started at 2:00 a.m. as a light mist. It turned to a steady sprinkle by three and became a full-fledged downpour by the time they reached Myrtle Beach around four in the morning. Many of the roads were flooded and it was only the Jeep's high undercarriage and four-wheel drive that allowed them to press on.

The sky was just lightening to a muddy gray as Ollie pulled into the parking lot at the Ocean Dunes Club. He turned off the engine and the four of them sat in silence, watching the angry surf pound away at the Carolina coastline. Huge waves battered the low breakwater, sending columns of seawater high into the air before cascading onto the fairways that lined the ocean.

"I don't know about this," Ollie said.

"Will you relax?" Jason shot back. "If the weather nerds are correct we're right in Bertha's path." He looked at his pals with excitement. "All we have to do is sit here and ride out the storm until the eye passes over. And then it's *FORE!*" Jason turned and high-fived Pete in the back seat, then looked over at Mitch, who was frowning at a row of cypress trees listing in the wind.

"What's eating you?"

"You heard what the reports said," Mitch replied. "The storm grew stronger during the night."

"So?" challenged Jason.

Mitch shrugged his slim shoulders and stared at the plywood nailed over the clubhouse windows. He glanced up at the Jeep's canvas top. "I just hope we're not in over our heads."

"Don't be such a wimp, Mitch," Jason said as a sudden gust rattled the window next to him. Another blast, this one much harder, rocked the Jeep and made an eerie moan as it infiltrated the chinks in the vehicle's armor.

Mitch noticed a slight tingling in his fingers and toes. He wiggled them. "I say we pull up closer to the clubhouse and get out of the wind."

"I second that," Ollie said and fired up the engine. He rolled the Jeep over the curb and up against a low wall close to the lee side of the building. It provided some protection but only a marginal amount. As the power of the storm increased the wind came at them from every direction, swirling and eddying and buffeting the vehicle with heightening violence. Ollie popped a cassette into the stereo and turned up the volume until the grinding beat of the music drowned out most of the hurricane's fury.

Mitch looked out and saw the rain falling horizontally, an infinite barrage of liquid bullets that ricocheted off his window, in a loud staccato that even the Rolling Stones couldn't quite mask. Palm fronds, sand, driftwood and all manner of debris filled the air and flung itself heedlessly against the tempered glass. A steel trash can appeared out of nowhere—cartwheeling across the grass before glancing off the front fender, careening into the sky, and disappearing again into the storm. It was raining so hard that he couldn't see the clubhouse only ten feet away.

The tingling sensation had spread up Mitch's arms and legs. He rubbed his thighs and shook both arms, trying to restore the circulation.

"You all right?" Pete asked.

"Yeah…I think all this sitting around is putting my arms asleep."

Out of the corner of his eye, Mitch saw something fly past the window. He was trying to process what he had seen, when another sailed past…then another…then half a dozen at once. He was about to shout out a warning when a concrete tile from the clubhouse roof slammed through the windshield, just missing Jason and Ollie. Another tile hammered onto the hood. Ollie cursed and threw the stick into reverse. He gunned the engine and the Jeep bounced backward toward the parking lot. The air suddenly became alive with concrete projectiles tossed in the hundred-mile-an-hour wind as easily as leaves.

Jason and Ollie had a lap full of glass from the shattered windshield, and a torrent of water was drenching their clothes. A hard gust hit the Jeep and ripped its rag top completely off. It sailed away across the parking lot like a black ghost, leaving the boys fully exposed to the force of the hurricane.

"We've got to get out of here and find some shelter!" Pete cried, trying to make himself heard above the wind.

Ollie and Jason tumbled out of the Jeep and ran for the nearby clubhouse. Pete flung open his door but the wind slammed it back shut, nearly crushing his fingers. He pushed it open again and turned to Mitch, who was hunched up on the seat, hugging himself and shivering violently.

"Mitch!" Pete shouted.

Mitch didn't respond. The stinging had turned into burning; a red-hot series of impulses shot through his extremities. Pete was alarmed to see the whites of Mitch's eyes rolled up under his fluttering lids.

"Jason, get back here!" Pete called.

"What is it?" Jason cried, as he dashed back to the Jeep.

"Something's the matter with Mitch!"

Jason leaned into the door. "Come on, let's get him out of there."

The two big youths pulled Mitch out of the Jeep and carried him toward the clubhouse. Most of the roof had blown off but stray tiles were still flying about with lethal randomness. One just missed lopping off Pete's head as they struggled against the wind. Ducking under the eave, they set Mitch down and he slumped against the wet stone wall.

Pete crouched and looked at him. "We should get him out of the storm!"

Jason and Ollie tried to pry open a gap between two sheets of plywood that covered the windows, but they had been secured to the frame with three-inch spikes.

"I can't budge it!" Jason yelled. "We'll have to find someplace else!"

But there was nowhere else to go, so they cowered against the stone wall and each of them offered a private prayer of deliverance. Sometime during the last hour the storm had crossed over the line between inanimate and animate. To Jason, Pete and Ollie it was now a living thing, a malevolent being with a breath that could snuff out their lives in a single flicker of their hearts. But to Mitch the wind had a voice, and it called him by name.

He began to recover as the morning wore on. The burning sensations regressed to a tingle, the tingle to a warm feeling that washed over his whole body. Mitch sat up with his back to the wall and Pete leaned close to his ear. "Welcome back to the land of the living."

"Is that what you call this?" Mitch replied looking at the devastation in Bertha's wake.

"You OK?"

Mitch nodded. "I think so." He peered out at the rain. "How much longer is this going to last? It's been hours."

"I don't know," Pete said glancing at the sky. "It can't be much longer until the eye passes over."

"This is crazy. I'm gonna kill Jason for talking me into this."

"The line forms behind me," said Pete. Mitch gave him a weak smile and turned to face Jason.

"Happy now?" he roared into the wind.

"What do you think?" Jason replied miserably.

"Not quite the rush you thought it would be, is it?"

"Stuff it, Mitch."

"You'll be lucky if we don't stuff you and hang your head on a wall."

"Hey!" Pete called from behind them. "I think it's letting up."

Mitch looked and, sure enough, the storm was showing signs of lessening. He could see farther, for one thing, and the rain was more vertical than horizontal in its fall. It was amazing how quickly the tempest subsided; in just minutes it went from a category two hurricane to a mild tropical storm.

Jason stood and pointed up at a patch of blue. "It's the eye!" he said excitedly. "Let's get our clubs!" He turned and ran out into the squall.

The other three gaped at him in disbelief and Pete said to Mitch, "Can you walk?"

"Yeah." Mitch got up to follow Pete and Ollie. They walked up behind Jason as he was pulling his bag from the back of the battered Jeep.

"Put 'em back, Jason," Pete said. "We're getting out of here."

Jason wheeled around and frowned at him. "Are you nuts?"

"No, you're the crazy one, remember?"

"You guys aren't serious." Jason noted the set expressions on his friends' faces. "You mean to tell me we came all this way and rode out the hurricane just so you could chicken out *now*?"

"We almost got killed," Ollie said, climbing behind the wheel.

"That's all the more reason to make it worth our while," insisted Jason.

"You coming or not?" Pete asked as he buckled in.

"You're forgetting something," Jason said, grinning at them through the missing windshield.

"And what's that?" Mitch asked irritably.

"You're in the eye, so no matter which direction you drive, sooner or later you'll hit the storm again."

Pete frowned. "He's right."

"Then we'll just drive until we find some shelter," Mitch said.

"You could," nodded Jason sagely, "but everything's probably boarded up tight—you'd risk getting caught out in the open."

"What about Mitch?" asked Pete.

"What about him?"

"You saw what happened to him," Ollie said. "He might be sick."

Jason glanced at his roommate. "He looks fine now. How 'bout it, Mitch?"

Mitch thought for a moment. He felt better than just fine. In fact he had never felt better in his entire life. He was almost giddy with energy. But the agony he had experienced during the storm was still vivid in his mind and he had no wish to relive it.

"Start it up," Mitch said. Ollie turned the key but nothing happened.

"Ignition must be wet," he said.

Ollie tried again but all they heard was a series of dry clicks.

Mitch sighed and looked around the parking lot. "We'll just have to build some shelter here."

Jason laughed. "Out of what…palm leaves and coconuts?"

The rain and wind had completely stopped and an eerie calm took their place as the eye of the storm moved overhead. Bertha whirled counter-clockwise around them, her towering structure a visible wall that spanned all 360 degrees of the compass.

"Come on, guys, or we'll miss the boat!" Jason said. "The storm's moving around twenty-five miles an hour, and the eye is anywhere from twenty to thirty miles across, so that gives us only about an hour-long window." He grabbed his clubs and dashed for the 1st tee.

Ollie shrugged and jumped out of the Jeep, while Pete looked across the seat at Mitch, who was staring at his hands.

"You sure you're all right?" he asked.

"Uh-huh. I just feel…funny."

"Funny how?"

Mitch shrugged. "Just funny, is all."

Pete climbed out of the Jeep. "You coming?"

"Yeah…sure. Why not?" Mitch opened his door. He hopped down onto the pavement and shouldered his bag.

Jason had already teed off with a 270-yard drive. "I've got five dollars burning a hole in my pocket and begging somebody to try and outdistance that."

Pete and Ollie each tossed him a bill and prepared to swing in unison.

"One, two, three!" they cried, and both swung at once, sending the balls soaring down the fairway but short of Jason's effort. Jason hooted gleefully and pocketed the money. He didn't bother asking if Mitch wanted in on the wager.

"Let's see you come close to that, Mitchell, my man!" he said.

Mitch smirked at him and teed up. He was typically the shortest off the tee and therefore the target of many a wager and good-natured ribbing from his teammates. But as Mitch addressed the ball he felt strangely galvanized, and when he unfurled his swing it was faster and more fluid than he was used to. The ball sailed high over the debris-strewn fairway and landed twenty feet past Jason's.

"What the…?" Jason said. He came over and playfully felt Mitch's bicep. "You been hitting the weights, Mitch?"

Mitch laughed and pulled his arm away. "Nope. Steroids."

Jason let out another loud whoop as they walked down the fairway.

"Ain't this something?" His eyes were wide with thrill. "Here we are playing golf in the middle of a hurricane! How many people can say they ever did that?"

"I gotta admit, Jason," Pete said with a grin, "this is kinda cool."

Jason dropped his bag on the fairway. "Five bucks says I get it within ten feet."

"You're on," Ollie said, tossing a fiver at his feet.

Jason's shot sailed in high and buried into the rain-soaked green about twenty feet from the pin.

Ollie picked up his bill and held out his hand. "Pay up."

"Double or nothing you can't get it closer," wagered Jason.

Ollie laughed and proceeded to loft a beautiful eight-iron that landed inside of Jason's ball.

"Like candy from a baby," he said as he lightened his friend's wallet.

After Pete pulled his shot into a greenside bunker, Jason turned to Mitch. "Your turn, Mr. Longball."

Mitch had about 120 to the middle of the green. He pulled out a wedge and astounded everyone, including himself, by hitting it 30 yards past the hole.

"What's up with that, dude?" Ollie yanked the club from Mitch's hand. "What were you using…a seven-iron?" His eyebrows shot up when he saw the "W" stamped into the stainless steel head. He showed it to the others.

"Only Daly hits a wedge 150," Jason said. "What's the joke, Mitch?"

"No joke," Mitch replied, holding up his hands. He was just as surprised as the others. All Mitch knew for sure was how incredible he felt. His whole body was on some sort of high, every sense and sinew tuned to a sharp clarity that he had never known.

The foursome finished out the hole and hurried to the next tee. The eastern wall of the hurricane stood noticeably closer and they wanted to card as many holes as possible before it overtook them. Jason studied the sign next to the tee box.

"OK...par-four, 435," he said lining up his drive. "Five says I clear the fairway bunker."

Pete surveyed the gaping trap that lay two-thirds of the way to the hole. "No way, that's out 280 at least."

Jason shrugged. "I feel lucky."

"Then put your money where your driver is," Pete said.

"I'll take a piece of that," Ollie said.

"Me too," added Mitch.

Jason laughed. "Your confidence in my game is heartwarming." He took his stance and clubbed a screaming drive that landed just short of the hazard and rolled in.

"Figures," he muttered. He turned to his companions. "Five more says you won't make it, either."

Pete shook his head. "Forget it."

"Not a chance," agreed Ollie.

Mitch stared down the fairway. "Make it twenty and it's a bet."

"Twenty bucks?" Jason gestured toward the tee. "By all means, hit away."

Mitch gripped his driver. A feeling of untapped power coursed through his arms and hands, confusing and exhilarating him at the same time. He took back the club with slow deliberation until it was across his shoulders and pointed at the trap, then brought it down with lightning speed.

The ball didn't just jump off the clubface—it was launched off it, rocketing over the bunker and straight for the distant flag.

"Holy..." Ollie started to say, as he and the others watched the flight of the ball in stunned disbelief. It finally came down near the front of the green and bounced onto the putting surface.

Jason wheeled around and got right in Mitch's face. "You trying to rip me off by using some sort of hopped-up ball?"

Mitch looked up at him and tried not to laugh. "No. I swear. Just my regular Nike."

"Like hell," Jason said. "Here, hit one of mine." He fished a ball from his bag and tossed it at Mitch.

Mitch swung again, this time clearing the green entirely and landing his ball in the rough beyond. Jason stood gaping down the fairway as Mitch shoved the driver back into his bag. "I'll take my twenty bucks now."

"I didn't just see what I just saw," Ollie said. "Nobody can hit a ball 450 yards."

"You mean nobody *used* to be able to hit a ball 450 yards," Mitch said, enjoying his newfound strength.

"I don't like it," Pete said, frowning at Mitch. "It's not...natural."

"Well, I like it." Mitch picked up his clubs and started down the fairway.

"Come on," Jason said, shouldering his own bag, "I wouldn't miss this for the US Open."

They played out the hole and then Jason, Pete and Ollie stood back to see what Mitch would do next. The 3rd was another par-four, which Mitch easily reached in one with a five-wood. On the 4th hole he took out his sand wedge and casually hit a towering 190-yard chip to the center of the green. But on the par-five 5th he outdid all of his previous feats by actually driving the green and holing out his putt for a 2.

The wind started to pick up as they stepped to the 6th tee.

"We ought to think about finding some cover," Pete said. He nervously eyed the approaching wall of darkness moving in from the sea.

"Not until I find out how our little friend here went from meek-and-mild Mitch to one of the *X-Men* in a matter of minutes," Jason said, his eyes fixed on Mitch.

"I'll tell you what I believe," replied Mitch. He pointed his driver at the hurricane. "It's the storm."

"What do you mean?" Jason asked.

"I told you yesterday, hurricanes carry with them megatons of potential energy. Somehow I've tapped into it."

"Come on." Ollie gave an uneasy laugh. "That's impossible."

Mitch looked over at him, his eyes wild. "Is it? How else do you explain the power that's rushing through me right now?" He held out his arms and closed his eyes. "I tell you I can actually feel the blood coursing through my arteries, feel every nerve ending in my body alive with anticipation." Mitch raised his voice: "I can feel the energy pass right through me, feel it lifting me to a higher plane. I am an oracle. A receptacle. A cosmic channeler!"

"Geez," Pete said. "He's flipped out!"

"I'll say," laughed Jason. "All right, Zeus, time to climb down from Mount Olympus." He gently took hold of his roommate's elbow but Mitch wrenched it away from his grip.

"I'm not going anywhere," he said.

The first drops of rain began to fall around them and Pete took a step forward. "Don't kid around, Mitch, we need to get out of here."

"Then go." Mitch waved them away. "I have a round to finish."

"Don't be an idiot!" Jason said, beginning to get angry. "You'd get killed out here."

Mitch eyed him with a level gaze. "Nothing can harm me in this state."

"That's it," Jason said firmly, "time to tuck Superman in for the night." He picked up Mitch's clubs but didn't even have time to *think* about making off with them before Mitch was on him. With a violent tug, he ripped the bag from Jason's shoulder and shoved him away with one hand. The push was so hard that the force of it momentarily lifted Jason off his feet. He hit the ground eight feet away, rolled two or three times and lay with the wind knocked out of him.

Jason struggled back to his feet and stood glaring at Mitch. "You asked for this, buddy," he said in a controlled voice. He pointed as he cautiously approached Mitch. "Pete you go for his left. I'll take his right side. Ollie, you be ready in case we need any help."

Mitch showed no sign of defending himself as the three of them came for him. He stood with his arms straight out at his sides and his feet pressed together, watching with an amused smile as his friends edged forward. All three reached for him at the same moment. Pete took hold of one arm and Jason the other while Ollie stood ready. Each of them outweighed Mitch by a good thirty pounds.

Bertha's force was building again, sending down sheets of rain and gusts that made it difficult to stand. "This is for your own good, Mitchell," Jason yelled over the rising wind. "The storm's done something to your mind as well as your body. Now be a good boy and come along quietly." He gave Mitch's arm a tug, and a moment later both he and Pete were dangling with their feet off the ground. With two quick jerks of his arms Mitch flung them to the wet turf. Ollie rushed at him and, as easily as if Ollie were a toddler, Mitch scooped him up and tossed him twenty feet into a greenside pond.

As Pete ran to fetch Ollie, Jason hunched in the howling storm and watched his roommate prepare to drive off. "Mitch!" he shouted. "Come back with us!"

Mitch smiled as he teed up a ball. "No can do, my friend," he said. "I have a course record to break."

"Please, Mitch…the storm will rip you to pieces!"

"I have to do this, Jason," Mitch said, his eyes momentarily returning to normal and pleading for understanding. "You've always been blessed with strength; this might be my only chance to know what it feels like."

"You don't have to prove anything to me, Mitch!" Jason cried.

"Then maybe I need to prove it to myself." Mitch took his stance. "You guys had better find some cover."

When Mitch swung he generated so much clubhead speed that he was just a blur. Pete and Ollie stumbled up to Jason's side and they watched their friend disappear into the hurricane.

"We have to stop him!" Ollie yelled.

Jason looked at the huge waves crashing on the beach and hung his head.

"We have a better chance of stopping Bertha," he said sadly.

*   *   *

They were back at the stone wall again, having failed at finding any safer haven from the storm. Bertha raged on, lashing the coast with all her pent-up fury, almost as if she were angry at having to leave behind the sea that had given birth to her destructive life.

Jason sat with his back against the wall and watched with detached interest as the winds ripped off the roof of a metal maintenance building and sent it soaring like a paper airplane. With the roof gone the rest of the structure came to pieces until nothing remained except its iron skeleton.

"He can't survive in this!" cried Pete.

Jason hugged his shoulders. "He can't drive a par-five either, but he did."

The hurricane began to lose steam after the violent eyewall had chugged past, its outer winds lessening to sixty miles per hour as the land sucked up its energy. Still, it was another hour before Jason and the others felt brave enough to venture away from the clubhouse wall.

Rain continued to pound the course as they searched for Mitch. On the 10th tee they came across their first sign of him: just the grip and shaft of his driver lying in the grass. The club's graphite tip shattered where the head had apparently snapped off under the enormous strain generated by Mitch's newfound strength. On the 14th they found his bag with most of the clubs strewn about the fairway. The three wet and tired youths pressed on to the 18th green but found no further clues to Mitch's whereabouts.

As darkness fell they gave up the search and went back to the Jeep, where Ollie spent a couple of frustrating hours under the hood. He eventually managed to dry out the electrical system and they drove for the nearest emergency station, which had been set up at a local high school. The place was in complete chaos, full of rain-slickered police and volunteers, all of them rushing about and shouting orders as vacant-eyed storm victims looked on in numb silence. No one would listen to their story. Jason finally placed himself in the path of a female sheriff's deputy. "Excuse me, but we need some help. My friend is missing."

"Lots of friends are missing," the deputy said as she tried to brush past with an armful of blankets. "You'll need to file a report at the desk."

Pete stopped her with a hand. "We tried that, but we couldn't get through."

"Look, I'm sorry," the young woman said, "but there's nothing I can do."

"Please," pleaded Jason. "He wouldn't be out there if it wasn't for me."

The deputy searched his face for a moment and sighed. "OK, where did you last see him?"

"Out on the Ocean Dunes Golf Course," Ollie replied.

She gave them a look of surprise mixed with reproof. "What were you doing out there?"

"Playing golf," Pete said sheepishly.

"Excuse me?"

"We were playing golf in the eye of the hurricane," explained Jason.

The deputy's eyes widened. "Come with me."

"Crazy macho idiots," she said under her breath, leading them down a long hallway. She glared over her shoulder. "It's a wonder you're not all missing. What were you thinking?"

"Obviously we weren't," mumbled Pete.

"Obviously," agreed the deputy as she burst through a pair of double doors and into the gymnasium. The huge space had been set up as a makeshift infirmary, with rows of cots and volunteer medical personnel tending the injured as they straggled in. The deputy walked up to a nurse.

"I think these *boys* might know who our John Doe is," she said condescendingly, even though she was at best only a couple of years their senior.

The nurse escorted them to a cot in the far corner of the gym. There, curled up in the fetal position and clutching a one-iron, was the small form of Mitch. He was in a deep sleep, dressed only in a pair of gray sweats and a borrowed fire department T-shirt that hung off him like a tent.

"Know him?" asked the deputy.

Ollie smiled affectionately. "Yeah, it's Mitch."

"We picked him up about thirty miles from here," she said. "Just wandering down the road—half naked, no ID, and carrying that golf club."

Jason knelt beside the cot and gently shook his friend's shoulder. "Mitch?" he said quietly. "Mitch...can you hear me?"

Mitch opened his eyes and Jason was relieved to see plain old Mitch looking back at him.

"Jason?" he said in a weak voice.

"Right here, buddy."

"I'm so tired, Jason," Mitch said, blinking at them in the harsh fluorescent glare.

"What happened to you?" Ollie asked.

Mitch raised up on one elbow and rubbed his eyes. "I did it, guys," he said, his eyes alight with pride. "I finished the round—all eighteen holes."

"Then what?" asked Pete. "Why didn't you come back to the clubhouse?"

"Bertha moved inland, and…I just went with her," Mitch said, struggling to stay awake.

"Doing what?"

"Just hitting my ball and running after it," Mitch replied with a yawn, and lay back down.

"In the middle of a hurricane?" asked the deputy in disbelief. "That's impossible."

Jason smiled and looked at Mitch with admiration. "You'd be surprised at the things that are possible."

"What do you think stopped him?" Pete asked, watching Mitch drift back to sleep.

"I dunno, maybe Bertha herself." Jason looked down at his roommate's serene features. "Hurricanes weaken the farther inland they go so maybe Mitch weakened with it."

"And now he's burned out," Ollie concluded. "He'll probably sleep for days."

"I wonder if he knows how much of a legend he's gonna become on campus once this gets around," Pete said.

Jason shrugged. "I don't think that's why he did it."

"Why then?" Ollie asked.

"Mitch just needed to grow a little in his own eyes," replied Jason.

He bent over and gently removed the club from Mitch's hand. "I wonder what he shot," he said softly.

"What?" asked Pete.

"On the course," Jason said. "I wonder what his score was."

"Fifty-three," mumbled Mitch, as he slipped into peaceful oblivion.

A GENTLEMEN'S GAME

G. GUILFORD BARTON

Those that know me well also know I'm a bit of a Civil War buff. Perhaps it's because my father took me to all the famous battlefields on our yearly sojourns down to Florida when I was a lad. Gettysburg, Bull Run, Antietam, Shiloh, Chickamauga, Chancellorsville…wherever blue and gray armies once grappled, I would stand and ponder the conflict that spilt so much blood on the soil beneath my feet. So many heroes, so much bravery, so much tragedy. The story that follows, though admittedly farfetched, postulates a way in which that epic struggle might have been changed by a different kind of warfare—not one of guns and lead, but balls and clubs…*A Gentlemen's Game.*

A GENTLEMEN'S GAME

June 1864 – Cold Harbor, Virginia

Captain Thomas Goree sat on his mud-splattered horse as it slowly picked its way along the soggy road. He was not an imposing figure even on horseback, having his father's slight build and studious features. He looked very much like what he was—a lawyer trying desperately hard to be a warrior.

Beside him rode a much bigger man who wore a gray felt hat pulled down low to hide his steel-blue eyes. His name was Major General James Longstreet, but to almost everyone in the Army of Northern Virginia he was simply known as "Old Pete."

Lean, sunken-eyed men stood to watch as the two Confederate officers passed through the camp. Some of them lifted their hats and cheered but most were either too tired or too hungry to muster the effort in the damp weather. The rations were low, the marches hard, their uniforms ragged and unrecognizable. It was an army in decline, an army on the run, and Thomas knew that it could only run so far.

Goree was self-conscious in the saddle. As a graduate of a college other than West Point, he knew that he was something of a rarity in the army and he tried to look dignified despite the frayed state of his uniform. He was a prideful man who firmly believed himself destined for greatness. His law degree had earned him the post of aide-de-camp to Longstreet, but the twenty-nine-year-old Texan lusted for an opportunity to shed his clerical duties and prove himself in battle—to gain fame as a leader of men rather than the glorified messenger that he had become.

But time was running out on Thomas. He had long surrendered any hope for a Southern victory. The North was simply too strong and its seemingly endless supply of manpower was wearing the Rebel Army to paper thinness. His comrades in gray would argue that they had *always* been outnumbered but Goree knew it was only a matter of time before the disparity became too great to overcome.

The road wound along the bottom of a series of hills, and Old Pete spurred his mount up the slope in an effort to shorten the ride back to his headquarters. As they crested the rise Longstreet reined his horse and leaned forward in the saddle, peering down into a wide valley nestled between the forested hills.

"What do you make of that, Captain?" he asked Goree.

Thomas followed his gaze and saw two men standing alone in a grassy field. One was dressed garishly in a red tunic, while the other wore a black sweater and what appeared to be a patterned knee-length skirt. Both carried a long, oddly-shaped stick. As the officers watched, the man in the tunic took hold of his stick with both hands and swung at something lying on the grass. Whatever it was, it flew away from the two men and landed 100 yards or so down the pasture.

"I believe that is Colonel Freemantle, sir," Thomas said.

"The Englishman?" Longstreet asked.

"Yes, sir." Thomas smiled, fondly recalling the odd little officer and his almost feminine manners. And yet there could be no doubt that he was a first-class soldier—no one enjoyed a fight more than Colonel Freemantle of Her Majesty's Coldstream Guards.

Old Pete nodded at the other man. "Who's that with him?"

"A Major MacTavish, sir."

"I don't know him."

"He's Scottish, sir. Just arrived in camp a month ago."

Longstreet frowned from his mount. "What are they doing?"

"I'm not sure, General, but I would like to reconnoiter."

"By all means, Captain," Longstreet replied, urging his steed onward. "Report to me in the afternoon."

Thomas rode down into the valley and cantered to where Freemantle and his companion stood surveying the ridge before them. The British officer turned as the Texan approached and offered a smile of uneven teeth.

"Good morning, Captain," he said.

"Mornin', Colonel." Thomas dismounted and stood holding the reins. He could now see what Freemantle had struck with the stick: a tiny ball made of pale rubber. Goree doffed his hat to MacTavish. "My compliments, Major."

"Welcome, laddie," replied the Scot in his highland burr.

"May I ask what you gentlemen are doing out here?"

"Aye," answered the major. "We're playin' golf, man."

"Golf?" Thomas shot them a puzzled look. "What's golf?"

"It's a game," Freemantle said.

Thomas frowned; he had never been much of a gamesman.

"What sort of game?"

MacTavish grinned. "The only way ta answer that is ta have ye play it."

The Rebel captain shrugged and listened to MacTavish explain that the sticks they were carrying were called clubs and that the ball was called a gutty. The Scot demonstrated how to grip the club and swing it at the ball, then pointed at the distant ridge. "See tha' flag oot yonder?"

Thomas nodded, noting a distant pennant fluttering in the breeze.

"Aim fer it."

Thomas took hold of the club as they had taught him and spread his feet. He brought it back and swung clumsily at the little sphere, sending it skittering across the grass.

"Nae, nae, nae," chided the major. "Yer noot digging a latrine, lad. Think o' it as assailin' an enemy position."

Goree retook his stance and gazed up at the flag poking out of the ridge. He looked back down at the ball—poised to be launched like a bullet—then at the club in his hand, the warm leather in his grip, caressing his palm. He swung again, this time smoothly. The gutty shot off the club and soared straight over the flag, landing some ways over the ridgeline.

Freemantle looked at MacTavish, and they both smiled in delight. "Yer a natural, lad," boomed the big Scot. "Come...play with us fer a wee time."

Thomas spent the remainder of the morning with the two foreign observers, growing more enamored with the game the longer he played it. He returned to headquarters in a contemplative mood, something Longstreet had grown used to.

"What's on that mind of yours, Captain?" he asked, as he sat whittling on a campstool outside his tent.

"Do you recall the conversation we had over supper last week, sir?"

"You mean about finding another means of ending the war?" Longstreet asked, keeping his eyes fixed on the knife in his large hands.

"Yes, sir."

Longstreet looked up from his whittling. "What about it?"

Thomas hesitated for a moment. "I may have found a way, sir."

"And how is that, Captain?"

Thomas began to explain to the general about the game he had learned and its many intricacies. When he had finished, Old Pete smiled and returned his attention to the remains of the stick in his hand. "Captain Goree, are you about to suggest that we challenge the North to a game?"

"There is some precedent, sir."

Longstreet's knife paused on the stick. "Oh?"

"Yes, sir. MacTavish and Freemantle told me about how the Scots once resolved a feud between clans in such a manner. The two sides had been fighting for decades and finally settled their differences by sending their best man to play a game of golf. A match, I believe they called it."

The general grew silent as he slowly reduced the stick to a pile of shavings. Goree knew that Longstreet also believed the war to be a lost cause and secretly hoped for a swift end to the senseless slaughter. When he had run out of wood, Old Pete clicked shut his knife and rose from the stool.

"Let us pay a visit to our foreign visitors."

* * *

The rain had begun again but it was only a half-mile or so to Lee's tent. The commanding general relied heavily on Longstreet's counsel and therefore rarely camped very far away. Lee's young aide, Major Taylor, rose from the fire as they approached and took hold of the reins of Longstreet's horse.

"Afternoon, sir," he said. "May I inform the general of your arrival?"

"No need for us both to do what I can do for myself," Old Pete said, brushing aside the protocol and making for the largest tent with Thomas close behind him. Just as they reached it the flap was thrown back and a tall figure emerged.

Robert E. Lee allowed himself a rare smile. "General, it is good to see you well."

Lee's posture was erect, his gray hair and beard framing a face that was a mask of dignity. Thomas knew him to be a man of immaculate manners and grace, a devout man, a man without vice who lived his entire life by the strict code of honor. Each time Goree saw Lee, he was alarmed at how old he appeared. The heart attack from the previous spring had taken a heavy toll, but it was more than the strain of command that was wearing Lee down. He had sent too many brave men to die, seen too many fine leaders wasted in the cause. The bloody years had slowly eroded his will until the gray eyes no longer burned with the light of victory.

Thomas saw the signs and knew that the time was ripe.

"Freemantle was in camp today," Longstreet remarked casually.

"How is the good Colonel?" Lee wondered out loud. He clasped his hands behind his back and they began to stroll through the rain toward the horses. Thomas followed the two generals at a respectful distance.

"He brought another officer with him," Longstreet said, "also a foreign observer—a Scotsman by the name of MacTavish."

Lee nodded firmly. "Fine fighters, the Scots. Rank and unit?"

"A major with the Black Watch."

Impressed, Lee raised his brows. "And what does Major MacTavish think of our position?"

"He does not find it enviable," replied Longstreet.

"Indeed?" Lee said. They reached the horse corral and a beautiful gray stallion trotted over. Lee reached out and gently patted Traveller's nose as Longstreet motioned for Thomas to join them.

"MacTavish told Captain Goree and me an interesting tale," Old Pete said.

Lee continued to stroke the horse's face, patiently waiting for the news to unfold just as he had so often waited for the Federals to show their hand in battle.

"Mind you," added Longstreet, "it was just campfire talk."

"Yes…of course."

Longstreet hesitated and glanced at Thomas, who cleared his throat. "The major told us that back in the 1600s two warring clans settled a fight by one-to-one combat."

"You mean they fought a duel?"

"Not exactly, sir," replied Thomas. "There were no weapons used; instead they played a game."

Lee frowned. "What sort of game?"

"They call it golf."

"Golf?" said Lee. "An uncouth name. How is it played?"

"Well, sir, from what I have gathered the game employs an assortment of specially-shaped sticks like this one." He pulled a niblick from beneath his coat and offered it to his commander.

Lee politely studied the club for a few moments before handing it back. "What is it used for?"

"To strike a small ball and send it flying." Goree produced a gutty and tossed it into the air between them.

Lee deftly caught it, turning it in his fingers. "Toward your opponent?"

"No, sir." Thomas shook his head. "The object of the contest is to propel the projectile with as much accuracy as one can manage."

"At what target?" Lee asked.

"A small hole in the ground that is usually placed three to four hundred yards away."

Lee grew silent and Goree suffered an uncomfortable moment as he realized just how absurd his description of the game must sound.

"That seems an unlikely achievement," Lee finally remarked. "How is the winner determined?"

"Allow me to explain, sir. Each player is allowed more than one attempt. He strikes his ball then follows it to where it lands and strikes it again. The objective is to get the ball into the hole with the least number of attempts. A contest, or match, is made up of eighteen such 'holes.' The ultimate victor is the player who wins the most holes in the match."

"Interesting," Lee said as Traveller nuzzled his beard.

Goree nodded. "An uncouth name, as you say, but a gentlemen's game nonetheless. One based on codes of conduct and honor."

Lee turned to look at him. "Honor?"

"Yes, sir."

"Captain Goree," Lee said with a half-smile. "Have you come here to suggest that we settle our dispute with the Federals by a contest of skill?"

Thomas looked to Longstreet for reinforcement. Rather than respond directly, Old Pete resorted to a flanking maneuver.

"Grant keeps getting stronger," he said, gazing past the horses to the vast Federal camp across the North Anna River. "My scouts report columns of fresh troops arriving almost daily, while we have not been reinforced in over a year. Supply trains grow few and half-empty. Sherman is moving on Atlanta. Sheridan and his cavalry wreak havoc in our rear while Grant pushes us farther and farther…"

"Do you have a point to make, General?" Lee asked sharply.

"We cannot hope to prevail."

Thomas gasped. There it was, stated flatly—what so many refused to face in the open and secreted away in their hearts. *Lee will most likely relieve him,* he thought despairingly.

But the old general shocked both officers. "I am aware of that." He pulled a lump of sugar from his pocket and fed it to Traveller. "But perhaps if we can hold out a little longer, maybe another winter, the North will lose their patience and pressure Washington for an armistice."

Longstreet eyed Lee sternly. "You must know that Lincoln will see this through!"

Lee sighed. "There will be an election soon; perhaps he will lose it."

"Perhaps," agreed Longstreet, "but you and I have been soldiers too long to rely on political solutions."

Lee fell silent again and Longstreet pressed the advantage. "General Lee, the day will come when you will have to ride hat in hand to Grant and surrender your sword. I, for one, do not wish to see that day arrive. There is still a chance to avoid it, an opportunity to win the field, but we must move quickly."

"And why would General Grant agree now to nullify his vastly superior advantage in favor of single combat?"

"There is no guarantee that he will," conceded Longstreet. "But they say he took the slaughter at Cold Harbor hard, very hard, and that he's fallen into a dark mood because of it. I know Sam Grant. He can suffer periods of doubt, but they are fleeting and his resolve will soon return twofold. Approach him with an alternative *now* and he might entertain it. Wait, and the opportunity will most likely be forever lost."

Lee gave Traveller's nose a few thoughtful strokes and turned to Thomas.

"Captain," he ordered, "please locate Colonel Freemantle. Give him my regards and request that he and Major MacTavish join me for dinner this evening."

"At once, sir," Thomas said, trying to cover his excitement. He quickly mounted his horse and the Confederate generals watched him disappear into the mist.

*   *   *

*Lieutenant General U. S. Grant, United States Army, Commanding:
3 P.M., June 24, 1864.*

The results of the past months have left me to ponder the wisdom of continuing engagements between our two forces. Therefore, I regard it as my duty to shift from myself the responsibility for any further effusion of blood, and respectfully request an immediate cessation of hostilities, in order that we might meet to discuss terms for the swift resolution of our conflict.

I am, respectfully, your obedient servant,

R. E. Lee, General, CSA, Commanding

*   *   *

They approached the Federal lines just after dark. Old Pete had urged waiting until morning but Lee was impatient to have it done. Thomas rode at the head of the column with one of the scouts, nervously searching the shadows for the first sign of the enemy. Lee and Longstreet followed close behind Goree while the irrepressible Freemantle and his Scottish colleague brought up the rear, dressed in garish uniforms that seemed like party costumes to the meagerly clad troops. The blue pickets were alert and ready, appearing suddenly out of the gloom and calling for the party of horsemen to halt and identify themselves.

The five officers were escorted into Grant's camp but remained mounted—edgy and ill at ease in the midst of their long-fought antagonists. Ulysses S. Grant stepped from his tent and approached them. Thomas found it odd that the commander of all the Northern forces would appear in an ordinary private's overcoat and cavalry boots. This was the man the papers were calling "The Butcher," and Thomas studied him for signs of his reputation. But Grant appeared just as apprehensive as the Rebels as he offered Lee a stiff salute.

Lee returned it smartly. "General Grant, we thank you for our safe conduct through your lines."

"You are most welcome, sir," Grant said. He grinned at Longstreet and tipped his hat to his old friend. "Evening, Pete."

"Sam," Longstreet said, with a nod. "It's good to see you."

"Circumstances could be brighter, General." Grant eyed the foreigners curiously and waved an arm toward his tent. "Will you gentlemen please be kind enough to join me inside?"

Thomas and the other Confederates followed Grant into the warm glow of his tent, where a table was spread with a steaming platter of fried chicken and gravy.

"Help yourselves, gentlemen," instructed Grant as he took a chair. Seated with him at one side of the table were John Rawlins, his chief of staff; Union Cavalry General Phil Sheridan; and Major General George Mead, commander of the Army of the Potomac.

Thomas eyed the food hungrily but waited for a cue from Lee.

"I was pleased to receive your message this afternoon, General Lee," Grant said cordially, "but I must say it took me by surprise."

"And why is that, General?" Lee asked, helping himself to a drumstick. Thomas eagerly dug into the feast as Sheridan entered the fray.

"What General Grant means to say," the slightly built officer said, "is that we thought you Rebs still had some fight left in you."

Thomas bristled at the bald insult and felt Lee stiffen beside him.

Grant glared at Sheridan. "That is not *at all* what I meant to say."

Lee held up a hand. "I hope you are not under the misconception that we have come here to surrender."

"Your message referred to terms," Meade said. "What other meaning could it have?"

"I believe the message read: *terms for the resolution of our current conflict…*" interjected Longstreet.

The fiery Sheridan rose to his feet. "There can be no other solutions except the complete and unconditional…"

"General!" Grant snapped and the cavalry officer clamped shut his mouth and returned angrily to his seat. Grant glanced over at Lee. "What *are* you here to offer?"

Longstreet spoke for his commander. "A contest."

"What kind of contest?"

"A one-on-one rivalry between two handpicked men from each force. Whoever prevails wins the war for his side."

There was a moment of stunned silence before Sheridan burst into laughter.

"Are you mad?" he roared. "We've routed you and your army out of the North, pushed you over the Potomac and chased you halfway across Virginia. We've whipped you in the Shenandoah and Sherman's about to cut you off from the Deep South. You're outmanned, out-gunned, out-supplied, and soon to be outmaneuvered. This army will be dancing in the streets of Richmond by Thanksgiving!"

Thomas knew it was not his place, but he could no longer hold his tongue. "Or lying dead in the Virginia mud by Christmas," he retorted with a cold-eyed stare.

The air in the tent crackled with tension which Meade tried to diffuse with a soft chuckle. "Surely you gentlemen are joking."

Longstreet turned to him. "Do you think we would cross your lines in the dark just to pass along a joke, George?"

Grant leaned forward. "Are you suggesting that we fight a duel?"

"No," responded Lee, "we are suggesting a competition."

"What kind of competition?"

"A game of skill," replied Longstreet. "It's called golf."

The Union officers exchanged confused looks and frowns until Grant surprised everyone by saying, "I've heard of it."

"Have you, sir?" Lee asked.

Grant nodded. "When I was stationed in San Francisco I knew a gentleman who traveled extensively abroad. He told me about witnessing an extraordinary game where a tiny ball is hit into a hole in the ground. A Scottish invention, if I'm not mistaken."

"Aye," MacTavish said from down the table. "We Scots dreamed it up many years ago."

"My apologies," Lee said. "May I present two of our foreign observers: Major Ian MacTavish of the Black Watch." The big Scotsman rose in his tartan kilts and black woolen sweater and gave a quick bow of his head. "And Lieutenant Colonel Arthur Freemantle of Her Majesty's Coldstream Guards."

The British officer smiled. "An honor to be in your company, gentlemen."

"And this is Captain Thomas Goree," Lee added, "the officer who initially brought the matter to my attention."

Thomas reddened and nodded to Grant, who eyed him curiously.

"If memory serves me right," continued Grant, "the game requires the use of rather unique clubbing instruments."

"Aye," answered the Scot, "but I brought me cloobs with me." He grinned down the length of the table. "That was before I discovered that ye had nae courses in yer country."

Grant produced a cigar from inside his coat and lit it slowly. "And where would this contest be played?" he asked, leaning back in his chair and blowing a column of smoke up toward the peak of the tent.

"I cannot believe what I am hearing!" Sheridan shouted and banged his hands on the tabletop, startling Thomas and causing Freemantle to drop the chicken wing he was eating. "Why are we entertaining this nonsense?"

"Another outburst like that, General," Grant said, "and I'll be forced to ask you to leave the conversation."

"Outburst? I'll give you an outburst," the furious officer said to Grant. "It is treasonous to even consider it."

"That will be enough, General Sheridan," Grant said sternly. "You are dismissed."

Sheridan rose and Thomas watched in satisfaction as he stormed from the tent.

Grant turned to Lee. "My apologies, General. He is a fine officer but outspoken in his passions."

"None are necessary. I have suffered many such displays from similarly minded officers who believe that combat is the only honorable means of solution." Lee paused and offered his counterpart a frank look. "But I believe there has been enough bloodshed."

Grant nodded and turned back to MacTavish. "The good major was about to explain where this contest might be held."

"There is a grand expanse o' pasture not far from 'ere," the Scot replied, "where the Colonel and I have laid out a makeshift set o' holes. There's nae much ta them, mind ye, but it's playable in a pinch."

"So you play the game, as well?" Grant asked Freemantle.

"Oh yes, a rollickingly good time," he replied with a grin. Then he frowned. "But bloody difficult as well."

Grant took another long pull on his cigar and stared up at the smoke that filled the tent. "An interesting proposition, gentlemen. Of course, I will need to confer with my superiors."

"Of course," Lee nodded solemnly.

"Do you feel that Washington will be receptive, sir?" Thomas asked anxiously.

"One can never tell with Mr. Lincoln." Grant smiled, then added, "And Richmond?"

"We are here entirely on our own authority," stated Lee.

A murmur of surprise spread down the Union side of the table. Grant allowed it to dissipate before asking, "And do you, in fact, have such authority, General?"

"President Davis has given me full command on the battlefield. This will simply be another form of battle, albeit a bloodless one."

The answer seemed to satisfy Grant, who rose to signal an end to the parlay. "There has indeed been too much killing," he said. "I will recommend your proposal to the president."

*   *   *

The moment Thomas saw Lee coming down the road on Traveller he knew that the news was favorable.

"Dear God," he whispered, and rushed to help his commander dismount. Thomas escorted the general into Longstreet's tent and watched as Lee pushed the message across the desk. Old Pete slowly digested its contents as Thomas tried to contain his excitement.

"So Lincoln has agreed," Longstreet said, halfway through the note.

"With certain stipulations," remarked Lee. "Read on."

"He requires that the contest be changed to a unit format composed of four men from each army," read Longstreet. "Each man will compete against his counterpart on the opposing side with the winner of each contest determined by the man who wins the most number of holes. Each unit is to be comprised of one infantry private, two officers, and…"

"Continue," Lee urged.

Longstreet looked down into Lee's face. "...and the commanding general of each army."

Thomas was stunned by the proposal but Lee's eyes were full of humor. "It would appear that General Grant has a flair for the romantic."

Longstreet handed back the message. "Are you going to agree to the terms?"

Lee rose from his chair. "What choice do I have? He makes it clear that the terms are final. It's either accept or return to the trenches."

"Who will you choose?" Old Pete said. Thomas felt a pang of sympathy for his commander, knowing that Longstreet wished to participate. But an almost fatal neck wound he received in the Wilderness had left the general's right arm virtually useless.

"I have given it much thought," Lee said. "I am intrigued by the inclusion of an ordinary enlisted man. What mischief do you suppose those people are up to?"

Thomas suppressed a smile as he listened. Lee insisted on referring to the Federals as "those people."

"From what I've heard of Lincoln," Longstreet mused, "it would not surprise me if this were a symbolic gesture on his part."

Lee nodded thoughtfully. "Yes...quite possible." He looked up at Thomas. "Find me a marksman, Captain. A good eye and steady hand might prove necessary."

"Yes, sir," Thomas replied and sat down to write the order.

Lee stood and began to pace the floor of his tent. He paused at one end. "An artillery man. We need someone who understands trajectory." He turned to Longstreet. "Do you recall the name of the officer at Fredericksburg who defied orders and held off Meade's division with a single battery?"

"Colonel Pelham, sir."

Lee allowed a smile. "Yes, he will do nicely."

Pelham! Thomas fumed in his chair, barely able to control his tongue. The whole venture had been his idea; if anybody deserved to represent the South it was Thomas Goree.

"Jeb Stuart would've been a good candidate," Longstreet said of the flamboyant, but dead, cavalry commander.

A moment of pain crossed Lee's features and he nodded agreement. "If only Jackson were still with us."

Jackson! stewed Thomas. *He's just as dead as Stuart.*

"So few left to choose from," lamented Lee, staring at his hands.

Longstreet glanced at Thomas, writing diligently at the desk. "What about young Goree, here? Freemantle says he has a knack for the game."

Thomas looked up in surprise and Lee nodded. "Of course—I am ashamed for not thinking of it myself. My apologies, Captain Goree; this was your strategy, after all."

"None required, sir," Thomas said, thrilled almost to tears. "It will be an honor to serve the cause." He bowed and added. "If you will pardon me, sir, I will circulate the request for a marksman to all commands."

Lee nodded.

"That's it, then," Longstreet said as Thomas left with the dispatch. "Pelham, Goree and yourself. Now all we have to do is find a private."

* * *

Thomas leaned against the rough bark of a tree and watched the private cook the squirrel over the open fire. He had searched for nearly two days for the right man, listening to amazing tales of marksmanship from company commanders eager for personal recognition. Most of the leads ended in a literal dead end, with the soldier in question killed or missing somewhere along the path the weary army had made during its retreat from the North. Thomas had finally settled on the young Virginian before him after listening to a sergeant tell how the sniper had taken the very critter he was roasting on the spit.

The private pulled off a leg and ate it with obvious hunger. He had probably eaten nothing but hardtack for weeks. The animal disappeared quickly and when the meal was finished Goree stepped into the ring of firelight.

"Your name Eustice Riley?" he asked.

"Yes, sir." The private wiped his face on his dirty sleeve and quickly jumped to his feet.

Thomas nodded at the remains of the squirrel. "They tell me you shot that from better than 200 yards."

"Could be; hard to tell in the half-light of dawn."

Thomas suppressed a grin. "You are to come with me, soldier."

"Now?" Riley asked.

"At once."

Riley picked up his rifle and shuffled after Thomas. "Shouldn't I tell my sergeant?"

"He has already been informed," Goree assured him.

"What's this all about, sir?" Riley asked. "Where are we going?"

"To see General Lee."

"General Lee!"

"'Fraid so," Thomas replied with a nod that Riley could not see in the dark.

*   *   *

An hour later Thomas escorted the bewildered private into Lee's tent. Riley stood at rigid attention as Robert E. Lee slowly looked him over: the ragged clothes, the gaunt features, the unshod feet. Lee turned to an orderly.

"Please bring Private Riley some food," he ordered. "And a proper uniform."

"At once, General." The sergeant saluted and left the tent.

"At ease, Private," Lee said in a kindly tone. "Please have a chair."

Riley sat down stiffly on a nearby stool.

"Where are you from, son?"

"Spotsylvania, sir," Riley said.

"Have you seen much action?"

"Yes, sir. I've been with General Pickett since before Gettysburg."

A shadow clouded Lee's eyes, and Thomas knew he was recalling the bitter memory of Pickett's division as it was cut to pieces over that long mile of open ground below Cemetery Ridge.

Lee cleared his throat after a moment's pause. "Captain Goree assures me that you are one of the finest sharpshooters in my army."

Riley blushed. "I don't know about that, Marse Robert, but I do reckon myself a pretty fair shot."

"We will need your skills in a very important contest," Lee said. "One that may decide, not only the outcome of the war, but the fate of the entire Confederacy."

"A shootin' contest?"

Thomas shook his head and carefully explained the circumstances to the young private. When he finished Riley sat staring at them in numb silence. Finally he blinked his eyes twice and whispered, "Lord have mercy."

"Yes," Lee agreed soberly. "May God have mercy on us all."

*　*　*

Thomas stood on the porch of a stately manor and studied the column of approaching horsemen with his field glasses. Gray cavalry led the procession as it wound down the dusty road from Petersburg, and he could easily make out Grant and Rawlins riding close behind. Following them was a pair of brigadier generals that Goree was not familiar with.

One was tall and handsome, with a long thick mustache. Although not awkward on horseback it was obvious that he was not at home there, either. Thomas would have felt a kinship with the officer had he known of his scholarly background. The Federal was an ex-theologian and college professor who had shocked his family and colleagues by volunteering for military service at the start of the war. He would shock them again by becoming one of the most extraordinary soldiers in the history of the United States Army. Wounded three times in battle, once almost fatally, he had been promoted to the rank of general posthumously when his superiors had assumed the worst. But Joshua Lawrence Chamberlain lived to return to the battlefield and gain a reputation that would have made Goree envious.

Thomas swung his glasses to the other officer. One glance told Goree that this was a professional soldier and his casual ease in the saddle was that of a cavalryman. His uniform was well-tailored and somewhat gaudy, his hair long and curly. He, too, was bound for fame but it would not find him for several years and far to the west. Thomas guessed correctly that Grant had chosen the horse soldier to appease the angry Sheridan, but Grant also knew the officer to be brash, bold and daring, a man who never shied away from a fight—the same qualities that would later lead George Armstrong Custer and his 7th Cavalry to their fate along the banks of the Little Bighorn.

Close behind the two generals a canvas-covered wagon bumped and rattled over the uneven roadway.

What have they got in there? Thomas wondered as the parade came to a halt in the yard. The Federal party dismounted and climbed the steps of the mansion, whose brick facade and graceful columns bore the telltale signs of neglect, the residents having long abandoned their home as the tide of war rolled toward them.

Grant nodded to his counterpart. "My compliments, General Lee. It is a fine day."

"It is indeed," agreed the Confederate.

Grant turned to his officers. "May I introduce Generals Custer and Chamberlain."

Both men bowed and Lee said, "You gentlemen are most welcome. Allow me to present Captain Goree and Colonel Pelham."

Thomas offered a salute but Pelham remained leaning against the porch rail.

Lee held out an arm. "And this is Private Riley of the 7th Virginia Volunteers."

Riley stepped hesitantly forward in his new uniform and bowed awkwardly.

Lee looked past Grant's shoulder. "And may I ask after your enlisted man?"

Grant signaled to the wagon and a tall, muscular infantry private emerged from beneath its canvas cover. He wore the baggy red trousers and tasseled fez of the 165th New York Zouaves. As he approached the porch a ripple of shock crossed the faces of the Confederates. It was not the color of his outlandish uniform that stunned Thomas, but the color of his skin.

"May I present Private Gideon Moore," Grant said soberly as the black soldier snapped to attention at the bottom step.

Thomas waited for Lee—or even Longstreet—to speak up. Surely they would not allow this. But Lee's face remained expressionless and Longstreet merely chuckled softly. "As you said, Sam. One can never tell with Mr. Lincoln."

"Actually, this is my idea," corrected Grant, "although the president supported it enthusiastically."

Pelham fidgeted at his commander's side. "Yes, Colonel?" Lee asked.

"If I may speak freely, sir," the gunner said. Lee nodded.

"I believe the Federals are making a mockery of this solemn occasion by the inclusion of a colored contestant." Pelham shot a haughty glance at the Zouave. "As gentlemen, we must refuse to participate in any endeavor where the opposition is of obvious inferior origins."

Thomas nodded. As a free Texan he did not believe in slavery but neither did he believe in emancipation, feeling as many did in the South that the Negro was not yet ready for the responsibility of freedom.

Lee looked over at Longstreet, who simply shrugged noncommittally. He turned to face Riley. "It is our young private who will be pitted against the Negro," Lee said, "therefore we will let him decide the issue."

Riley stared at the black soldier, whose eyes had remained to the front throughout the discussion. "It will be a pleasure, sir, to give the Federal the whippin' he deserves."

*　*　*

Thomas rode with the other contestants to the same wide valley where he had come across the two foreigners almost a month beforehand. Ringed by deep woods and carpeted with sheep pasture, the vale was dotted here and there with a number of ponds and traversed by a maze of creeks. MacTavish and Freemantle had spent two hard weeks preparing the course for play. With the help of a Tennessee regiment they had cleared away the rocks from the fairways and made use of modified wagons to smooth out the greens. Eighteen holes had been devised in a roughly circular layout, with each tin can cup sporting a captured Union regimental battle flag hanging from its wooden pin—a special touch that had Thomas and the other rebels grinning.

Grant had the wagon rolled up and its cover torn off. Inside lay a stack of eight wooden crates, each containing a set of golf clubs manufactured in the industrial North and patterned after Colonel Freemantle's clubs. Thomas opened his crate like a Christmas present, removing the freshly-oiled clubs one at a time and carefully placing them in a polished leather bag that had arrived with the crates. Using the new equipment, the teams underwent two days of intense instruction and practice under the watchful eyes of the foreigners. Thomas and the other Southerners worked with MacTavish on the front nine while Freemantle guided the Northerners around the back. Goree developed a quick bond with the big Scotsman, who recognized the Texan's talent and took him under his wing.

"Ye've got a gift fer the game, laddie," MacTavish told Thomas as he and his teammates hit scores of practice balls. "But don't be lured into believing that ye've mastered it—or that ye'll ever master it. Golf has a way of humbling even the most gifted o' players."

Humbling was exactly how the Americans found their introduction to golf's fundamentals:

"Ye're not allowed ta attack yer opponent or his ball under any circumstances!"

"You can't hope to control your swing, General, if you insist on gripping the club like a saber."

"Nae, nae, nae, Private! Stop swingin' yer driver as if it were a bloody musket!"

"The idea, my colonial friends, is to loft the ball toward the green, not propel it low and straight as if it were a Minié ball and then flag the enemy."

"The object is ta keep yer ball out in the open, in the middle o' the fairway, not under the cover o' the trees or behind the fences, nae matter how safe it may feel."

"I don't care how tempting it might appear, General Custer, it is still not allowed to swing your club from horseback."

And yet, aided by the rigors of their military discipline, the newcomers displayed a marked improvement after two days of constant practice. As twilight touched the course on the end of the second day it was Goree and Chamberlain who stood head and shoulders above their comrades, with Pelham, Riley and Moore occupying the second echelon, making the South a clear favorite going in. Thomas slept little on the eve of the match and was already up practicing when the morning dawned bright and clear. Freemantle and MacTavish addressed the teams on the dew-blanketed course as the sun climbed high over the treetops.

"Gentlemen," began the Englishman grandly, "the day is upon us. The pairings for the matches will be as follows: First off will be General Ulysses S. Grant, USA, vs. General Robert E. Lee, CSA. Following will be General George A. Custer, USA, vs. Colonel John Pelham, CSA. Next will be General Joshua L. Chamberlain, USA, vs. Captain Thomas J. Goree, CSA. Lastly will come Private Gideon Moore, USA, vs. Private Eustice Riley, CSA."

Thomas regarded the dashing Chamberlain with some trepidation, having recently learned that this was the same brave officer who had led his heavily outnumbered regiment in a desperate bayonet charge that saved the Union's left flank from collapse at Gettysburg. How the Federal would perform on the course Goree could not guess, but he was determined to remain on the lookout for any surprising maneuvers.

"Colonel Freemantle and I will serve ta ensure that fairness and order are abided by," added the burly MacTavish.

"Like Provost Marshals?" asked Thomas.

"Aye," replied the Scotsman. "We'll be acting as marshals and arbiters o' the rules."

Freemantle stiffly scanned the American faces before him. "Are there any questions before we begin?"

Lee cleared his throat. "I have had some…difficulties of late," he said, obliquely referring to his heart attack. "Is it allowed for someone to carry my bag?"

Freemantle and MacTavish conferred for a moment. "It is acceptable," the Englishman said, "providing that all who wish to have their bags carried are allowed the same advantage."

Major Taylor stepped to Lee's side. "General Lee, it would be an honor to carry your bag."

"I am grateful, Major." Lee handed the young aide his clubs.

Thomas was surprised to find Old Pete standing behind him, holding his bag. "Please, sir, it won't do to have a major general carry my clubs."

"Nonsense," replied Longstreet gruffly. "Besides, what better way to follow the developments?"

"We will proceed by order of rank," Freemantle said to Lee. "You and General Grant will play first."

"Very well, Colonel." He turned to Grant. "After you, sir."

"No, General," Grant replied, pointing his club at the ground. "This is soil which you have defended admirably. If it is to be struck, let a Virginian strike it first."

Thomas nodded approvingly at the well-spoken words and Lee bent to scoop a handful of sand from the teebox. With it he constructed a small mound and placed his ball on the crest. Taylor handed him his driver and Lee waggled it once over the ball before staring intently down the fairway. His swing was controlled and graceful, but the ball was badly topped and bounded a few dozen yards like a wounded rabbit.

Thomas groaned inwardly and turned to watch Grant study the hole as he chewed on a cigar. The Federal commander set the half-finished stogie on the ground and took a wide stance. The tails of his infantry coat, unbuttoned and open, swayed comically with his rapid and abbreviated swing. His ball flew farther than Lee's but was hooked sharply and vanished into the woods on the left. Rawlins shouldered Grant's clubs, and the final battle of the Civil War began in earnest.

It came as no surprise to Thomas that Lee's game was one of stratagem and opportunity. His genius in battle was his consistent ability to perceive the lay of the land and use it to his advantage. Likewise, in golf Lee learned to assess a hole quickly and make good use of the knowledge. Ball placement and timing, along with knowing when to take risks and when to be defensive, were the hallmarks of his tactics, and Goree felt a sense of pride watching the heroic figure maneuver around the links.

On the other hand Grant's style seemed to be one of intuition and bullheadedness. He displayed a talent for finding a hole's weakness and attacking it without mercy, propelling his ball onward more by the power of his will than by any physical gifts. Neither man excelled at the game, and shots more often sailed wide than found their mark. Lee played well enough to jump out to a two-point advantage by the time they made the turn, but Grant applied a steady pressure on the back nine that slowly eroded, and eventually overran, the Confederate's lead, giving the first match to the Federals 2 and 1.

The second match was not as hotly contested as the first. While Custer charged boldly around the course, Pelham countered with a more methodical approach. His artillery instincts for range and windage combined with a deft sense of touch had him lobbing balls at the flags all morning. The steady barrage forced Custer into a spiraling display of recklessness and Pelham claimed the match 5 and 4.

Thomas and Chamberlain squared off in the third match and the Federal established himself early as an inspired choice. Thomas could not help but grudgingly admire his opponent as he watched Chamberlain apply his intellect to the task—first reducing the holes to a series of problems, then solving them one at a time with clever, and sometimes unorthodox, shots that confounded Goree and had him pushing to hold his ground. Thomas made a brief run on fourteen and fifteen with back-to-back bogeys, but the turning point came on the 17th hole when he followed Chamberlain's fine drive with an atrocious slice into the middle of a pond. Chamberlain holed out for a bogey and the match was over, with the officer in blue up by two points.

The final pairing proved to be an intriguing contest and Thomas was able to watch much of the seesaw struggle from his position a hole ahead. Moore played a power game, clubbing breathtaking drives and approach shots that got him into serious difficulty almost as often as it got him to the greens. Goree noted that, although Private Riley's efforts traveled nowhere near as far as those of his Union foe, his marksman-like patience and subtlety around the greens more than made up for his lack of strength. The sharpshooter ended up winning the match by a stroke with a long putt on the 18th green as Thomas and the others watched from the fringe.

"What happens now?" Thomas asked MacTavish, after the contest had ended with the forces even at two matches apiece.

"We were prepared fer the possibility o' a standoff," the Scotsman replied. "Following a rest and a break for mess call we shall return ta the 1st hole and draw lots ta determine new pairings. The first pair will then play the hole ta determine the outcome."

"And if there is no outright winner," added Freemantle, "we will proceed to the next hole, where the second pairing will take a turn. This will continue until an eventual victor is decided."

*　*　*

It was mid-afternoon when Thomas noticed the first Southern troops emerging like gray ghosts from the forests that surrounded the course. It is an old adage that military secrets are by far the most fleeting, so it did not take long for the news to spread through the rank and file of both armies. An hour later he saw the blue uniforms begin to straggle in.

Thomas was thrilled to see them arrive—thrilled that they were coming to see *him*, Thomas Goree, take a hand in deciding the great conflict that had torn a nation apart. By the time Goree and the other contestants reconvened on the 1st tee, the split-rail fences that lined the fairways were filled with battle-worn men who had come to witness the end of their long struggle. By an unspoken accord they lay aside their muskets, until the meadow beyond the woods resembled a field at harvest time dotted with triangular stacks of iron rather than cornstalks. Both sides then settled in and waited to discover what the day would reap.

As MacTavish and Freemantle prepared lots, a carriage flanked by a strong contingent of Federal cavalry rolled to the edge of the course. From beneath its shadowy interior emerged a tall thin man dressed somberly in black. The horse soldiers tried to form a protective screen around him, but the lanky figure pushed past and strode with long legs to the top of a nearby knoll.

Thomas gaped at the famous profile and Lee said, "It would appear that Mr. Lincoln is impatient for news of the outcome."

"Then let us not keep him waiting," responded Grant. MacTavish held out his tam filled with eight folded slips of paper and each player picked a number. Thomas presented his to Freemantle and waited anxiously as the English officer compiled the results.

"The first pairing will be General Chamberlain vs. General Lee," Freemantle announced.

Thomas' shoulders sagged at the news. Not only was he disappointed at not being chosen, he also felt a sense of dread regarding the outcome. Chamberlain had performed brilliantly during the morning round, and given Lee's spotty play there seemed no reason the dominance would not continue.

The handsome Federal stood on the tee and regarded the long hole before him, his dark eyes roving the terrain, seeking opportunity. He chose to aim to the right of a small hillock that dominated the center of the fairway, and his shot was short but relatively accurate, landing near the knoll and rolling along its edge.

Before playing, Lee took a moment to confer with his teammates.

"Any advice regarding strategy, gentlemen?" he asked.

"Stay close to him," urged Longstreet.

Thomas nodded his head vigorously. "Yes," he said, "shadow him and look for an opening."

Lee drove off, and his ball ended up farther to the right than Chamberlain's but close enough to give the Confederate essentially the same second shot as his opponent. Chamberlain stepped up to his ball and fired a brassie well down the fairway. It appeared to be a fine play until it took a bad hop and trickled into the long grass that bordered the course. Lee answered with a shot that managed to stay in the fairway just a dozen yards behind the Federal's ball.

Noting Chamberlain's thick lie, Lee launched a bold offensive of his own. A narrow finger of woodland poked across the fairway and guarded the green that was mostly hidden behind it. Lee considered the obstacle and turned to the nearby Pelham. "Distance, Colonel?"

The gunner frowned at the hole. "One hundred and forty-five yards, sir."

The safe play was to the right around the trees, but Lee decided to gamble and shoot straight for the flag. His high approach was over the green but effective.

"Brilliant stroke, sir," Thomas beamed. "He'll have no choice but to try and follow suit."

Hindered by his poor lie, Chamberlain's third shot also landed long and each officer took another three strokes to hole out.

On the 2nd tee Freemantle studied the paper in his hand and cried out: "General Grant vs. Colonel Pelham!"

Excellent, thought Thomas, wishing again that it had been his name called, but pleased with the results. *Surely Pelham holds the advantage.*

Grant must've felt the same. He grumbled as he took his stance and stroked a low shot that never got more than a few feet off the ground. It bounced down the middle of the fairway and came to rest halfway to the green.

"A fine shot, sir," Rawlins said encouragingly.

The Federal commander shoved his cigar back into his mouth. "Merely the first thrust, John. We must wait and see what the opposition does."

Pelham countered with a high drive to the left that avoided a small hollow filled with dense shrubbery guarding the right-hand approach.

Goree smiled and swelled with pride as he followed the twosome up the fairway amidst cheers and hoots of encouragement from the troops in the gallery.

"Teach that Reb a lesson, General!" a blue soldier close to Thomas shouted while the Rebel leaning over the fence beside him hollered, "Yeah, like the quickest way back across the Potomac."

Each officer mishit his next attempt and Grant followed with a vicious hack at his ball for his 3rd stroke. It quickly bled to the right, barely missing the hollow and disappearing into a patch of deep grass well to the front and right of the green.

As he had done all day, Pelham took careful aim and followed with a wonderfully hit niblick that landed near the front of the green and rolled all the way to the back edge. A number of the Confederates let out a loud whoop that slowly gained strength as more and more took up the cry. It soared to an eerie high-pitched crescendo that sent a chill down the spine of every soldier in blue— the Rebel Yell.

Rawlins was clearly shaken, having never been so near the infamous battle cry. But Grant merely produced a new cigar from his coat and calmly lit it. He tossed the spent match to the ground and went off to look for his ball. When it was not immediately found a search party was formed to comb the long grass.

"I think we have them, sir," Thomas remarked to Longstreet as the blue forces foraged through the thick turf.

"That is what the Federals have said about us time and again," Old Pete replied, "only to be proven wrong."

Thomas looked up the hill to where Lincoln stood still as a statue, his arms clasped behind his back. Here was a fellow intellectual, a lawyer like himself. Goree could only wonder what was going through the man's head as he watched the ebb and flow of the match from the high ground.

Grant's ball was eventually found and he stood behind it staring intently at the flag blowing in the gentle breeze. He had about 10 yards of knee-high grass to escape from, and then another 20 yards of uneven ground that rose in a steep slope to the edge of an elevated green whose putting surface slanted sharply away from him.

"Gentlemen," he said, "the enemy is on both flanks and it would seem that drastic measures are called for."

Chamberlain stepped forward. "May I suggest a direct assault, sir?"

Grant looked toward the green. "You mean charge the hill?"

Chamberlain nodded and Grant smiled. "My thought exactly."

He asked Rawlins for the cleek and eyed the grass to his front, searching for an opening. Using the strength in his stocky shoulders the Union commander swung the club as hard as he could. The ball sliced out of the tall grass and struck the side of the berm that cradled the right side of the green. It bounced high into the air, landed on the edge of the putting surface and rolled to a stop just eight feet from the cup.

Thomas shook his head as the Union troops surrounding the green burst into joyous shouts of "Huzzah! Huzzah!" He looked back up at Lincoln but saw no change in the stoic posture. It gave Thomas a moment's pause. So much was at stake for Lincoln and his precious Union, yet Goree sensed only a quiet watchfulness from the great politician—a faith that the outcome was in larger hands than his.

Pelham proceeded to lag his ball to the same area of the green as Grant's and both managed to get down in two from there.

Thomas joined the others on the 3rd tee and waited to see who would be next. He was stymied again as Colonel Freemantle called out, "Custer vs. Riley."

For the second hole in a row it appeared that the odds were in favor of the South, but Riley opened with an inglorious slice into the rough. Custer, well aware of his opportunity to secure a place in history, followed by clubbing a heroic shot down the left side of the fairway, leaving him in perfect position to take the hole. To his credit Private Riley showed no sign of panic. The young marksman calmly launched a towering volley that impacted on the upper tier of the green and bounced off the backside. Custer then counterattacked with a mashie hit directly at the pin, which stood at attention on the lower tier. The ball struck the flag square on and fell a mere foot from the cup.

Sensing that all was lost, Thomas gloomily stepped on the green to tend the pin as Custer preened shamelessly before the roaring crowd of blue troops. He bowed low and swept his hat along the ground. Goree eyed the short distance between Custer's ball and the hole, then turned to survey Riley's tricky downhill pitch.

"Can you make it, son?" he heard Lee ask the private.

Riley snapped a crisp salute. "I will endeavor to make Virginia proud, sir."

"I have never asked anything more from my men," Lee replied. "Carry on."

The sniper gauged his line with care, stalking the length of the green twice before stepping to his ball. It was more than forty feet across the upper tier and another twenty to the cup itself. Using his wedge, Riley lobbed the ball high over the green. It hopped twice, then settled down to roll smoothly across the short-trimmed grass. Thomas watched it reach the slope that divided the two tiers with barely enough speed. It trickled over the ridge and quickly shot down the embankment, carving an accurate arc for the target. He pulled the pin just as the ball fell into the tin cup for a 3.

Thomas tossed his hat high in the air, and the keening warble of the Rebel Yell filled the valley as the dazed Custer tried to recover himself. Lee eventually quieted the troops and Custer tapped in the short putt to halve the hole.

Both teams huddled on the 4th tee, the officers in two groups with the privates standing respectfully, just outside their counsels. There was no need for Freemantle to announce the next pairing; everyone realized it would be Thomas against the big Negro private.

"You should have an easy time of it against the colored boy," Pelham remarked confidently.

Old Pete frowned. "I believe Private Riley would likely tell you that the Federal proved a worthy adversary."

Pelham dismissed the comment. "Begging the General's pardon but I have yet to meet a colored who was worthy of anything other than hard labor. Besides, Riley is a mere farmer; there's not a Negro alive who can beat a Southern gentleman on equal terms. Ain't that right, Goree?"

Thomas did not reply. He knew that this was not an issue of race. It was no longer even a matter of North vs. South. After four years of horrific battles and more than a million men dead or wounded it had all come down to just two individuals. Thomas had spent those four years craving the chance to make a difference, never once daring to dream that he would someday stand on the cold knife-edge of history waiting to see which way the blade would slice. He glanced back up the hill. Lincoln knew the immense pressure Thomas was feeling—so did Grant and Lee.

"It's yer play, lad," MacTavish said in a kindly tone, snapping the Texan out of his reverie.

Thomas stared down the fairway. The fourth was a long, curving hole with woods crowding the left side, and a large pond on the right that bloated into the fairway just short of the green. Moore had been hitting tremendous drives, and Thomas knew that he needed a satisfactory one in order to keep up with the powerful Zouave. He swung and, thankfully, made solid contact, sending his ball well down the fairway and close to the trees on the left. Moore responded by hitting his drive hard but fat. The skyrocketed result traveled only 50 yards and Thomas had to fight back a grin. Moore, anxious to make up ground, followed his unfortunate first shot with an even worse second, slicing his ball toward the lurking pond. It landed short of the water and looked for a moment as if it might stay dry, but the pond was sunk into a deep depression in the valley. The ball rolled to the rim and slipped over the side into the murky water.

Thomas and Longstreet walked to his ball, with the youngster brimming with confidence. He lay only one and was almost even with the Federal who, if Goree understood the rules correctly, was faced with an impossible task. The Southerner played a safe second shot up the middle of the fairway and wandered to within earshot of where his opponent stood conferring with Freemantle and Chamberlain.

"You'll have to take a penalty stroke and a drop from this side of the pond, where you'll be playing four," the British colonel informed Moore.

Thomas looked to the green and the body of water that spanned to within yards of its edge. The way in which the pond took a massive bite from the fairway left Moore no alternate means of approach. More than 200 yards of still water stood between him and his goal, and the Zouave had no choice but to find a way across it in a single shot or the war was lost.

"Do you think you can reach it?" Chamberlain asked the black soldier.

"I can only try, sir," Moore replied, not taking his eyes off the green.

"If you end up in the pond again."

"What pond would that be, sir?" Moore asked.

Chamberlain grinned. "It's your battle, Private."

Moore nodded and set his heavy jaw as he took his stance. Thomas could almost feel the energy coiling in the Federal's limbs as he stared fiercely at his ball. When he swung, the club made an almost musical sound as it sliced through the air, just as the impact with the ball reverberated with a clear note that left no doubt it had been struck with perfection. It soared for the green, tracing a glorious arc that Goree could only watch in complete fascination. The rubber sphere landed a bare foot from the shore of the pond, took a high hop onto the green and came to rest on the far side of the pin.

Thomas was dumbfounded. A moment ago he was in total command of the field. Now he needed to reach the green in order to maintain any advantage. Suddenly he understood what it must be like for the field commanders who seem about to overrun a position, only to have the enemy appear out of nowhere on their flank.

"Steady now, son." Longstreet lay a large hand on Thomas' shoulder. "A good soldier learns not to flinch under fire." Goree swallowed and nodded. He saw Lee and Pelham watching from a distance and felt as if a row of Union cannons were pointed at him. His ball lay well up on the grass; he had a clear shot at the flag. All Thomas had to do was loft it onto the green.

He knew halfway through his downswing that it was offline but he was powerless to stop its momentum. The left to right action sent the ball on a long, bending flight into the forest. The horrified young Confederate did not turn around, had no wish to see the recrimination in Lee's eyes. Old Pete shouldered the clubs and together they silently trudged off beneath the canopy of trees.

There was a long search for his ball in the dense underbrush, but Longstreet finally discovered it lying beside a thicket of blackberries forty feet from the fairway. The position left Thomas little to work with. A shot toward the green was a virtual impossibility, and even the "safe" play straight to the open fairway was wrought with peril. He looked in the direction of the distant flag where a gauntlet of stout trunks stood between him and the green like a full brigade of Federal infantry.

Longstreet stood mutely a dozen paces away, a subtle signal that he had no advice to offer his troubled subordinate. Goree gripped his mashie and peered down the columns of trees that barred his way. There was only one opening that was more generous than the rest, a place where an older tree had fallen and the forest had not yet had time to close ranks and fill the gap. But it was a hopeless task. He looked down at his ball lying in the dead leaves and when he looked up again Private Riley was at his shoulder.

"Find a mark, Captain," the sharpshooter said, "something well toward the target."

Thomas looked and saw a pinecone hanging from a green-needled limb just past the opening in the trees. "Found one," he said.

"Now, stare at it until it's all you can see. Focus on it until nothing else exists in this here woods except you and the target," whispered Riley. "When you reach the point where it's still there when you shut your eyes...look down and swing."

Thomas stared at the pinecone until his eyes began to water with the effort. He shut them tight and it dangled in his mind like an icicle. Bringing the club back slowly, he held it up high for a moment before releasing his shoulders and letting his body uncoil. The ball made a sound like a bullet as it zipped through the woods, whistling and ticking off leaves as it found the chosen breach, just missing the nose of the pinecone. It sailed clear of the forest and floated toward the green, alighting just a few feet from the hole and rolling a handful of yards away.

Thomas could not believe his eyes. He gaped at the club in his hands and turned to thank the infantryman but Riley had slipped away just as quietly as he had come.

Lee was the first to reach Goree as he emerged from the trees. "Magnificent shot, soldier!" he said. "Absolutely superb!"

"Thank you, sir, but there is still work to be done." Thomas soberly surveyed the green. "The enemy has yet to leave the field."

The Federal had the slightly longer putt but far easier terrain to navigate. Moore settled over his ball and stroked it firmly toward the hole. It rolled true to its line, and Thomas felt his heart sink as it dropped into the center of the cup. All Goree could hope for now was to halve the hole and continue the match. He had eight feet of sloping grass to the cup. Make it—and it was on to the next tee. Miss—and the North wins. He looked at his hands as they gripped the putter, realizing that it was his own destiny he was taking hold of. Fate funneled down to a point in time as he lined up over his ball, and Captain Thomas Goree felt it pressed sharply against his throat.

Every man stood stock-still. Total silence filled the valley and surrounding woodland as if the tortured countryside itself held its breath in anticipation. Thomas softly tapped the ball and it immediately began to pick up speed and slide to the left. Too late he realized that he had aimed high and the ball would miss on the uphill side. But a foot from the hole it encountered a patch of uneven turf and kicked to the left. Not much, just a degree or two, but enough to correct its course and steer it toward the target. *It was in!* Thomas thought with glee. *They would live to fight another hole!* The ball skirted the edge of the cup, rolled completely around the rim and lipped out to lie impotently on the green carpet.

* * *

The Civil War was over. But instead of the wild cries of the victorious or the anguished wails of the vanquished, only silence remained. Perhaps it was a moment to recall the dead who would never return home, or perhaps a moment to mourn the living who must somehow carry on amid a vast storehouse of haunting memories. Whatever the purpose, it passed in a respectful hush that was finally broken by a cry of rage from Colonel Pelham.

The Confederate gunner stormed up to Goree. "You, sir, have shamed the South and the very uniform you wear," he roared, red-faced. "How dare you allow yourself to be beaten by a colored boy!"

Thomas felt a remarkable sense of calm, almost a relief. For good or bad the South's inevitable fall would be forever tied to him. He looked down the fairway at the crowding mass of foot soldiers and thought of the lives that would be spared—of the happy faces of the wives and children, and in many cases the mothers and fathers who would welcome these men home. If that was to be Goree's destiny, could a man ask for a more honorable one?

Thomas pulled himself to attention. "You're wrong, Colonel. I was beaten by a fellow *man*. And if there is to be any shame let it be directed at our long-held ignorance."

He turned to Lee and gave a short bow. "My apologies, sir."

Lee shook his head. "You fought well." He gazed out over the land and the sun dipping toward the tree line. "Virginia may weep, Captain Goree, but she remains proud." He glanced up the hill to where Grant stood beside Lincoln. "If you gentlemen will excuse me."

Longstreet trailed Lee up the hill and Thomas turned to follow. When he went to retrieve his bag he noticed the two privates standing on the edge of the green, where they seemed to be trading tips on the game.

"I just wanted to thank you for your help back in the woods," Thomas said to Riley.

"Just doing my duty, sir," replied the marksman.

"And I'm much obliged," Goree said and turned to face the Zouave, who carefully watched his face. "You played well, Private."

"Thank you, Captain," Moore replied. "As did you." Thomas was surprised to hear a voice that was rich and educated.

"That ball you hit over the water," Thomas said, "I didn't think a shot like that was humanly possible."

Moore smiled a wide infectious grin. "To tell you the truth, sir, neither did I." He laughed and extended a hand. Thomas stared at it for a moment, then clasped it with his own.

"God go with you, Captain," Moore said.

"And with you…sir," replied Thomas. Riley offered Goree a nod and then he and the Federal joined the procession of men, both blue and gray, who had already begun the impossibly long journey back to the lives they had left a lifetime ago. Thomas hurried up the slope after Lee. As he neared the brow of the hill he saw the Confederate leader remove his hat and bow to Lincoln.

"I regret that we have yet to broach the terms of our surrender," Lee said as he felt for his sword and, not finding it on his belt, awkwardly turned his driver around and handed it to the president, grip first. "Until we do so, I must consider myself your prisoner, sir."

Abraham Lincoln looked down at the proffered club and shook his craggy head. "No sir…you *must* consider yourself, once again, my countryman."

A look of gratitude passed over Lee's features. He bowed again. "With your permission I will return to my headquarters. There is yet much to do."

"By all means, General," replied Lincoln.

Lee spotted his aide standing nearby with his clubs slung over a shoulder. "May I keep these, General?" Lee asked Grant, pointing to the bag.

Grant grinned and turned to his coal-black charger. He flipped aside a canvas flap to reveal his own clubs strapped to the side of the horse.

"Consider them a souvenir of war," he said past his cigar.

* * *

Lee and Longstreet waited at the bottom of the hill as a horse was brought for Thomas. He mounted and the three men rode slowly back toward the camps. Long lines of gray troops parted to make way for the trio, many reaching out to touch Traveller as he passed by, their tear-streaked faces mirrored in their beloved commander's eyes. Some patted the flank of Goree's horse as well, offering him a look of respect that caused the young aide to sit taller in the saddle.

"It was well fought," Old Pete said.

"Yes," nodded Lee, keeping his eyes forward, "there can be honor in this."

Thomas smiled to himself and thought, *Honor is where one finds it.*

"An interesting exercise, this game of golf," Goree remarked as he rode between the two generals.

"Indeed," Lee said, turning for a last look at the dusk-shadowed course. "It is well that I am so terrible, lest I should grow too fond of it."

Author's Note

To the many Civil War buffs who have undoubtedly noted that one or two of the characters may or may not have been in action during the time in question, thank you for allowing me a wee bit of literary leeway. And for those who do not recognize the final sentence, it is taken from the lips of Robert E. Lee himself when, after watching 8,000 Federal infantry slaughtered in front of a stone wall at Fredericksburg, he supposedly said to Longstreet: "It is well that war is so terrible, lest we should grow too fond of it."

THEY PLAY GOLF IN HEAVEN

G. GUILFORD BARTON

What *will* heaven be like? Will the streets really be paved in gold? Will there be no sun or moon—the only illumination provided by the radiance of God himself? We do know that it will be a place free from sin and sorrow and death, where the saints will revel in God's holy presence forever and ever. But what else will we do there? After all…forever is a very long time. So here's a whimsical take on what the afterlife might be like for anyone who's ever wondered if *They Play Golf in Heaven*.

THEY PLAY GOLF IN HEAVEN

T he truck loomed out of the San Franciscan fog like a lost ship. It bore down on Reverend Francis Mulroony and struck him squarely on the left side, sending him tumbling across the damp pavement. The next thing the minister knew he was standing at the curb, watching with detached interest as a small knot of bystanders formed around the spot where his crumpled body lay. Someone dashed off to call 911 while another kindly soul removed her coat and gently covered him with it. The simple act of compassion touched Mulroony, who noted with irony that he had been en route to offer similar comfort to an ailing member of his flock.

*   *   *

Francis found it odd that what disturbed him most about the scene was not the blood flowing so freely into the gutter but the way his limbs were so carelessly left in an undignified state—arms flung over his head and legs bent at odd angles. He had an urge to bend down and straighten them out but the light from the corner convenience store distracted him. It flooded out the door to lap and tug at his feet—warm and bright and so inviting that he turned from his broken flesh and stepped into the light....

*   *   *

He found himself in a tiny wood-paneled room with a beamed ceiling and golden sunlight pouring through the many-paned windows. In the middle of the room sat an ancient table, and in the middle of the table lay a huge book, and in the middle of the book a man followed a line of text with his large-knuckled index finger. He was a giant of a man, dark-haired, bearded and rough looking. The leather-like texture of his skin spoke of many years spent working beneath a scorching sun, yet his thoughtful brow betrayed an even longer term of devotion to a far different calling. He wore a white golf shirt that displayed an arching rainbow over a rising sun on one side of his barrel chest. Beneath the logo, stitched in golden thread, was: *Paradise Gate Golf Club.* Over his other breast it read simply: *Pete.*

"May I help you?" he asked, keeping his eyes fixed on his reading.

"Um…I'm not sure," Francis answered uncertainly, looking around the room. "Is this heaven?"

"Yep. Do you have a reservation?"

"Well…I hope I do."

The big man finally looked up and eyed him carefully. "Let's just consult the book, then, shall we? Name, please?"

"Mulroony. Francis James Mulroony."

Pete flipped forward a few pages and ran his finger down the wide white surface crowded with peculiar-looking text. "Hmmmm, Mulroony, Mulroony…odd, nothing under that name."

He raised a hand to his face and stroked his thick beard as he studied the newcomer. "But now that you're here what shall we do with you? Ah, now I remember.…He pointed a finger to the sky and turned to the back of the book. "You're in luck; we had a late cancellation this morning. You tee off in twenty minutes."

"Tee off?"

"Yes, you do play golf, don't you?"

"Well…yes. But I don't have my clubs." Francis looked down on his striped boxer shorts. "In fact I don't have any clothes, for that matter."

"Of course not," Pete said gruffly. "Did you think we were just kidding with that *you can't take it with you* stuff?"

The minister pointed to his undergarments. "What about these?"

"We let you keep 'em." Pete waved his huge hand. "You'll find that fig leaves are hard to come by and not very practical in any case." He pointed to the floor and said, "Just follow the white line and you'll find everything you need."

Mulroony wanted to pose a few more pointed questions but the saint had already turned back to his study of the perplexing tome. With a sigh, Francis walked along the narrow line and passed into the adjoining room where he froze in wonder. Before him stood a vast storehouse of every kind of club and golf accessory ever made. Display upon countless display, aisle upon endless aisle, stack upon stack upon stack, piling up until they vanished in the murky distance high overhead. The minister stood gazing upward when a smiling face popped out from behind a stand of golf bags.

"Be with you in a moment," the face said cheerily before disappearing again.

Being a bit of a historian, Mulroony thought he recognized the neat features. Stepping into the neighboring aisle he found the man setting up a row of putters. He was dressed in a pair of light gray plus-fours, yellow knee socks, a tweed cap and the same type of shirt as Pete, except that this one proclaimed his name to be Harry.

"Welcome, friend," the man said warmly in a clipped British accent. "Can I help you find a set of clubs?"

"You're the great Harry Vardon!" Mulroony stammered, pointing like a five-year-old.

The man waved away the minister's homage like a pesky fly. "Tut, tut. Around here, I'm just plain old Harry." Vardon chuckled and cast a dubious eye on Mulroony's boxers. "May I suggest we start in the trouser aisle?"

The legendary golfer sat Francis down in front of a gilded mirror and instantly produced a pair of sporty checked slacks. "How do these grab you? They're the latest rage on the greens."

"Hmm…do you have anything in khaki?" Francis asked hopefully.

"Khaki?" shouted Harry. "Say no more!" He wheeled out a long rack of trousers and Mulroony picked out a pair that fit snugly around his ample waist. Next he selected a powder blue shirt emblazoned with the club logo. Much to the minister's surprise he found his name already embroidered on it when he pulled it from the rack. In fact every shirt he modeled had *Frank* sewed on the chest in golden letters. He completed the ensemble with argyle socks and a pair of black, wing-tipped spikes. Harry proclaimed it a smashing outfit but Francis frowned as he studied his image in the mirror.

"You know I don't have any way to pay for all this."

"Frank, old bean," Harry admonished, snapping his fingers under the minister's nose. "Root of all evil? Render unto Caesar what is due Caesar? Ringing any bells in the old steeple?"

"Oh...right."

The Brit gave a wide sweep of his arm as he led Mulroony off to survey a staggering selection of clubs. "This whole lot is free for the taking. Take your pick of anything we have in stock, which just happens to be everything. You name it, we've got it. Traditional design, cavity back, offset, steel shaft, graphite, boron, stainless steel, titanium, persimmon head, metal wood, oversized—the whole kit an' caboodle."

As Francis gaped in indecision, Vardon reached out and grabbed a nearby mid-iron. "May I suggest these little beauties? Personal favorite of mine, swing like a dream, with a huge sweet spot. In fact the whole face is one big sweet spot—can't help but catch every shot perfect."

Francis looked at him. "You're joking?"

"Hey, this is heaven, remember?"

"Oh...right," repeated Mulroony, as he selected a white leather bag to carry the clubs in. Like the shirt his name was already stitched along the side.

"Now, in terms of putters," Vardon continued, "I've played every course from the Horsehead Nebula to this side of Purgatory and you'd have to go a lot farther than that to find anything that beats this little number." He held up an elegant hickory-shaft putter and twirled it like a baton. "Just get a load of these slim lines," he bubbled. "Now feel it. Is that light as a feather, or what?"

Francis nodded and placed the exquisitely balanced club in his bag. "I'll need some balls."

"Balls!" bellowed the Englishman. "Say no more." He grabbed hold of the minister's wrist and dragged him to a next aisle where the dimpled orbs stretched for as far as the eye could see. "Balls!" Harry repeated unnecessarily. "What's your pleasure? One piece, two piece, wound, solid or liquid core, Surlyn cover, Balata, low trajectory, high compression, white, orange, yellow, glow-in-the-dark? We've even got some old gutta-percha and featheries if you insist on being a masochist about it."

"I'll take a box of Tour Balata 90s," Mulroony said without hesitation.

"Excellent! Nothing like a chap who knows what he wants," Harry cried, fetching an armful of sleeves and stuffing them into Mulroony's bag.

"There, you're all set. Just follow the white line out to the 1st tee," Harry said with a wave. "Cheerio and good luck!"

*   *   *

As Francis followed the meandering path through the unfathomable warehouse he spotted many other souls like himself being outfitted and gently eased into the afterlife. Eventually he came to a huge pair of intricately carved doors. On the marble header were the chiseled words, PASS THIS BLESSED PORTAL AND KNOW PARADISE. Next to the door was a smaller sign that read *Members Only*.

So Reverend Francis Mulroony stepped past the blessed portal and knew paradise.

Before him stood the ideal 1st tee, beyond that the ideal 1st fairway and beyond that the ideal 1st green shining in the sunlight like a small emerald star. A rushing stream flowed down the left side of the fairway, laughing and singing gaily as it went. Trout leapt from its depths and smiled at him before falling back into the milky froth. Two gazelles lowered their graceful necks for a long drink as a pride of lions lounged indifferently nearby. Birds filled the air with wings and song. Insects droned hypnotically but kept a respectable distance. Francis immediately sensed that he was in a place that knew no pestilence, no sorrow, no fear, no death. It was joy that coursed along the streambed, not water—clean and clear and eternally fresh.

On the tee were three golfers waiting to drive off. Ben Hogan practiced chipping while Bobby Jones chatted away happily with Babe Didrikson, who had been a childhood friend of the minister.

"Mildred?..." he said uncertainly.

"Francis!" Didrikson exclaimed bounding over and hugging him tightly. "At last you've arrived."

"Decent of you to come on such short notice," Jones said in his soft, Southern drawl.

"Well, I really don't see as I had much choice in the matter..."

Babe laughed delightedly. "That's a good one, isn't it, Ben?"

Hogan just nodded as he studied his take back.

"So this is Heaven." Francis drank in the sights and sounds around him. He lowered his bag to the ground and looked about him. "Where are the carts?"

Hogan froze in mid-swing.

Jones paled noticeably.

Didrikson looked stricken.

"I know it's you're first day, dear," she whispered, "but some things are just not spoken of. In heaven, *everybody* walks."

Mulroony blushed. "Sorry."

"Hey, Francis," said a tall, golden-eyed young man, who Francis could have sworn had not been present an instant beforehand. The youth took Mulroony's bag and slung it over his shoulder. "My name is Damien. I'll be your caddie."

"Damien is your guardian angel, Francis," Didrikson said.

The minister chuckled. "You're not serious."

Damien placed his hands on his hips. "What's the matter? Don't you believe in guardian angels?"

"Well, I..."

"Who do you think gets you mortals through a typical day without being hit by a truck?"

"In my case, nobody," Francis said.

Damien rolled his golden eyes. "All right, bad example, but I had orders not to interfere. And don't think for one minute that it was easy to hover around and do nothing."

Mulroony shook his head and stifled a laugh, earning a glare from his protector. "I'm sorry, Damien, I guess I just considered you fellas a product of someone's whimsy."

"Whimsy?" cried the angel. "Remember that charity tournament you won at Pebble a few years back?"

Francis nodded. "Yeah, what about it?"

"Well, it wasn't whimsy that kept your errant drive out of the ice plant on seventeen, pal."

"That was you?" Mulroony exclaimed. "I said at the time it was a miracle the ball stayed in play."

"You bet it was, buster." Damien leaned forward. "And by the way, you're welcome."

"My belated thanks," Francis said peering over the angel's shoulder. "What happened to your wings?"

"Oh, that's just a bunch of nonsense cooked up by the artists' guild during the Renaissance. Can you imagine the havoc those things would wreak with my backswing?"

Babe motioned Mulroony over to the tee. "Why don't you hit first, Francis?"

"But I haven't had a chance to warm up yet."

"No need for that," Jones said, playfully jabbing the minister in the chest. "You no longer have a body in the same sense you used to. This one doesn't need limbering up or any other sort of preparation."

Francis nodded toward the diligent Hogan. "Then why hasn't he stopped practicing since I got here?"

"Because he's Ben Hogan, dear," Didrikson answered sensibly.

"Oh…right."

Francis teed up his ball and swung at it with his heavenly driver. It roared down the fairway like a rocket, landing close to 300 yards down the track.

"Wow!" he cried. "That felt fantastic!"

"Of course it did, Frank," Damien said, returning the club to the bag. "You're in heaven now; things are different."

"You mean to say that every shot will be…you know, perfect?" Francis asked in wonder.

"No," Bobby Jones replied, preparing to swing. "A poor shot is always a possibility, but it won't be due to any flaws in your physical mechanics. Your body, mind, and soul are one now, in perfect harmony."

"No more lapses in your timing," Didrikson said. "No more last-second doubts or visions of impending disaster that can cause you to decelerate through impact."

"However one can still fall victim to adverse circumstance, poor club choice, misread greens and, of course, just plain bad luck," Jones said, finishing his sentence and follow-through almost simultaneously.

"Luck?" the minister asked, watching Jones' drive sail past his own. "In heaven?"

"Certainly," said Babe, "it would hardly be golf without luck, now would it?" She stroked a beautiful shot and turned to Francis. "And you'll find that the score somehow doesn't matter as much here. Isn't that right, Ben?"

Hogan clubbed the best drive of the bunch, caught his tee in midair, grinned broadly and marched down the fairway. Francis sniffed the air as he trailed after him, detecting an odd sulfuric odor coming from somewhere nearby.

"What's that unpleasant smell?" he asked.

"Brimstone," Jones replied, gauging the breeze.

"Brimstone!" Mulroony glanced warily to his right and noted a line of white stakes running along the edge of a deep chasm. A few wisps of smoke billowed up from its depths. "You mean?…"

"That's correct, Francis," Babe nodded, "plays hell with one's left-to-right game."

"Definitely OB," added Jones.

"Stroke and distance," Hogan warned.

"You see, Francis, all mortals, both those that know God and those who don't, come to this place at first," explained Babe. "It's just that the nonbelievers never make it past this point in the journey. They all slice their drive into the abyss and are then irresistibly compelled to follow after it. Once there, they can never return."

Francis took a step backward. "What's it like?"

"We'll never know for sure, thank the Lord," Babe said with a shudder. "Only that it's a place totally devoid of God and golf."

"And as bad as that sounds, what makes it even worse is that they've been *here*, albeit ever so briefly," Jones said, "leaving the image of paradise forever burned into their souls."

"Serves them right for not taking the righteous fork in the road of life," Hogan said curtly.

Didrikson pursed her lips at him and gazed sadly toward the line of stakes. "We can only but dimly imagine their wretched existence and the depths of their suffering as they wander eternally in search of a ball they'll never find."

*　*　*

Francis parred the 1st hole, birdied the next three, eagled the 5th and then found out just what Jones had meant about luck on the 6th when his ball struck a rhinoceros roaming near one of the fairway bunkers. It caromed off the brute's armor and into the adjoining woods. Francis peered beneath the canopy of leaves and hesitated. Unlike the surrounding landscape this place had a brooding quality to it, and even though he could make out a multitude of clearings and glades within, there was a lingering sense of darkness that the slanting shafts of sunlight could not dispel.

Damien walked up beside him. "That's the forest of original temptation."

"I think I'll just take a drop," Mulroony said.

"No, Francis," the angel said, "you have to go in and face the music."

"Why?"

"Why do we do anything in life? To serve the Creator," Damien said. "But don't worry, I'll go with you."

"Watch yourself in there, Francis," Babe cautioned as he and Damien stepped into the trees. "Remember how close you are to the abyss!"

"I'll look in this direction," the angel said pointing to his right, "and you go that way."

"Wait," Francis said in a panicky voice, "you said you were coming with me."

"I won't be far away. Have faith, Mulroony."

*   *   *

Francis wandered about for a few minutes, poking his wedge into the luscious undergrowth. About 20 yards into the forest he found his ball hard against the trunk of a large tree with a huge snake coiled around it.

"Hello, Francisssssssssss!" it hissed.

"Hey," the minister said warily, "you're not supposed to be here."

"Sayssssss who?"

"M...m...m...me," Mulroony stammered, "now get out of the way so I can play my shot."

"You're not *really* going to play it where it liesss, are you?" the snake asked silkily as it coiled tightly, pushing the ball up onto its head before letting it funnel back to the ground. "All you have to do is kick it over a few feet and you'll have a clear shot."

Francis looked, and sure enough a series of clearings aligned themselves to offer an open shot to the green, if only the tree weren't standing in the way.

"Are you suggesting that I cheat...in heaven?" Mulroony asked incredulously.

"Why not?" hissed the reptile. "No one's watching." Francis sensed that it would have shrugged if it had been able to perform the maneuver. "Besides," added the adder, "you've done it before."

"That...that was different."

"Oh?" the serpent said, inching closer. "How sssso?"

Trapped, the minister toed the ground meekly. "It just wouldn't be right."

"Don't be a naive fool," said the snake, "*everybody* does it. It's all part of the game. It's expected!"

As Francis considered the snake's argument he saw a man approaching from the direction of the parallel fairway. He was short and sturdy looking, with plain, even features. Mulroony was struck by his ordinariness and by the fact that he liked him instantly. The stranger stopped in front of the minister and smiled warmly.

"Hello," he said, his eyes dancing with good humor, "you in here, too?"

"Yeah," Mulroony replied guiltily. He glanced down but the serpent was nowhere in sight.

"Looks like a tough lie," the man commented, following Mulroony's gaze. "What are you going to do?"

"I haven't decided yet."

"It's a difficult choice, isn't it?" the man said. "On one hand you can take the risk and play the shot as it lies, while on the other you take a drop and accept the penalties and setbacks that go along with it. I suppose you could even choose a third direction and decide to bump the ball for a clear shot. I know that I've been tempted on occasion to take the easy way out."

"What did you do?"

"I took the hard road, my friend, the path of righteousness and never looked back," he said, wincing slightly, as if recalling some long ago pain.

"Well, I'd better be getting back. It was nice talking to you," the man said as he continued his search. "Give me a holler if you come across a Titleist 4. And watch out for that snake," he called over his shoulder.

"Whew!" said the snake, slithering out from under a nearby rock. "That was closssse. Now where were we? Oh, yessss, you were about to nudge your ball into a better lie."

"No," Francis said firmly, "I was *not*."

"There you are, Frank," Damien said, fighting his way through a screen of ferns. He quickly reached down and grabbed the snake as it was trying to escape. It writhed in his hand and tried to bite his arm.

"Oh, stop fussing, Lucifer. You've had your fun. Time to go." With his foot the angel lifted a large boulder. Francis had a moment to notice that there was nothing beneath it—no earth, no hole, no air, no…nothing. "Going down!" the angel shouted and tossed the reptile into the nothingness. Then he let go of the rock, cutting off a bloodcurdling shriek of rage.

After consulting with his caddie, Mulroony decided the wisest course of action was to take a drop back on the fairway. Normally he would have been miffed by the calamity and the loss of a stroke, but Didrikson had been right—somehow it didn't matter. Nothing seemed to matter. For the first time in either life Francis realized a true sense of peace and embraced it fiercely.

"Do you get to play every day?" he asked as he breathed in the sweet smell of freshly cut green.

"Francis, dear," Babe said, "we get to play *all* the time. After this eighteen there lies another, and another, and another after that. One fabulous course after the next, stretching out in an endless line into high heaven. You can play forever."

"Forever?" Francis repeated, awestruck by the idea.

"His kingdom shall have no end, remember?"

"Oh…right. But don't you ever get tired?" Babe rolled her eyes and he quickly added, "I know, I know…this is heaven."

"And there's no more waiting to tee off," Jones pointed out. "No more slow play. No more greens under repair, no more duffers. Just golf, golf, golf and more golf!"

Francis laughed. "Are the other heavens as wonderful as this?"

Jones glanced at Didrikson, who shrugged. "How's that, Francis?"

"The other heavens," he repeated. "This is just golfer's heaven, right?"

His companions stared at him blankly. "Surely there must also be a heaven for rock climbers, and skydivers, and marathoners, and all the other enthusiasts who, you know…qualify?"

"Oh no, dear," Babe answered gently. "I'm afraid that all of those other pursuits are misguided. This is the one *true* heaven."

The revelation stunned Mulroony.

"Surprised?" Didrikson asked from across the green. "You shouldn't be—the Bible is full of references to the game."

"It is?"

"Sure," she said, bending over her putt. "What did you think David was referring to when he wrote about being made to *lie* down in *green pastures?*"

"Or being led *beside* still waters?" Jones added.

"His cup ranneth over all right," cracked Hogan, pointing at Francis with the handle of his putter, "with twelve-footers for birdie."

Babe retrieved her ball from the hole. "Remember in the book of Genesis where it says that on the seventh day God rested?"

"Of course," replied the minister.

"Well, it lost something in the translation," she said. "What it should have said was that on the seventh day God had a tee time."

The minister looked at her skeptically, and Jones said, "Want proof? See that foursome waiting to tee off on the next hole?"

"Yes."

"And see that fellow addressing his ball?"

Francis looked and saw that it was the same guy he had encountered earlier in the woods.

"Yes."

Hogan crouched to survey his line. "That's Jesus."

"What?!" roared the minister as he watched his Redeemer produce an appalling swing, topping his drive into the rough. "But he's terrible!"

"Yes, that's true," Babe said sadly. "His form's never been quite the same since He became a man. He says that His hands no longer feel right on the club. Hasn't broken a hundred in almost two millennia, the poor dear."

"But He doesn't really mind," Jones said. "He claims that the high scores are a necessary reminder of mankind's suffering and that on Judgment Day His game will be renewed along with the rest of Creation."

At the back of the tee stood an extraordinarily tall man. His long red hair glowed like fire, sending out little wisps of flame as he laughed and nodded at something Jesus had said.

"Who's he?" Mulroony asked.

"That's the Holy Ghost," replied Jones, "but we just call him H.G."

At this, H.G. turned and waved, giving Francis a jaunty wink. Then He addressed His ball and uncoiled a gorgeous swing, sending the shot far down the fairway. This effort was applauded by two men making their way up the path from the snack bar. One of them Francis didn't recognize, but the man sporting kilts and downing a hotdog caused him to exclaim in shock, "Good heavens, when did Jack Nicklaus pass away?"

"That's not Nicklaus," growled Hogan, "that's God with John the Baptist."

Mulroony gasped in disbelief. "God looks like Jack Nicklaus?"

"No, Frank," chided Damien, handing him his putter, "Jack Nicklaus looks like God."

The minister slowly digested this information as he gaped at the Supreme Being. "Please tell me that He doesn't *sound* like Nicklaus, too."

The others, except Hogan, who was stalking the green like a cat, burst into laughter, and Babe slapped her old friend on the back. "Oh, Francis, you *are* precious. Isn't he, Ben?"

Hogan grunted his assent as he plumb-bobbed his putt for a third time. Francis was away but he could not take his eyes off the preceding group. He watched in fascination as John the Baptist sent a towering drive toward the green. When the ball began to wander to the right he pointed at it and bellowed, "Repent!" It immediately straightened out and landed safely in the center of the fairway. Now it was the Big Guy's turn. He wiped a smear of mustard on his kilts, took hold of his driver and delivered a whopping drive that sailed well past the other two balls. As God admired His shot, a chorus of cherubs popped out from behind a passing bank of clouds and yelled, "You the Man!" God grinned at the cloud and a faint tittering could be heard as the holy foursome drew away.

"Have you ever played a round with them?" Mulroony asked in wonder.

"Of course," Babe replied. "Bobby and I played a match with J.C. and His Father just last week."

"Beat 'em 5 and 4," Jones added.

"What are they like?"

"Francis!" Didrikson scolded, "I'm disappointed. You of all people should know the answer to that question, being a man of the cloth and such."

"Well...yes, of course," he stammered, "but praying and reading the scriptures has its limitations. To actually play golf with God would be...well, rather illuminating."

Bobby Jones grinned. "It's somewhat difficult to describe, actually. To say that they're remarkable people is like saying the course is green; it doesn't even begin to capture their complexities."

"Jesus is an absolute dear," Babe said. "One can talk to Him for years on end and never tire of it—He tells the funniest stories!"

"Which is quite extraordinary considering that He's holding the universe together at the same time," Jones said.

"I guess if I had to sum it up," Jones said thoughtfully, "I'd say that They complete us."

"What do you mean?"

"We were not created as whole beings, dear," Babe said. "Why else do you think we spent so much time on Earth asking questions like: *Who am I? Why I am I here? What's it all mean? Is this all there is?*"

"It's not until we come face to face with our Creator that we realize the answer to all those questions," explained Jones. "Turns out that we all have a God-shaped hole inside us that only He can fill."

"It's a lot like the first time I scored a hole in one," Ben Hogan said as he deftly rolled his ball into the cup. "That feeling of perfect oneness with my surroundings."

"And They all just adore the game," Didrikson said, "although God does sometimes tinker with the rules."

"How so?" Mulroony asked.

"About a month ago," began Jones, "He and I were teamed up in the All Saints four-ball tournament against Adam and Eve..."

Francis did a double take. "Adam and Eve play golf?"

"But, of course!" Babe replied. "And talk about a formidable twosome."

"Like they were made for each other," agreed Hogan. "Eden had a 72-hole track, you know."

"And a driving range," added Didrikson.

"It was a real paradise until Adam had to go and sin," sighed Jones. "At any rate, we were playing the south course when He pulled His shot off-line on the 14th. There was a big oak tree between Him and the green, so He decided to move it out of the way. I carefully pointed out the rule prohibiting the removal of any living obstacles, and do you know what His response was?"

The minister shook his head. "No, what?"

"He nodded His understanding and promptly sent a bolt of lightning down on the tree, splitting the trunk in two. Then He picked up the portion that had toppled onto the fairway and tossed it into the rough, claiming it was a loose impediment."

"All technically legal," Hogan pointed out.

"But hardly what the Royal & Ancient had in mind when they wrote the rule book," said Didrikson.

"I mentioned that and He just laughed," Jones explained with a shrug. "He said that there are higher authorities than the R&A."

Babe pulled out a five-iron and lined up her shot on the next hole, a gorgeous par-three with its green nestled between a pair of waterfalls. "And don't forget the time He kept parting the waters on the Lake Course last summer."

*   *   *

They trailed after God and His remarkable playing partners for the remainder of the round, which Francis finished with an astonishing 74—the first time he had come close to breaking 80. On the 1st tee of the next course, which happened to be an exact replica of Augusta National, they found the Trinity waiting for them. The Holy Ghost strolled over and took the minister's hand in his cool grip. At close quarters Francis was astounded to see that His hair actually *was* fire.

"Francis, how are you?" He asked. "Have you enjoyed your round?"

"It's been splendid," gushed Mulroony.

H.G. led him over to where the Son of God was using the ball washer. "Francis, this is Jesus."

Jesus nodded at the minister and offered a wry smile. "We've met. I see you made it out of the woods safely."

Mulroony grinned and glanced toward Damien. "I had a little help."

When he was introduced to God Himself, Mulroony wanted to fall to his knees but the Lord shook his head. "Now, now, Mulroony, you'll soil your nice new slacks. I trust you've had a good round?" He asked, putting an arm around the minister's shoulder. "My boy's been telling me good things about you, Mulroony. Good things. Keep up the nice work; we need more like you on the front lines."

Francis glanced about in confusion. "I don't understand. How can I continue my work while I'm up here?"

"Didn't Pete tell you?" asked H.G.

"Tell me what?"

"That you're only here on a temporary basis to fill out our morning foursome," Didrikson replied.

"There was no way we were gonna get 'Champagne' Tony Lema out of bed at this hour," added Jones.

"You mean I have to go back?" the minister asked in horror.

"Sorry about this, Francis," Jesus said, "but it's only for a little while."

"Good-bye, Francis," Babe said, "I'll save you a locker next to mine."

"See you in church," waved H.G.

"Come on back now," drawled Jones.

"Chin up and all that, Mulroony!" God encouraged.

"Work on that follow-through!" ordered Hogan.

And Francis felt himself begin to slip away. At first it was a lazy sensation, a slow-motion tumble down a padded elevator shaft. But as he quickly picked up speed Francis lost all sense of himself and his surroundings, until his whole existence was reduced to a regular pattern that passed before his eyes: Light, dark…light, dark…light, dark…

…light, dark…light, dark…fluorescent light, ceiling tile…fluorescent light, ceiling tile…

He was lying on a gurney moving rapidly through a hospital corridor. Someone was running beside him calling his name softly. "Reverend…Reverend Mulroony, can you hear me?"

Francis looked into the anxious face of a young nurse who held an IV bottle as she jogged alongside him.

"You're going to be all right," she said. "The EMS boys got there in time and revived you in the ambulance. There's some damage and we're taking you into surgery now—but you're going to make it!"

It was all a dream, Francis thought with immense sadness, beginning to drift off again, *just an illusion brought on by the shock of the accident.*

The last face Francis Mulroony saw before they wheeled him into the OR was that of the paramedic who had miraculously saved his life.

Damien grinned and gave him a big thumbs-up.

GANYMEDE GOLF & COUNTRY CLUB

G. Guilford Barton

Continuing the Series

GOLF IS NO ORDINARY GAME!

Thanks to the foresight of astronaut Alan Shepard golf has already been introduced in space. I've just taken it the next logical step with this tongue-in-cheek look at what the game might be like in the far distant future. Fellow fans of science fiction are sure to note my humble tribute to the genre's many heroes.

cup in the first place. Jimmy Cerk is back as this year's captain and he's assembled what may be the best team ever."

"Can't argue there, Johnny. Cerk's fresh off his romp through the field at the Intergalactic Open, and Roddenberry, Azimov and Kubrick should give him some strong support. Stir Ripley, Bowman and Lucas into the mix and you're cooking nothing but trouble for the Galactic squad. Is there anyone, or might I add, any*thing* that could give the humans a run for their money?"

"Don't get me wrong, Zorphon: The Galactics have talent. Their Normanian captain captured three tour victories in the past year. But as a group they just can't hang with the home team."

"Let's go out to Gort Gertway covering the 10th hole, where I understand things have already begun to heat up in the alternate shot competition..."

"Right you are, Zorphon. The Galactics have gotten off to an unfortunate start, down in three matches and barely even in the other. Nimoy and Azimov have played brilliantly, already up by four holes, they're on the verge of sending their alien opponents to an early sulfur bath. There's a steady breeze blowing in off the ocean, and with the condensing units working overtime to provide a dampening mist, the middle holes have offered stubborn resistance to par throughout the week's practice rounds."

"Nimoy has just hit a perfect drive down the middle and now Nhoj from the planet Daly is preparing to answer. It's a gorgeous sight here at Pebble Beach, with the ocean crashing on the beach below the bluffs to provide a stunning backdrop for the competition."

"Now here's Nhoj stepping to the tee. The hulking Dalyite has been crushing his ball of...my word, he got all of that one, sending it sailing high into the fog. Keep in mind that Ganymede's mass is significantly less than that of Quillian 3—the gravity here being approximately a third of the original course—so the balls have been modified to weigh three times what they would normally weigh on Quillian 3. Let's go to twelve while we wait for it to come down...."

"Thank you, Gort, and good afternoon. I'm Skye Ranchwalker and I'll be covering the action here on the 12th, where Eneg from the planet Sarazen has just pulled another drive into the rough leaving his Watsonian partner with little or no chance of reaching the green. Eneg's problem is obvious to all. Blessed with two heads, he's having a devil of a time keeping them both still through his swing and consequently the going's been rocky. Now back to the 10th…"

"…where Nhoj's ball has just fallen from the mist and struck a spectator. Oh my…I'm afraid it's hit one of the gelatinous blobs from the Orion system and imbedded into its uhh…body. The spectators are in play, of course, so unless Nhoj and his partner Neb from Hogan can find a way to dislodge the ball their team will be assessed a two-stroke penalty and a formal apology to the Orion delegation. Here they come now and they don't look too happy. The Dalyite seems to be having a heated argument with the Blob. Now here come the officials for a ruling. The ball can clearly be seen just under the surface of the creature's umm…shoulder. The officials are talking to the Blob; it appears to be nodding its errr…head. Now they're in conference with the Galactics…and they're going to play it from there! Johnny, have you ever seen anything like this before?"

"Not since Nicklaus the CCDIV played his miracle shot from the tank of a water-breathing Gillslider to win the 2665 Masters."

"And who can forget *that* shot? OK, now it appears that the Blob is spreading out across the ground to give Neb a better lie. Looks like he's going with a seven. Wait, he's stepping back—the Blob had begun to quiver. Now it's settled down again. The Hoganite swings and sends the ball and a large divot of the Blob sailing toward the green and…it's in the hole! He's holed it! What a shot! But wait… something's coming out of the hole! It's the piece of the Blob slithering back to its owner! Neb has run up to the green…he's reaching down into the hole…and he comes away with the ball! The gallery is going crazy! Hole to the Galactics. Back to you Zorphon…"

"Do you think this could light a fire under the Galactics, Johnny?"

"It just might ignite their booster rockets, Zorphon, and they're going to need them in order to catch the Quillian team."

"Let's head back out to the course and Ben Wrong…"

"Thank you, Zorphon. Ben Wrong here to bring you the action on this most majestic of golf holes, the 431-yard, par-four 8th here at Pebble Beach. Players are required to hit their approach over the yawning, ocean-filled chasm into a tight green that is well defended by a multitude of gaping bunkers. Ripley has just landed a beauty within twelve feet of the cup, and now it's the Vulcan's turn to answer. He's a cool one, plays a very logical game, never shows any emotion on the course; in contrast, his Wookie partner seems in an almost constant state of agitation. The two appear to be debating over club choice at the moment. The Wookie is pointing to his partner's bag but the Vulcan and his caddie are shaking their heads—they're sticking with their club. The Wookie throws up his hands as the Vulcan addresses his ball. He swings, cutting a precise arc through the salt air. The ball has cleared the abyss but it's fallen well short of the green's upper tier and is rolling back down and off the putting surface. Looks like the...hold on! The Wookie has grabbed the Vulcan's bag and tossed his clubs over the cliff. The Vulcan's caddie is trying to stop the hairy brute and...the Wookie's has thrown *him* into the sea as well! Now he's gotten hold of the Vulcan by the throat and is dangling his playing partner over the edge of the cliff. The officials are rushing in. This is the Wookie's third outburst on the front nine and there's bound to be yet another lengthy delay. Back to you, Zorphon."

"Startling developments out at Pebble, Johnny. The ex-Earthlings quickly bolted out to an early lead, but we've started to see some inspiring play from the Galactics as the day wears on, especially from Yrag of the planet Player."

"That's right, Zorphon. This is the first year the Players have been allowed to compete since they were caught using psycho-kinetic energy fields to guide their putts into the hole. The subsequent invention of the psychometer is keeping them honest, but Yrag has certainly proven he can hang with the rest of field without resorting to mind games. Dressed in his traditional dark garb, the man in black has been tearing it up of late."

"He's teamed with Sandy Doones from the desert planet of Arrakas. Doones feels very much at home in the sand, and therefore relies on the extremely unorthodox technique of playing his shots from one bunker to the next as he progresses toward the hole. Now let's head out to Augusta, site of the four-ball matches, and our commentator, H.G. Swell."

"Hello, this is H.G. Swell, your guide through the treacherous turns of Amen Corner. Our journey begins here on the 10th, where the insect-like Thing from the planet Ping is preparing to play his tee shot. Always a crowd favorite, the multi-armed Thing is one of the few players on tour that does not use a caddie. In fact he doesn't even use a golf bag, choosing instead to carry all fourteen clubs in his multi-joint appendages. He's stepping to his ball now… he swings and sends a booming drive that bisects the fairway nicely. That certainly put a wide grin on his slavering mandible. As he scuttles up the fairway he's being greeted with the customary 'You the Thing!' from his adoring followers in the gallery. To fifteen…"

"…where Luke Lucas is lining up for his birdie putt…and he's done it again! This is the third time he's stepped up to his ball and dropped his putter. He's partnered here with Hal Kubrick against the team from planet Palmer. The Palmerites have long been suspected of possessing the ability to influence the thoughts of other beings. Relative newcomers to the game, they've recently won two tournaments under suspicious circumstances when their opponents exhibited inexplicable behavior down the stretch. In last year's Andromeda Open, Herbert Frank was leading the field with one hole to play when he suddenly decided to hit his approach to the 18th green while balancing on one leg. Consequently, he pulled his shot well off-line and lost to his Palmerite competitor by a stroke. Quite a stink was put up but the allegations of synaptic tampering have never been proven. Lucas is back over his ball and now it appears that's he's trying to putt with the wrong end of the putter! There's scattered hissing from the gallery but the Palmerites have remained poker-faced throughout this embarrassing display. Lucas strikes the ball with the club handle sending it careening across the green and into the bunker. Kubrick is protesting but the match will go to the Palmerites. Let's head over to the 8th and Cap Neemoh…"

"This is the impressive Regit Swood of the enormously affluent Nike system striding up the 13th fairway where his ball lay in perfect position for his second shot. Some of you viewers are noting for the first time that Regit plays without clubs in the normal sense. As a shape-changer he was born with the unique ability to rearrange his molecular structure and contort his body into any form of his choosing. He's arrived at his ball, and it looks from here like he's morphing his arms and hands into a three-iron. He takes his stance and hits a rocket that lands past the green and rolls into the dense woods beyond. A tough break for the young Swood—he'll never get up and down from there. Now hold on a moment…the trees are moving! Oh ho! It would appear that I've mistaken a group of Root Walkers for an ordinary grove of magnolias. My apologies to the planet Arboritus. Now the marshals are herding them back away from the green…and there's Regit's ball lying safe and sound. Another break for the Galactic squad. To Balley Hoo…"

"…Zeugirdor of the planet Chi-Chi preparing to hit his drive here on the par-four 11th. He and his partner, Yont from Lema, have kept within striking distance of the Quillian team of LeQuin and Roddenberry, down only 2, with 7 to play. The diminutive Zeugirdor will need a prodigious drive in order to put his team in good position. And he's hit a high shot that's slicing toward the rough…hang on…now it seems to be changing course and curving back toward the fairway. That's the third hole in a row where he's played a slice *and* a hook on the same shot, and the human team has got to be growing suspicious. Yes…they've just called for a conference with the officials. Now one of the officials is motioning for the Chi-Chian caddie to hand over Zeugirdor's bag for inspection. They've gone through the pockets and come up empty. Now they're looking at the clubs themselves and—clever, very clever—it's a miniature tractor beam ingeniously disguised as a one-iron. Zeugirdor had been making such subtle use of the device that I don't believe anyone suspected a thing until the 9th green, where his putt appeared to break *uphill* on its journey into the cup. Of course it means an automatic disqualification for Zeugirdor, which will surely hamper the Galactic cause. Back to you Zorphon…"

"Zeugirdor thought he could pull a fast one, Johnny."

"Reminds me of the time the great Jobby Bones got caught using a cloaking device to hide his opponent's ball in the middle of the fairway."

"And yet, despite all the shenanigans, an afternoon of rallying has put the Galactic squad in surprisingly good position to challenge for the cup. With just two of the singles matches left to be decided the upstart Galactics are down by a single point. It promises to be a memorable finish at our final venue. To St. Andrews and Brad Rayberry…

"…where Shar-ek of Norman and Jimmy Cerk are preparing to do battle here on the 18th hole. Even through the first seventeen, the two captains have waged a bitter see-saw struggle throughout the day. The wind is howling in off the Firth of Clyde…and it's just blown Cerk's ball well off course and into the right-hand bunker. The Normanian has reached the green safely but has left himself a long and difficult putt for birdie. Here's Team Captain Cerk now… and he's played a marvelous sand shot to within two feet of the cup. That should put the pressure on Shar-ek as he stalks the green using his three eyes to triangulate the distance. He's over his ball… the putt is on the way, and it's rolled well past the hole, eliciting a groan from the Galactics in the gallery. He's left with about four feet downhill and he'll need to make it to keep the Galactic hopes alive. The gallery has gone deathly quiet as they await the Normanian captain's fateful stroke. Shar-ek steps away from his ball to consult with his caddie for a moment. Now he's ready…and he's missed it on the short side! All Cerk has to do is sink his tap-in and the cup is…Zounds! His ball has just been vaporized on the way to the hole by what appears to be a disrupter beam! Zorphon, what's the news?"

"We've just gotten word that a Normanian battle cruiser in a tight orbit around Ganymede is claiming that their sensors clearly indicate that Cerk grounded his club in the trap. They're demanding a review by the officials or they'll lay waste to the entire course. Johnny, such a thing hasn't happened since a seemingly innocuous two-stroke penalty escalated into the exceedingly bloody Ryder Cup Wars of 2469.

"And if the accusation stands it'll give the match to the Normanian.

"The officials are huddled in the holo-replay booth surrounded by a crowd of anxious fans. The tension here is thicker than the atmosphere on Rigel 4. The officials have reappeared…and they're going to penalize Cerk! Which means the Ryder Cup will be decided by the final group! To seventeen, where Vern Jules is on hand to bring you the climactic action…"

"There he is, the dreaded Gorse. The mere mention of his name can send an entire gallery stampeding in panic. Openly hostile, ravenously carnivorous, outrageously deadly, not to mention shockingly rude, the Gorse are the terrors of the known universe—every sentient species' living nightmare. Trouble is, they also happen to be some of the best golfers in the galaxy, showing a remarkably deft touch around the greens. Heavily armed guards monitor their every move, and their caddies are exclusively droids by necessity since any flesh and blood version would most certainly be devoured the first time it misjudged the yardage. Luckily we've had only one unfortunate incident in the early going when a spectator on the 2nd coughed during the Gorse's backswing. It took three burly security guards to overpower the tentacle the despicable beast wrapped around the woman's throat. But now all seems forgiven following his tremendous drive here on the infamous Road Hole that cleared the trainyard and put him in perfect position for his approach to the tiered putting surface.

"Bowman has answered with a booming effort of his own and now it's up to the Gorse. What a hideous sight he is—all talons and writhing tentacles and venomous fangs—but such a lovely swing. He uncoils his loathsome mass and sends a low sizzling shot that lands short of the green and rolls up the slope to stop just inches short of the hole. It'll all boil down to this next shot for Bowman. He'll need to get it close for any chance to halve the hole and keep the cup for the ex-Earthlings. And things would've been even worse for the Quillian team had the Faldonian not chosen to use an experimental dilithium crystal driver on the 12th tee sending both the ball and himself into an unstable wormhole. He ended up lying two with 400 light years to the green!"

"Bowman's over his ball. The fate of the cup hangs on this shot. He takes his swing and hits a lofting approach that bounces once… twice…and a third time right over the Gorse's ball and into the hole!

"The Ryder Cup remains with the Quillians! The gallery is going crazy…and so is the Gorse! He's dispatched three of his guards and has just eaten Bowman's caddie…and now he's after his opponent! Oh my God, this is horrible! The remaining security guards have opened fire and disintegrated the monster but not before he managed to gobble up the victorious Bowman. Uhhhh…Zorphon???"

"Thank you, Vern, for that riveting account. Well, that about wraps things up here at Ganymede, Johnny. Looks like it's back into the deep freeze for you."

"Been a pleasure, Zorphon. See ya next time, folks."

"Stay tuned for *Galactic Idol,* over most of these same stations…"

AT THE TURN

G. GUILFORD BARTON

Continuing the Series

GOLF IS NO ORDINARY GAME!

I have always been somewhat fascinated by mysteries. Are there really UFOs? What happened to Amelia Earhart? What were the final moments like at Custer's Last Stand? As a teen I couldn't get enough of the Bermuda Triangle or Area 51. What's all this got to do with golf, you ask? Well, you won't know the answer to that until you read this tale about love, destiny and most of all…hope.

AT THE TURN

They boarded the Winsome *in the early calm before dawn. Beth immediately began to check the sails and riggings as Alex loaded the golf clubs and supplies they would need for the hundred and forty mile voyage to Grand Bahama Island. Karen went below to organize the kitchen and help stow the supplies. Each time Alex brought down a new load Karen's heart would skip a beat. She closed her eyes as he brushed past and only began to breathe normally again after he had climbed out of the cabin. Up on deck Alex paused to help Beth with the rope, hoping to somehow connect with her, but her restless gray eyes seemed to look right through him as she gazed longingly out to sea. The fifty-five-foot schooner cleared the breakwater just as the rim of a peach-colored sun peaked over the horizon. The forecast called for a week of fair weather and gentle seas.*

Neither the Winsome *nor her crew of three were ever seen again.*

"This is awesome," Alex said as he stood scanning the waves. It was his first open-ocean sail and he was overwhelmed by the vastness of the sea.

"'Awesome' doesn't even scratch the surface," Beth replied from behind the helm. She had just turned thirty the previous week. Tall and tanned and blonde, she looked so natural at sea that it was hard to imagine her as wa s one of the LPGA's top caddies. Karen, who had known her since high school, swore she was part mermaid.

Alex turned and regarded Beth for a moment; she had that same distant look toward the rolling horizon. "You really are in love with the ocean, aren't you?"

"Hard to say, seeing that I've never been in love," she said.

Karen joined them on deck and immediately sized up the situation: Alex's incessant infatuation, Beth's steady indifference. Angry, she stepped beside her friend and made note of the heading.

"You're a degree off course," she snapped. "Stop staring dreamy-eyed at the damn ocean and pay attention to the helm."

"Hey," Alex interjected, "give her a break."

Karen wheeled around. "And when was the last time you sailed the Seven Seas, Ishmael?" She shoved a finger into his chest. "FYI: We don't have to be off course by much to sail right past the Bahamas and into the middle of the Atlantic. Now why don't you make yourself useful and start dinner?"

Beth laughed as Alex's face grew red. "Aye, aye." He waved a sloppy salute and stomped down the ladder that led to the cabin.

Karen sighed. She was just making matters worse but she couldn't help it. The man was infuriating! She turned back to Beth—it wasn't her fault. "Sorry, B," she said.

"Hey, you're the skipper, and besides you're right. I need to pay better attention."

Karen nodded and walked toward the bow. She had known Alex for about a year. They had been paired during a charity golf tournament near West Palm Beach, and she quickly found herself smitten by his boyish good looks and a pair of sky-blue eyes that he continually flashed in her direction. He was intelligent and funny, but what tickled Karen most was his status as an up-and-coming tour pro.

Karen had been playing golf ever since her grandmother, one of the first LPGA professionals, had bought her a set of clubs when she was five. There had hardly been a day since when Karen did not have a club in her hand. She was the star of her high school golf team, an all-American at Florida State, and had been caddying for six years in hopes of one day earning her own tour card. Alex was between regular caddies when they met, but by the time they had finished the tournament he had someone new to carry his bag around the course.

They toured together for the last half of the season, and for a brief time Karen thought he might begin to reciprocate the feelings that she was barely able to keep below the surface. Then Alex met Beth at a party Karen threw for her fellow caddies. Afterward all he could talk about was Beth this and Beth that and wasn't Beth something else? He even had the nerve to ask Karen if she would fix the two of them up. Karen had to face the fact that maybe all she was to him was his caddie, and maybe not even that for much longer.

This trip was going to be her last effort. Time to fish or cut bait. A full two weeks cruising the Caribbean and playing the lushest courses it had to offer. Karen had planned on just the two of them but then Alex asked if Beth might want to come along—with Beth standing right there! What was Karen supposed to say to her friend's giddy acceptance of the invitation? *No, I want him all to myself.*

"Damn!" Karen shook her head and whispered, "It's not her fault." It had become a private mantra she had to repeat over and over to keep from ripping out her best friend's hair by the roots. She looked aft and saw Beth's gaze fixed on the waves, her eyes rising and falling with the hypnotic rhythm of the swells. Karen wondered if she even knew what was going on.

*   *   *

"Karen!" Alex shouted from the helm. "Get up here quick!"

Karen scrambled up the ladder, not sure what to expect. They had been at sea for almost three hours before she had finally given in to Alex's constant pleas to be allowed a turn at the helm, reluctantly leaving Beth to keep an eye on him while she went below to catch an hour's sleep. They were near the shipping lanes, so maybe a freighter was bearing down on them. Or worse, maybe Beth had fallen overboard. *One can always hope,* Karen thought morbidly. Then she mentally kicked herself. *It's not her fault!*

Both Beth and Alex were standing at the wheel when she came on deck.

"What's up?" she asked calmly.

"Look at the compass," Alex said. "It's freaking out."

Karen glanced down and saw the digital display putting up random headings in an erratic fashion.

"How long has it been doing this?" she asked.

Beth shrugged. "A few minutes."

"Probably just an electronic glitch," Karen said. "I'll check the Loran."

She went back below and checked the navigation device to make sure it was working. But the numbers Karen saw were nothing but gibberish. She climbed back topside and nudged Alex aside.

"Well?" Beth asked.

Karen took hold of the wheel. "It's not working either."

"So what does that mean?" Alex asked.

"I don't know," Karen said. "I've never had it happen before."

Alex shoved his hands into his pockets. "Well, that's just super! How are we supposed to find our way to Freeport?"

"Relax, Alex," Beth said. "Karen knows what she's doing." Then she raised her eyebrows in Karen's direction as if to add: *Right?*

"No need to panic yet," Karen replied. "Our heading was almost due east. We'll just follow the sun for a few hours and see what happens."

Alex plopped down onto the gunwale and crossed his arms obstinately. "Super."

Karen laughed and tossed him a bottle from the cooler next to the helm. "Have a beer, Alex."

"I think I'll join you," Beth said, grabbing one for herself.

* * *

"What the hell is that?" Alex asked almost three hours later.

"What?" Karen was a good foot shorter and could make nothing out from her vantage point.

Alex pointed over the bow. "That white line straight ahead."

Beth, who was almost as tall as Alex, peered forward. "Fog."

Soon it was visible to all three—a wall of cloud that rolled over the surface of the waves. The compass and Loran were still acting up. Karen studied the fog bank for a few moments.

"No way I'm taking us in there without navigation. I'm going to bring her about."

"Don't bother," Beth said, looking aft. "It's all around us."

Karen turned and saw a ring of low cloud rapidly shrinking to engulf them.

"All right if I panic now?" deadpanned Alex.

"Shut up, Alex," Beth said. She stood next to Karen. "What do you think?"

"I think we're screwed," Karen said as the first wisps passed over the mast. "Get on the radio and call the Coast Guard for the forecast. Tell them our situation."

"Got it." Beth disappeared below. Five minutes later she was back, her tanned face deathly pale. "There's nothing but static."

"That's not possible," Karen said. "Did you try…?"

"I tried the whole friggin' dial," Beth shot back. "There's nobody there."

Karen picked up the cell phone next to the helm and turned it on. The screen came to life, and all three watched as it blinked the message *Cannot Locate Satellite.*

"I need another beer," Alex said, pulling up the cooler lid.

Karen slammed it closed. "Settle down. It'll be dark soon; we'll need to keep our heads."

The three of them sat in silence, watching as the noose of fog tightened above them, shutting out the sun completely.

*   *   *

They heard the surf long before they saw it. The wind died as soon as they entered the fog. Karen had the sails furled and they just drifted in the eerie calm, figuring that the slower they were moving the slower they'd run into trouble. But trouble found them sooner rather than later. It had been dark for only an hour when the first ominous roll reached their ears. Karen reached down and pressed the starter for the inboard motor. It turned over but refused to catch.

"Crap!" she shouted and stared past the bow toward the sound. A low line of foam soon appeared in the dark. It extended as far as they could see off either beam.

"What *is* that?" Alex asked.

"It's a coral reef," Karen replied with a calm she didn't feel.

Alex's eyes widened and he looked out at the line of breakers. "Well…do something!"

"There's nothing *to* do," Karen said. "The engine won't work. With no wind all we can do is drift and the waves will take us right onto the reef. Nothing to do now but wait."

"I can't accept that."

Beth smiled up at him. "You could always jump overboard and take your chances."

He glanced at the ocean for a moment, then grabbed the nearest life preserver and began to strap it on. "Better than sitting around here waiting to run aground."

"Of course, you'll probably be torn to pieces on the coral," Karen said dryly.

"Or carried out to sea," added Beth.

Karen nodded. "Not to mention the sharks."

Alex stared at the two of them, then sat down and started to unbuckle the life preserver.

"Keep it on," Karen said, tossing one to Beth and slipping her arms through another. "Beth, get in the bow and yell if you see an opening." Beth ran forward and Karen turned to Alex. "You stand by the mast and hang on." As he turned to go Karen almost blurted out a confession of love, but something stopped her. She shook herself and called out to Beth in the prow, "What do you see?"

"Hard to tell," she yelled back. "Looks to be about twenty yards!"

"Do you see any gaps in the reef?"

Beth hesitated. "No, nothing." But seconds later she shouted, "Wait...there's a break about thirty yards portside!"

There was no time to hoist a sail. Karen threw the helm hard left and the *Winsome* slewed into a lazy turn to port.

"Hurry, Karen!" Beth cried.

"I've got it to the stops!" Karen could see the gap now and they weren't going to make it. "There's no power! She won't respond!"

A wave slowly built up in the approaching shallows and lifted the *Winsome*'s stern, sending her rushing toward the reef. But the added speed also helped the rudder bite and steer them closer to the gap in the coral.

"Come on!" urged Karen. Another swell piled up behind them and the sailboat surged farther to the left. For a brief moment it looked like they might make it; then the keel struck the reef and the *Winsome* lurched to a sudden halt.

Karen was thrown violently forward, bashing her head hard against the wheel. Blood oozed down into her eyes and she struggled to regain her equilibrium. She heard Alex scream, "Beth!"

The jolt had sent Beth straight over the bow rail and into the sea. Alex rushed forward and leaned over the rail. "Beth! Where are you?"

Karen was about to shout a warning when a large wave broke over the bow and swept Alex off the deck. "No!" she shrieked. Every fiber of her body wanted to dive in after him, but she knew the best hope lay in staying with the boat. Another wave crashed over the deck propelling the *Winsome* farther onto the deadly reef. An ominous scraping sound resonated down the hull as the razor-sharp coral found its purchase. Karen quickly went below—the water was already ankle deep. She hit the switch for the pumps and was rewarded with a faint mechanical whir.

"At least something works," she muttered, grabbing the inflatable life raft and dashing topside. More breakers pounded the *Winsome*, dragging it across the reef. Another big wave buried the stern and carried off the raft. Karen lunged for it but it was gone before she could reach the gunwale.

The *Winsome* was foundering badly and there was little point of staying aboard while she broke apart on the reef. Karen reached over and flicked on the distress beacon. She popped two flares into the sky, grabbed the first aid kit and jumped into the seething surf.

Thankfully the water was warm. Karen kicked away from the *Winsome* as fast as she could, clearing the reef and coasting into the clear water beyond. The sky was pitch black, the only source of light the faint phosphorescence given off by the ocean itself. She spent a few futile minutes searching for the raft but could barely see as far as the next wave.

"Alex! Beth!" Karen shouted into the dark as she treaded water. "Where are you?"

Getting no response to several calls Karen spun around trying to orientate herself. She had no idea which way the shore was—or even if there was a shore, for that matter. Swimming blindly and aware that she was not far from exhaustion, she plunged through the swells as the sound of the receding reef was swallowed whole by the darkness. At one terrible point she felt something bump against her leg and turned in time to see the triangle of a large dorsal fin disappearing in the night.

"Ahhh, God," she moaned and swam harder. She remembered the gash from the helm and stopped swimming to feel her forehead. Blood on her fingers, blood in the water. She came very close to panic, whimpering and spinning around as she searched for the shark.

She took a deep breath and managed to calm herself. *Easy Karen, or you're just going to wear yourself out.*

She pressed on, each minute seeming like an hour as she waited for the bone-crunching strike to hit her. Then she heard it—the distant sound of breakers. Was it shoreline or just the reef again? More eternal minutes passed. There it was! A narrow band of pale beach just a couple of dozen yards away, waves breaking in the shallows and hissing up the sand.

Please, she begged. *Almost there.*

Her arms and legs felt like lead weights; only the life preserver kept her afloat. A wave buoyed her up and she bodysurfed halfway to shore. Another replaced it, then another, until she finally washed up on the wet sand. With her last reserve of strength, Karen crawled the final few yards to the tree line and collapsed into the dreamless sleep of the exhausted.

*　*　*

She awoke to the sound of a large bird squawking in the palm trees above her. It was like no bird Karen had ever seen. Large and yellow with a long sharp bill, it eyed her curiously from its perch before letting loose another shrill cry and flying off with a flap of its bright blue wings.

Karen sat up and shaded her eyes against the blinding glare of the white sand. She guessed it was late morning. A cloudless bowl of blue hung overhead and the ocean sparkled a delicious blend of aquas and vivid greens. She gazed out to the distant reef but the *Winsome* was gone, presumably scattered along the bottom.

Feeling refreshed from her almost-comatose slumber, she rose and walked along the beach, keeping a sharp eye out for Alex and Beth. A small white object caught her eye and she detoured to find a golf ball lying in the sand. At first she thought it might be flotsam from the wreckage but when she picked it up she noted that there was no brand stamped on its dimpled cover. She pocketed the ball and continued on with her exploration.

I wonder which Bahamian island this is. Karen kicked off her shoes and strolled barefoot in the warm sand. She rounded a point on the coastline and stopped short: there was the *Winsome* lying just yards offshore. Although listing hard to starboard she was miraculously still afloat, the pumps managing to keep up with the flooding until the tide had freed the boat from the reef.

Karen quickly swam out and climbed aboard. She started the engine and steered the sailboat into the shallows, then dropped the anchor and went below to look for her cell phone. She found it lying under a foot of seawater. Grabbing as much food and water from the galley as she could carry, Karen waded back to shore and turned to smile at the *Winsome*.

The only sight that would've made her happier would be to find Alex and Beth. Her thoughts went back to the cruising shark in the night and a wave of grief washed over her. Tears streamed down her face and she realized she didn't care if she stumbled on them making love on the beach, just as long as she found them—alive.

A path wound out of the trees on her right and Karen veered toward it. There were footprints along the sandy trail and hope leapt into her throat. She followed the path through the dense jungle for about a mile until the tracks vanished as the sand turned to hardpan. She plunged on, pushing past huge green fronds and wild tangles of vines. She was just beginning to wonder if perhaps it wasn't the Bahamas, when the foliage began to thin and she stepped out onto the edge of a golf course. And not just any course, but one of the most gorgeous she had ever seen.

A wide, gently-rolling fairway stretched off in both directions, bordered on each side by lush tropical forest and a narrow swath of freshly-cropped rough. To her left Karen beheld a distant green that sat jewel-like against the backdrop of the azure Caribbean. Parallel lines of towering palms marched toward the hole like gigantic runway markers, stopping just short of the two bunkers that guarded the approach, each with sand white as sugar.

Karen decided to head in the opposite direction, inland, toward the tee. The jungle stepped back as she neared the start of the fairway, letting her see more of the course. Directly in front of her stood a deep-blue lagoon with an island green that seemed to float on its placid surface. A river fed the lagoon and wound its way through a series of exotic-looking holes before coming to an abrupt end at the base of a cliff, where a waterfall cascaded from rocky heights and thundered beside a mist-shrouded tee box.

But it was not this outlandish sight that arrested Karen's attention. It was the airplane perched in perfect incongruity in the middle of a long fairway. It was large and ungraceful looking with an extended plastic canopy along its spine and a four-bladed propeller for a nose. There was no doubt that it was an old aircraft both in design and lifespan yet it appeared to be almost brand new. Its dark blue paint shone in the harsh tropical sunlight, the exposed metal of the engine free of any rust or grime. As she stared at the plane she heard a sharp clang. Karen jumped, looking around wildly, when the sound rang again and a golf ball glanced off the wing. It ricocheted over her head and down the fairway. She walked around the nose of the plane and saw a man standing a dozen yards away. He wore a khaki flight suit that hung loosely on his compact frame. A golf bag lay in the grass behind him and in his hand was what appeared to be an old wooden mashie. Strewn about the man's feet were a handful of golf balls. He swung awkwardly and sent one flying at the plane. It missed, falling short and rolling to a stop close to where Karen stood.

The man looked up and almost dropped his club in surprise. He took a few hesitant steps forward and paused to stare at her. "Dotty?" he said.

When Karen did not respond he smiled. "I knew you'd come!"

"Excuse me?"

"I knew that you would come."

Karen took a step backward. "I don't know what you're talking about."

The man stepped, almost staggered, a dozen paces closer and she could see his face clearly. He was in his middle-to-late twenties, nice-looking, with sandy blond hair and a full beard that he kept trimmed short. But his eyes…his eyes were those of a much, much older man. Pale gray, they regarded Karen thoughtfully before his smile faded. "I'm sorry," he said dully. "I thought you were someone else."

"Our sailboat was wrecked on the reef last night." Karen pointed the way she had come.

"Our?" the man asked, his strange eyes searching the immediate surroundings.

"I had two shipmates who were lost overboard: a man and woman. Have you seen them?"

The man shook his head. "Can't say that I have." He took another pace forward and peered at her intently.

"I wish you would stop looking at me like that."

"I'm sorry. It's just that you remind me of someone."

"Dotty?" she asked.

"Yeah."

"Well, my name happens to be Karen." She offered a hand. "Karen Holiday."

He smiled again…a warm lopsided smile that made his eyes look younger. "Charles Taylor," he said, shaking her hand. "But most people just call me Taylor." He nodded at Karen's forehead. "You're hurt."

She reached up and felt the ugly scab that had formed just below her scalp. It was still very sore.

"I'll make it," Karen said with a grin.

He gave her another off-center smile. "I certainly hope so."

"So what's with the old plane?" she asked, walking around one of the wings.

Taylor laid a hand affectionately against the propeller. "This is a Grumman TBF-1 Avenger."

"A Navy plane?" she asked, noting the markings on the wings.

"Yep," nodded Taylor. "Fighter bomber."

"You some kind of collector?"

He chuckled. "Not exactly."

Karen glanced around and then back at the plane. "May I ask what it's doing here in the middle of a golf course?"

Taylor shrugged. "Only thing around that qualifies as a runway."

She looked at him with amazement, noticing the wings sewn into his flight suit. "You mean you can fly this thing?"

"Of course I can fly it," he said in a wounded tone. He ran his hand along the fuselage. "This is my bird."

Karen laughed. "Don't they mind you landing on their fairways?"

"Doesn't who mind?"

"The folks who run this course."

Taylor casually flicked the club in his hand and knocked the ball at Karen's feet back toward his bag. "I'm not sure that anyone runs it."

She folded her arms across her chest. "Well…someone must."

"You see anybody around?"

For the first time Karen noticed that there was not another soul in sight. A chill worked its way up her spine, and she couldn't decide whether to take a step closer to, or farther away from, the stranger. "I don't understand," she said.

"That makes two of us," he answered in a tired voice. "I gave up trying to understand it a long time ago."

Karen's mind jumped back to the problem at hand. "Look, I need to try and find my friends. If you see them please let them know that I'm OK and that I went for help. Can you tell me where I can find a phone?"

"Aren't any phones."

"Then how about a car?"

"None of those around either," he said, searching the ground for more stray balls. "Or roads either."

Karen lost her patience. "Well, then, would you please just point me in the direction of someone who might be decent enough to help out a gal who washed ashore during the night and has lost two of her best friends in the process!"

Taylor looked up at her and his eyes were soft with sympathy. "I'm sorry Karen, but there *is* no one else. We are alone on this island as far as I know."

Karen took that step backward.

"You're crazy." She swept her arm around. "You can't have a golf course like this without people around to take care of it."

"As far as I know," he said mildly, "it takes care of itself."

"As far as you *know*…as far as you *know*," she mocked out of uneasiness. "And just how far is that?"

"I've lived here a long time," Taylor said patiently. "Visited every corner of this island. There is no one else here."

"I don't believe you!" she blurted in anger born of fear. "Where am I?"

"I don't know where *we* are."

"Stop it!" she cried. "Shut up!" She covered her ears and almost missed the faint "*Karen!*" drifting across the course. She turned and there was Alex running over the grass toward her with Beth just a few yards behind. Karen rushed at them leaping up into Alex's arms and hugging him fiercely. He twirled her around twice and the three of them beamed at one another.

"Am I ever glad to see you!" Karen cried with pure relief.

"We thought you were dead," Beth said.

"And I thought you were both gone." Karen embraced them both at once. "The *Winsome* is still afloat."

"We know," Beth said. "We spotted it just after we found your footprints on the beach."

"Isn't this place fantastic?" Alex cried with a broad smile. "It's like a course out of my dreams." He turned as Taylor approached the trio. "What's up with Wilbur Wright? He run out of gas or something?"

In the excitement of the reunion Karen had forgotten about Taylor. "Alex...Beth, this is Charles Taylor."

Beth shook his hand but Alex stood stock-still, the smile on his face replaced by a bewildered look. He glanced quickly at the plane and cocked his head in Taylor's direction. "Lieutenant Charles Taylor, United States Navy?"

"Yep," Taylor replied. "How did you know?"

Alex laughed uneasily. "Very funny. So what's your real name?"

Taylor gave him a steel-eyed look. "You just heard it."

Alex frowned and took a closer look at the airplane. "Dear God, that's an Avenger."

"Correct."

Alex walked down one side of the aircraft until he got to the tail, recoiling in astonishment when he saw the number 28.

"This...this isn't happening," he moaned walking in slow circles with his hands stuffed in his armpits.

"What's wrong?" Karen asked. "What is it?"

"What *is* it? It's Flight 19!"

"What's Flight 19?"

Alex stopped in mid-stride and gaped at her. "Only one of the greatest unexplained mysteries ever recorded. Everyone's heard of Flight 19. Didn't you see *Close Encounters*?"

Beth obviously had, for when Karen turned to her for help she found her friend gaping at Taylor and his plane.

"Well, I haven't," Karen said. "So why don't you enlighten me?"

Alex sat down on the grass and laid his forehead in his hands. "Flight 19," he began, "was a squadron of five Navy torpedo bombers that took off from Ft. Lauderdale in December of 1945. They were on a training mission off the eastern coast of Florida, and apparently their compasses malfunctioned—probably much like ours did. The flight leader radioed in his problem saying that he thought he was somewhere over the Florida Keys, and another pilot..."

"Lieutenant Cox," Taylor offered helpfully.

"Yes, thank you," continued Alex. "This guy Cox picked up the transmission and suggested that the Avengers fly north. As it turned out Flight 19 was nowhere near the Keys. They were probably over the Bahamas so the turn north took them farther out into the Atlantic instead of back toward the base."

He looked up at the lieutenant. "Let me know if I muck up any of the facts."

"So far, so good," Taylor said, engrossed in the account.

"At any rate as the afternoon wore on it became increasingly clear that the Avengers were hopelessly lost. The Navy sent out rescue planes and one of these went missing, too. Something like two hundred ships and planes searched through the night and the next day, but no trace of the bombers or the search plane was ever found."

"That's it?" Karen asked. "It doesn't sound all that mysterious to me."

Alex shrugged. "Maybe not, but the disappearance of Flight 19 is what kicked off the whole Bermuda Triangle mystery. Gallons of ink have been spilled linking the mishap to theories ranging from UFO abductions to the Lost City of Atlantis."

Karen looked up at Alex. "How do you know all this?"

He blushed and gave a slight shrug of his shoulders. "I used to watch *The X-Files*."

"Wait a second," protested Karen. "What has all this got to do with Taylor here?"

Alex swallowed. "The squadron was under the command of a Lieutenant Charles Taylor."

Karen burst out laughing and looked up at Taylor. "But that would make him close to eighty years old."

"What is today's date?" Taylor asked.

"June 2, 2000," replied Beth.

He thought for a moment and smiled. "I'll be eighty-four in three weeks."

"That's not possible," Karen said. "You barely look twenty-five."

He shrugged. "Nobody ages here; it was the same for all of us. I don't think time even exists in this place, at least not in the normal sense."

All four fell silent as the weight of Taylor's statement sank in. Finally Karen stirred. "So you're trying to tell me that we're lost in the Bermuda Triangle on the island that time forgot?" She shook her head violently. "I can't accept that. I've sailed these waters for close to twenty years and never seen any sign of the paranormal."

"Until now," said Beth.

Karen scowled at her and turned to Taylor. "So where are the others?" she asked. "What happened to the other four planes and their crews?"

"Five, counting the Martin Mariner search plane," he corrected. "They're gone."

"Gone?" Beth asked. "Gone where?"

"I don't know," answered Taylor. "One day, long ago, they all voted to leave…and they never returned."

"They didn't make it back to the mainland," Alex informed him.

Taylor sighed and gazed off in the distance. "I never had any doubt of that."

"Is that why you decided to stay?" Karen asked.

Taylor shook his head and frowned down the fairway. "No, I stayed behind for personal reasons."

Alex gave him a sly smile. "Like living forever?"

Taylor looked at him with his old eyes. "Immortality ain't all it's cracked up to be, junior."

"So we're supposed to believe that you spent the last fifty years just twiddling yours thumbs and eating coconuts?" Alex asked.

"I really don't care what you believe," retorted the pilot. "And as far as what I've been doing…well, there's always the *Course*."

All three newcomers turned and looked at the magnificent holes that surrounded them. "What's it doing here?" Karen asked.

"I don't know," Taylor replied. "All I know is that it was here when we arrived and it's available for play to any and all comers."

Alex pointed at the plane. "I'm guessing that you didn't bring your clubs along with you."

The pilot nodded past the Avenger. "There is a place near the 1st tee with all the necessary equipment."

Karen pulled the ball from her pocket and showed it to him. "Is this one of yours?"

Taylor examined it turning the ball over in his hand. "Yes, it's from the Course. You'll find that none of the gear has any markings on it."

Beth frowned. "But who put it there?"

"I don't know."

"You don't know much, do you, Taylor?" Karen said.

He smiled into her eyes. "I know a good thing when I see one."

Karen was surprised to find herself blushing. "What's so special about this place?"

"If you want an answer to that you'll just have to play the Course and find out for yourselves."

Karen cocked her head. "How did you know I was a golfer?"

"I didn't. But everyone who comes here picks up the game sooner or later."

"Well," Karen said, "I'm sure we'll have more important things to do, like repairing our sailboat."

Taylor shook his head. "It won't do you any good. You can't leave that way."

"What do you mean?" Alex said.

"If you try to sail away from here you'll just end up right back on the island."

Beth crossed her arms. "That doesn't make any sense."

"Do *I* make any sense?" Taylor asked. "Does this place?" He regarded the doubtful faces around him. "Look, play the Course and you'll understand."

Karen sighed. "What the heck. I guess it can't do any harm."

*　*　*

Taylor led them along three consecutive fairways until they reached the base of the cliff. The waterfall that thundered down its sheer face was at least two hundred feet tall. It fell into a deep pool whose surface was remarkably unruffled by the plunging torrent. They followed the pilot along the bottom of the cliff toward the waterfall. Just as Karen thought their guide was going to walk right into the cascade he veered left and disappeared into a cleft in the rock. It turned out to be more than a mere wrinkle in the cliff face: a deep fissure ran halfway up the precipice. Karen watched Taylor squeeze through the narrow gap, then did the same and found herself in a wide shallow cavern lit by an odd blue glow. She took a few steps deeper into the cave and discovered the source of the strange light. Through a wide breach in one of the walls she could see the back of the waterfall as it rained past. The roar it made was deafening in the tight confines of the grotto, echoing off the damp rock and making her ears ring.

"Over here, Karen." She heard Taylor call and turned to see him standing with Alex and Beth in the back of the cave. A row of golf bags leaned along the rough wall. Some of the bags appeared to be quite old. A few, like the bags of all wooden clubs, looked down-right ancient. There seemed to be equipment from every era of golf, even featheries and gutta-percha balls. It was like some sort of crude museum devoted to the game.

Alex pulled a dusty club from a leather bag and waggled it. "This is amazing. How did you stumble on this place?"

"It wasn't all that hard to find," the pilot replied. "We aren't the only ones who've been here."

"What do you mean?" asked Karen sharply.

Taylor shouldered his bag. "Play the Course…"

"…and we'll understand," Karen finished for him, selecting a set of clubs for a player about her size. "Let's get on with it, already."

Taylor led them back out of the cave to a tee that lay just out of reach of the shadows cast by the cliff. Spray from the waterfall caught the sunlight and made a series of miniature rainbows as it drifted overhead with the gentle breeze.

There were no tee markers, so they all hit from the same spot. Beth swung first, a long fluid stroke that sent her ball well down the fairway. Karen followed with her compact swing and managed almost as much distance. Next up was Alex, who clubbed a beautiful drive and then stepped aside to give Taylor room to hit. All three were curious to see how the pilot would fare, and he did not disappoint them. Taylor proceeded to produce a very unorthodox swing, consisting of an agonizingly slow take back, a distinct pause at the top and a lightning quick downstroke. The swing concluded in an awkward follow-through that left him somewhat sideways to the target. The results, however, were anything but awkward. His ball sailed almost as far as Alex's to land dead center in the fairway.

Alex laughed. "Who taught you that swing?"

Taylor gave him a sharp look. "No one. I've never had the benefit of lessons."

"You don't say?" cracked Alex.

Karen shouldered her bag. "Well, it seems to work."

And work it did, for Taylor put together a remarkable string of holes that had him one under after seven. It didn't take long for Karen to notice that, whether by design or by accident, Taylor always seemed to be nearby. He apparently played a game similar to her own, tending to place his ball in the same area of the fairway. Alex, on the other hand, did his best to stay as near to Beth as possible, even going as far as deliberately mishitting shots in order to ensure his close proximity. Oddly enough this didn't seem to bother Karen as much as it should have.

As they approached the 8th tee Alex said to Taylor, "They blame you, you know." The pilot glanced over at him and Alex added, "For the disaster, I mean; they concluded it was your fault."

"And so they should," Taylor said. "I was in command; it was my responsibility."

"So it's true then?" Alex pressed. "You screwed up and led the whole squadron in the wrong direction?"

Karen frowned, irritated at Alex's badgering. "Why don't you give the guy a break, Alex?"

He smiled and held up his hands defensively. "Hey, I'm just trying to establish the facts." He turned back to Taylor and raised his eyebrows with an air of inquisitive innocence. "Are the accounts accurate?"

"You mean did I lose my bearings?" the pilot asked. "Yes. Did I act out of bad judgment or negligence?" He shrugged. "Maybe…if you base it solely on the accounts you told me."

Karen was moved by the man's honesty and lack of evasiveness. "What really happened, Taylor?"

He looked at her gratefully and teed up a ball. With his driver Taylor hit another long shot down the right side of the fairway. "Flight 19," he began, "was supposed to be very much like playing a golf hole: just a simple flight between a series of points station to station." The others played their drives and Taylor continued as they walked down the fairway. "Things began normally enough. We left the air station at 1400 hours. The weather was fine, visibility good, all the planes flying smoothly. We reached Hen and Chicken Shoals on schedule and made our practice bomb runs. That's when things started to happen."

He stepped up to his ball. "The flight plan called for us to proceed east awhile." Taylor struck the ball and it continued its mission down the fairway. "That's when everyone's instruments failed at the same instant. Suddenly I had four green pilots screaming in my ear that every dial in their cockpits was going haywire. I managed to get the group turned around and headed back west into the sun." He paused and fell silent, his eyes seeming to look inward as he recalled the moment. "And then…the sun moved."

"What?" Karen asked in astonishment.

"It shifted," the pilot replied. "One second, it was at our twelve o'clock; the next, it was off my right wing tip."

"Last time I checked, the Earth doesn't spin in two directions," Alex said.

Taylor bristled with the first sign of anger. "You weren't there. At one point there were actually two suns visible."

"Come on," Beth said, "it had to be the moon."

Taylor wheeled on her. "I know the sun when I see it!" he shouted. He sighed and wiped his damp brow. "Or at least *a* sun," he added. "Who knows what we were really seeing? We were flying blind with no instruments and unable to trust our own eyes. Two of my students got vertigo and inverted. One of them panicked and dove for the ocean, thinking that he was gaining altitude."

Taylor stopped by his ball and shook his head. Karen was startled to see that he was crying. "I did my best to try and talk him straight," he said softly. "He took the bombardier and navigator with him, both of them screaming the whole way down. They were just kids, for God's sake…eighteen, nineteen at the most."

He slashed at the ball in anger. They watched it fly straight for a short while and then tail sharply off course.

"It was soon afterward that we found the island," he said.

"This one?" Karen asked.

The pilot nodded. "We saw the Course right off." Taylor smiled, remembering. "I was never so happy to see anything in my life. One of the other pilots suggested that it must be the Bahamas but we had already turned west, so I assumed it was the Florida Keys."

"So when Cox told you to fly north…" Alex started to say.

"We did as he suggested," finished Taylor, "and it made no difference. We flew straight away from this island only to have it appear in front of us again. We tried four times and ended up right back over it four times."

"So what did you do?" Karen asked.

"Nothing else we could do," Taylor said, pulling out his wedge and lofting a high shot that fell to the center of the green. "With the sun going down and our fuel low, we had no choice but to land."

"You said that we'd understand things better after playing the Course," Karen said, "but so far I've seen nothing enlightening."

"Wait a hole," was all Taylor would say. He seemed to withdraw into himself as they played the 9th, a tight hole made even narrower by the oppressive jungle, which gradually funneled them toward a tiny green almost completely surrounded by a wall of foliage. The foursome putted out and Taylor abruptly turned and marched off into the trees.

"What's eating him?" Alex muttered as they followed the pilot down a long tunnel of dense greenery.

"Beats me," shrugged Beth, eyeing the dark jungle around them.

"Can't you feel it?" whispered Karen.

Alex peered over his shoulder at her. "Feel what?"

Karen had no words to describe the sensation that had washed over her the moment they stepped off the green. A few strides later and she didn't have to, for the three of them emerged from the conduit of trees to behold a sight that defied description.

Directly before them was a long straight fairway that terminated at a distant green. Just to the left and right was another, similar hole. Next to that was another. And another after that. And then another, each radiating from the same tee box and lying one after the next in a hundred eighty degree arc that ended at the tree canopy. Karen turned her head and was assailed by a blur of overlapping images, all clamoring for her attention. She started to swoon and felt Taylor's arm on her own.

"Move your eyes slowly," he said, "and try and focus on one hole at a time."

She did as he suggested and was stunned to see that there were still more holes sandwiched between the ones she could see. Every fraction of a degree seemed to be crammed with dozens, hundreds, thousands of holes—each one alike yet slightly different from the next. To Karen it was like being inside a living kaleidoscope. Even Alex was uncharacteristically speechless. And there was a tension in the air around them, a tingling feeling that hinted at some great source of hidden power.

"What *is* this place?" Karen asked breathlessly.

"They call it *The Turn*," Taylor said.

"They who?" asked Beth.

"Those who use it."

"I don't understand," Karen said. "Use it for what?"

"I believe that this island—this Course—is a kind of portal."

"A portal to where?"

"Other worlds. Other systems. Other galaxies," replied Taylor. "Perhaps even another universe."

Alex laughed. "You're not serious."

"I'm dead serious—each one of these holes leads whoever plays it to a different place. It's like an old railroad turntable," explained the pilot. "Just choose a track and off you go."

"How does it work?" Beth asked, her eyes wide with wonder. "Do you just walk onto a hole and find yourself on another planet?"

Taylor began to shake his head, then changed it to a nod. "Yes, once you leave this tee you'll be in another world, but it's not so simple if you wish to stay there. You have to play the Course in order to successfully complete the transition—all the way to the 18th hole. Only when you sink the last putt are you allowed to continue on."

"But..."

"And don't ask me how or why, because I don't know," the pilot quickly interjected. "All I know is that golf is the key; it's the link that holds it all together."

Beth frowned. "How do you know all this?"

"I know because I've tried it. We all did."

"Where did you end up?" Karen asked, her mind trying to get a handle on the concept.

Taylor smiled at her. "It's not like they have road signs." He turned and searched for a moment, finally focusing and pointing down one of the holes. "If you were to hit a ball along this fairway you'd end up on a course with green skies and water the color of wine." He looked back at her. "I've visited worlds where there is no land or sea, only floating platforms in the sky, where the fairways and greens blow with the wind. I've been to the heart of the galaxy, where the stars are so thick in the night sky it's almost as bright as the day. I have seen wonders that no human was ever meant to see, things that could spark a million dreams." He bowed his head and turned away. "Or a lifetime of nightmares."

"Taylor," Karen said gently. "Where are the others?"

He looked up and nodded at the array of holes. "Out there... somewhere. Fifty years ago they decided to strike out as a group—to find freedom, room to grow and explore, maybe even a way home."

"But why didn't you go with them?"

"Because I couldn't go through with it," he said bitterly. "Something inside me wouldn't let me...hasn't let me finish each of the many times I've tried." He turned back to face them. "And so I come back here...to wait."

"Wait for what?" Karen asked. Then she quickly held up her hand. "Don't tell me—*You don't know!*"

"So you've been alone here for fifty years?" Beth asked, trying to imagine what that would be like.

"For the most part. From time to time someone like you is stranded here. And there are other times when I'll meet the occasional traveler who's using the Course as a means of transport. But sooner or later they all leave." He gave Karen a sad gaze. "Just as you will...in time."

Alex began to laugh. "I'm not going anywhere except Florida. I've got a PGA career to get back to."

"You're kinda slow on the draw, pardner," Taylor said to him. "There *is* no going home."

Alex stepped up to face the pilot. "Look, spare me the Twilight Zone crap and just tell us how we get back to the waterfall."

"Alex..." Karen began, but Taylor cut her off.

"It's OK," he said. "Just go back the way we came."

"Thanks," Alex said, grabbing his clubs and striding off the tee. He stopped and turned at the edge of the jungle. "You girls coming?"

Beth hesitated for a moment, then followed after him. Karen looked expectantly at Taylor.

"You go on ahead," he said in a kind voice. "I'll see you later."

*   *   *

Karen found Taylor later that evening sitting by a small fire he had started on the beach.

"Mind if I join you?" she asked.

"Not at all," he said. "Pull up a log."

Karen laughed and sat down in the sand across from him. The pilot looked somehow older in the firelight, as if the darkness temporarily dispelled his veil of youth, leaving the glow from the flames to reveal a flicker of his real age.

"How have you survived, Taylor?"

He shrugged. "There's plenty of food on the island and the climate is mild enough to allow sleeping outdoors year 'round." He jerked a thumb over his shoulder in the direction of the forest. "You should see the swell shelter I built out of salvaged aircraft parts. All the comforts of home," he grinned.

"I think you know that's not what I meant," she said softly. "How do you survive the loneliness?"

His smile faded and he silently gazed deep into the fire. Karen was about to apologize for the question when he began to speak.

"I was engaged to a gal named Dotty. We met in Miami during the summer of '45, after I returned from a tour in the Pacific. She was a golfer like you. In fact she was the one who first introduced me to the game. She used to watch me swing and say, 'You, sir, are a disgrace to that uniform. I think it's high time somebody taught you the proper way to play this here game.'"

He chuckled quietly and scooped up a handful of sand. "She was going to give me lessons after we were married," he said, letting the sand slowly sift through his fingers.

"She was a real beauty. I wonder whatever became of her."

Karen knew better than to say anything. She just let him get it all out.

"I've tried leaving the island. Filled up my plane with what little fuel was left in the other tanks and just took off. Didn't care which direction…just as long as it was away from here. I flew for ten blissful minutes before I saw the island ahead of me. I banked left and flew another forty or so miles until it appeared again…right in front of me. I try it every once in a while just to make sure."

Karen was about to ask him a question when Alex burst out of the trees and came running up the beach.

"Beth's gone!" He bent over, trying to catch his breath.

"Gone? Gone where?" Karen asked in alarm.

"I don't know. I went back to the *Winsome* for a few supplies and when I came back she was gone."

"Maybe she just took a stroll along the beach." Karen stood to go search but Taylor shook his head. "She's out on the Course."

"How do you know that?" Alex demanded. "Did you see her?"

"No, but the same thing happened fifty years ago. Guys would just vanish for a few days, then come back with stars in their eyes and incredible tales to tell."

Alex crossed his arms. "I don't believe you. Beth wouldn't run out on me like that."

"Don't you mean *us*?" Karen said in irritation. She turned to Taylor. "Do you really think so?"

"Didn't you notice the look in her eyes?"

Karen had—a quiet look of contemplation that had lasted all afternoon.

"We've got to go after her!" Alex cried in desperation.

"Don't be a fool," Taylor said. "You have no idea which direction she went. Beth could be anywhere."

Alex bent down and grabbed Taylor by the collar, lifting the smaller man roughly off the ground. "This is all your fault!" he shouted angrily. "None of this would've happened if you hadn't popped off with all that nonsense about other worlds."

Karen saw a flash of movement, too quick to catch in the dim light of the fire. Alex let out a sharp grunt and suddenly Taylor was standing over him.

"Beth would've found out about The Turn sooner or later," the pilot said. "You all would've found it so there was little point of me keeping it a secret. She'll be back, so the best thing we can do is get a good night's sleep and keep an eye out for her." He gave Karen a lingering look and walked away, disappearing into the night.

Alex sat up and rubbed his stomach. "Sucker punch."

"I'm going to find a place to crash," Karen said, helping him to his feet.

"I'd better come with you."

"No!" she replied sharply. He shot her a surprised glance. "Look…I'd rather be alone, is all."

Karen followed the pilot's tracks through the sand and into the jungle, stumbling in the dark until she saw the glint of starlight off metal. She took a step closer and saw the wing of a plane wedged horizontally between the trunks of a pair of trees. Beneath it was slung a canvas hammock, and in it lay a dark shape. Karen listened to the sound of Taylor's even breathing for a long moment, then wandered back to the beach and settled down for the night.

*   *   *

Beth was back. Karen woke to see her sitting at the edge of the surf line tossing shells into the waves.

"Welcome home," Karen said, sitting down in the sand beside her.

Beth looked over at her, a strange light in her eyes. "Home? This isn't home." She picked up another shell and tossed it into the sea without a word.

"Alex and I were worried sick," Karen said.

"I'm sorry," Beth said, "but I had to go and see for myself."

"And what did you see?"

Beth gazed out over the water. "A world where the ocean never stops," she replied in a dreamy voice.

"You've always been in love with the sea even more than you love golf," Karen said. "When are you leaving?"

"As soon as I can. I just came back to say good-bye."

Alex ran up from down the beach looking tired and disheveled. "Thank God you're OK. I couldn't sleep from worrying…"

"Beth is leaving, Alex," Karen said, wondering why the fact didn't elate her. She would have Alex all to herself with Beth out of the way.

It took a long time to explain it to Alex. He grew angry, calling Beth both crazy and selfish, but his attempts to dissuade her failed. "Fine," he said, "then I'm going with you."

Beth laughed. "Don't be an idiot, Alex. Why in the world would you want to go with me? I'm selfish and crazy, remember?"

"Maybe you are," he said with a smile, "but I'm going with you anyway. I won't let you do this alone. I love you."

Beth was speechless. The shock on her face uttered volumes, but there was gratitude, too, and that spoke even louder.

"What about your PGA career?" she asked.

Alex shrugged. "To tell you the truth, I'm kinda sick of being whipped every weekend by Tiger."

Beth turned to Karen. "Come with us," she urged. "There are people there, people like us. And clouds the color of lemons, and lagoons so clear you'd swear there was no water in them, and fish that *really* fly! It's beautiful beyond description."

Karen hesitated. "All right, I'll come have a look." She glanced toward the jungle. "You guys get the clubs; I'll meet you on the tee."

She searched the beach and Taylor's "house" but found no sign of him. Walking slowly to the 1st tee, Karen spotted Alex and Beth leaving the cave.

"Was Taylor in there?" she asked them.

"Nope," Alex replied.

"I really wanted to say good-bye," Karen said, searching the nearby tree line.

"Maybe it's better if we don't," Beth said.

Karen nodded. "Perhaps you're right."

She looked for him as they passed the Avenger on the 4th fairway, hoping to see him there with his ridiculous mashie. But the plane stood in mocking solitude. To Karen its mere placement appeared menacing, almost accusing—the twin machine guns pointing right at her and the wings spread out as if trying to bar her escape. She hit her second shot straight over the bomber and gave it a wide berth as she walked past it toward the green.

On the next tee Karen turned to look back. There was Taylor standing on one of the wings with his hands on his hips.

"You're up, Karen," Alex said after his drive. Karen wanted to go back, wanted to say a proper good-bye, wanted to say *something*. But Taylor raised his arm and waved a farewell, so she numbly mirrored the gesture, then took her turn on the tee. When she looked back again he was nowhere in sight.

The foursome reached The Turn close to midday. Beth pivoted slowly, searching the array of holes until she found the one she was looking for.

"You guys ready for this?" she asked.

Alex nodded and Karen took one last look around. "You lead the way, girl."

Beth teed up and hit a pretty ball down the middle, followed shortly by Karen and Alex. Karen picked up her clubs and trailed after Beth, not knowing quite what to expect. They stepped off the tee in unison and her first impression was one of disappointment. Nothing seemed to have changed. Then came a brief instant of disorientation accompanied by a sort of musical roar, and Karen found herself in a place that made no physical sense. She stood on a fairway that was fifty yards wide and as flat and straight as a highway through the desert. Except this particular desert was watery and boundless, stretching from horizon to horizon in a breathtaking sea of turquoise. The green surface beneath her feet was more like a short-napped fiber than actual grass, yet Karen was sure it was alive. It spread with unbroken uniformity, right to the water's edge, where it looked to have been evenly sliced by a knife of cosmic dimensions.

And then there was the ground itself. Although firm underfoot, there was something unstable about it. Karen knew intuitively that no rock lay below her. She had this verified moments later when, far off in the distance, she noticed a small ridge where there had been nothing but flat expanse just seconds before. As Karen watched, the ridge moved toward her, growing in size as it approached. She realized with a chill that it was a wave she was seeing, that the "land" she stood on was nothing but a thin layer adrift on the vast surface of the ocean, and therefore subject to that medium's fluidity. A thin layer of what, she could not imagine.

The wave came at them slowly. It reached the end of the hole, and Karen caught a momentary glimpse of the green as it rode up the wave's face and disappeared over the crest. Her instincts screamed *RUN!* But there was nowhere to go, so Karen widened her stance and waited as the eight foot wall of green bore down on them. She felt herself rise suddenly, her stomach giving a roller-coaster lurch as she was carried up the slope. Before she had time to breathe, she was riding the wave crest and able to see for miles. Then she was quickly plunging down the trough on the far side, to end up on the flat again.

The whole experience lasted no more than a few seconds, and Karen was left standing in the exact same place she had been before the wave had passed, like nothing had happened. But something *had* happened. It was one of the most exhilarating moments—yet at the same time totally alien—that Karen had ever experienced.

Things like that just didn't happen on Earth.

Beth let out a loud whoop and threw up her arms. "Wasn't that incredible?"

"Yes," Alex said breathlessly, clearly stunned by the wave's passing. "Does that happen a lot?"

Beth laughed. "All the time." Alex glanced at the horizon in anticipation, and Beth took hold of his hand and gave it a reassuring squeeze. "You'll get used to it."

"Yes…yes, I think I just might," he said with a broad grin.

Karen mutely watched this exchange and wondered again why it had no effect on her. Instead, her mind kept returning to Taylor, wondering what was going through his head as he found himself alone again on the island. She recalled the brief vision she had had while on the apex of the wave, the strings of holes linked one after the next until they eventually joined a larger "island" off in the distance.

"What happens when the Course ends, Beth?" she asked. "Do you know what's on that island?"

"That's where the people live," Beth answered, walking up to her ball and hitting it onto the green.

"And they're human?" Alex wondered.

"Now, how would I know that?" Beth replied. "I didn't get a chance to run a DNA comparison, but they sure *look* human enough."

"Did you talk to them?" Karen took her shot and landed inside of Beth's ball.

"No, but I waved, and some of them waved back."

Alex looked at her doubtfully as they made their way to his ball. "How do we know they're not cannibals or something?"

"Oh, for Pete's sake, Alex," Beth sighed. "Will you please just shut up and hit your ball?"

Another wave approached while they stood on the green. Alex suggested that they pick up their balls to keep them from rolling off, but Beth just smiled and told them to leave them where they lay, and watch. The swell rolled under them, turning the putting surface into a moving hill, with a break that no course architect could ever have imagined. Karen watched her ball as she was tossed first uphill then down. Amazingly, it never moved. She looked over at Beth, who laughed with delight.

"It's the grass, or whatever you call it," Beth said. "It somehow grabs the ball and keeps it from moving."

Alex frowned. "Then how can you putt?"

"I don't know, but you can."

As they played the remaining holes the three of them tried a variety of experiments, like trying to time their swings to coincide with the exact moment they crested a wave, adding many yards distance to their shots. Or hitting blindly over a wave as it rolled toward them and wagering on who would end up closest to the pin. Karen could not recall having so much fun playing a course in her life, but her mind kept jumping back to Taylor, picturing him where she had first found him—whacking balls off his Avenger's fuselage with maddening monotony. Waiting.

Waiting for what? she wondered to herself, realizing that she never got the chance to find out.

The sun was setting as they reached the 18th green, a great pink ball that melted into the endless sea. Karen could now clearly see a group of natives on the adjoining island. Beth waved at them and several returned the gesture enthusiastically.

"Seem friendly enough," Alex said, eyeing them carefully.

Beth rolled her eyes. "You're away, Braveheart."

He lagged his ball to within inches of the hole and looked up at the two women expectantly.

"Go ahead and finish," Karen said.

"Well," Alex said nervously, glancing again at the island before settling over his ball. "Here goes nothing."

He tapped it into the center of the cup and looked around dramatically, waiting for something to happen. He turned to look at Beth, who shrugged.

"I'm not sure," she said and stroked home her long putt for par, "but I don't think anything happens until we finish and walk off the green." Then the two of them stood on the fringe to watch Karen sink her final shot.

Karen lined it up carefully, pulled back the putter and sent the ball toward the hole. It rolled just past on the short side and the sudden sense of relief she felt almost took her breath away. She stared at the ball and the hole, then looked up at her friends. "I can't."

"Sure you can," Beth said. "Just tap it in."

Karen bent over and picked the ball up. She smiled, her mind settled. "I can't do it. I belong with Taylor."

"What?" Alex said. "But you hardly know the guy!"

"Maybe I'd like to get to know him," she shrugged. "Or maybe I've known him all my life." She laughed and threw her ball as hard as she could. It flew high into the darkening sky and landed in the sea.

Beth walked up and embraced her. "Are you sure?" she asked, looking her friend in the eye.

"Yes," Karen said, trying to fight back the tears. "You'll be happy here, Beth. I know you will."

When she turned to Alex, she was surprised by the knowing look in his eyes. Her jaw dropped. "You knew?"

He placed his hands on her shoulders. "I'm not stupid, Karen."

She hugged him tightly and whispered in his ear. "You take care of yourself."

Together, Beth and Alex stepped off the green and walked to where the group of people waited for them on the big island. Karen saw them welcomed by the small crowd and led inland, away from the Course. They turned and waved to her in the fading light and she waved back as another swell surged toward them. Karen watched as they topped the wave. By the time it rolled by her, they were gone.

"Good luck," she whispered, tears streaming down her cheeks.

*　*　*

Karen was surprised to find that it was still the middle of the afternoon when she stepped out onto The Turn. The walk back along the Course was a difficult one. What would she say to him? Did he even want her to stay?

As she neared the Avenger, Karen paused to search the canopy, thinking that maybe he was inside, watching her. She didn't notice anyone, but it was hard to see anything through the glare on the plastic. She climbed up onto the wing and peered inside. It was vacant. On an impulse, Karen slid it open and swung a leg over the lip of the cockpit, lowering herself down onto the leather seat. She sat for awhile staring at the complicated array of dials, wondering how anyone could possibly fly an airplane. In the shadows at the far left, a small black and white photograph had been wedged between two screws in the panel. Karen removed it and held it up to the light. It was a picture of a young woman sitting on a golf course bench. She smiled into the camera lens with her knees pressed together and a driver resting across her lap. Karen stared at the photo for a long time before climbing back out of the cockpit.

*　*　*

She found Taylor lying on his hammock with an arm flung over his face.

"Hello," she said.

Startled, he quickly lifted his arm and gaped at her with eyes red and wet.

"What are you doing here?" he asked. "I thought you went off with the others."

"I couldn't do it," Karen said. "Just like you, something wouldn't let me sink that last putt."

He sat up. "What was it?"

"Same thing that stopped you," she replied. She walked up next to him and held up the photograph. "I found this in your plane."

Taylor rose and took it from her hand, gazing at it with unmasked affection.

"Dotty?" she asked.

He nodded, still staring at the snapshot.

"Her given name was Dorothy Merril," Karen said.

The pilot's head shot up. "How did you know that?"

"She was my grandmother."

"What?" Taylor whispered in disbelief.

"I remember it all now," Karen said. "Grandma Dot used to sit me on her knee and tell me stories about her long-lost flyboy." She grinned, recalling it. "That's what she called you—her flyboy."

Taylor didn't know what to say. He just kept looking from the old photograph to Karen's smiling face.

"So now we know what you've been waiting for all this time," Karen said. "Funny how life sometimes gives you a second chance, huh?"

She adjusted the set of clubs slung over her shoulder. "You, sir, are a disgrace to that uniform," she said, adopting her grandmother's sweet Georgian drawl. "I think it's high time somebody taught you the proper way to play this here game."

Without waiting for an answer, Karen turned and walked away.

Charles Taylor grinned his lopsided grin. Gently, he lay the photograph down on the hammock, took one last look around, and eagerly followed her out onto the Course.

The Magic Niblick

G. Guilford Barton

CONTINUING THE SERIES
GOLF IS NO ORDINARY GAME!

R egardless of the title of this story, I do not believe in magic. I do, however, believe in miracles, and there is no greater miracle than a changed life. Much of my writing is metaphoric, and the magical club in this tale is a metaphor for the only thing that can truly change hearts: The Gospel of Jesus Christ.

The Magic Niblick

What's that you say, young fella? You want to hear the story of the magic golf club? Look around you, son. This is a pro shop, not a bookstore.... Yeah, I know it's been comin' down all day and business is slower than a foursome of duffers. And yeah, I could use the company, I suppose. Oh, very well. But take a seat — I'm not saying nothin' while you're standing there with one foot pointed toward the door. Comfy? Good, 'cause it's a long story.

Now, first off, it's not just any old club we're talkin' about here; it was a niblick.... What's a niblick? Don't they teach you kids anything in school? A niblick is the old name for what we call a nine-iron. Wish they never got rid of the old names, much more colorful than a bunch of numbers.

At any rate, see that fella over at the starter's hut looking out at the rain?...Uh huh, that's right, Arnold Remlap. Heck of a guy, Arnold, a real prince. But he wasn't always such a benevolent chap, no siree. There was a time when Arnold Remlap was the foulest member of our little club. Couldn't get a game to save his life. Spent his weekends roaming the course alone, he did. Just the mere mention of his name in the locker room would earn you a month's worth of undesirable tee times — usually directly behind a foursome that included the president's wife — and we all know what a hell *that* can be....

What was wrong with him? He was a perfectly vile man — that's what was wrong with him. Never had a kind word for anyone. The type who would step on your line without giving it a second thought. Even known to cheat on occasion. Yep, the very same Arnold we know and love. Whatever traits his so-called parents chose to invest in him, they negligently overlooked generosity, patience, empathy, charity and, most important, any semblance of a sense of humor. The man was a walking icebox, and we would have had him excommunicated at the drop of a tee if we could have found grounds for it in the club charter.

You don't believe me, eh? Think I'm lying?…Good, because I still pack a wallop, sonny—so watch yourself. What changed him into the angelic creature you see today, you ask? Well, if you'll pipe down for a few moments, I might get the chance to tell ya. It all has to do with the magic niblick.

You see, Arnold Remlap came marching into my shop some thirty years ago, madder than a wasp in a rainstorm. Didn't bother with the niceties (he never did), just slammed his clubs down on the counter and asked, "What'll ya give me for these things?"

Now, Remlap might have intimidated others, but he didn't scare me none. I looked at him right in the eye. "You want to sell your clubs, Arnold?"

"That's what I said, didn't I?" he jeered. "Are you hard of hearing, old man?"

"Just makin' sure, that's all. How much do you want for them?"

He waved his hand impatiently. "I don't give a hoot. Just get rid of them! I'm done with the game, I tell you, and good riddance."

Now, this news should have set me dancing and shouting down the fairways, but something deep in his lifeless eyes made me pity the man. I was so surprised to find that his rock of a heart could experience anything resembling pain that, against my better judgment, I asked, "Bad day on the course?"

"Bad day?! Bad day!" he bellowed in my face, spraying me with spittle. "What do you know about bad days? You sit behind your counter selling these, these…instruments of personal destruction to the unknowing, sending us fools out to meet whatever humiliating fate awaits us, while you and your cronies go out at twilight to shoot par and laugh at the rest of us poor sots laden with our impossible handicaps."

He paused and shoved his hands into his pockets, adding in a quieter tone, "I despise you and all your ilk."

"That's a rather damning statement, Arnold."

"So what if it is?" he asked defiantly. "Are you gonna do something about it?"

"As a matter of fact, I am," I answered. "I'm going to help you."

This caused poor Remlap to pause and blink at me as if he wasn't quite sure if he'd heard me correctly. Then he re-gathered his cloak of nastiness. "I don't need your help."

"I don't care if you need it or not, lad, you're gonna get it just the same."

Not used to being treated in this manner, Remlap just stood and gaped at me as I ducked into the back room and came out with a slim, wooden case.

"What's that?" he asked warily.

"It's a golf club," I said, opening the box to reveal an old, well-worn niblick with a hickory shaft and battered head.

"What's the big idea?" he snorted. "That thing must be a hundred years old."

"Three hundred, at least," I said. "It was made in the 1700s by a Scottish smithy who forged the head from a lump of metal that he alleged came from the sword of Sir Galahad. Local legend has it that the weapon was melted down after the virtuous knight returned from his successful quest for the Holy Grail, and the Scot claimed that a portion of these metallic remains had been handed down his family line for generations."

"How'd you get your hands on it?" he asked, picking up the old club and waggling it.

"By way of a…friend," I told him. "He was quite convinced that it is enchanted."

"What?!" Remlap cried, dropping the niblick as if it burned his hands. "Oh, I get it," he said acidly. "Trying to make of fool out of me, are you? I can just see your pals clutching their fat guts in helpless mirth as you tell them all about how you pulled a fast one on me. Well, I ain't buying it, old man. You've seen the last of Arnold Remlap."

"It's not for sale, Arnold."

He turned at the door. "What's that?"

"I said it's not for sale. I'm giving it to you."

Remlap cautiously wandered back to the counter. "Why?"

"I told you; I want to help."

"Nobody wants to help me," he said suspiciously. "What makes you such a Samaritan?"

"Let's just say that I'm repaying an old debt."

Arnold peered at the club with skepticism. He took hold of it again. "What's it supposed to do?"

"That depends," I said with a shrug.

"Depends on what?"

"On what needs doing. All I know for sure is that the club won't obey your will; it does what it sees fit to do at the time."

Remlap nodded. "OK, I'll take it. But it better work," he said menacingly, poking me in the chest with the worn leather grip. When he tried to pull the club back I grabbed it and held on tight. "There's only one condition."

"I knew it," he said with a steely-eyed glare. "What's the catch?"

"It's very simple: you have to pass the club along to someone else."

"You crazy old coot. If this club really *is* magical, why would I get rid of it?"

"Because you will find that you'll want to," I told him. "It's just how the club works."

"But who am I supposed to give it to?"

I smiled. "Oh, you'll know when the time comes."

So Remlap left the shop with the niblick in hand and promptly forgot about it. It wasn't until a week later, as he was on his way to play in the club's four-ball tournament, that he noticed it lying on the seat next to him. This came as a considerable surprise to Arnold since he was *positive* that he had tossed it into the trunk along with his other clubs.

When he arrived at the course he left the niblick on the front seat, grabbed his bag and shoes from the trunk and headed for the 1st tee. Remlap was slated to team up with Charley McDoon against the rather dubious pairing of Peterson and O'Maley, and for once he felt optimistic about their chances.

Now, Arnold Remlap was a terrible golfer. I know he may be the pride of the club today, but back then he was perfectly dreadful. He sported a herky-jerky swing and an appalling putting stroke that resembled a man poking at some distasteful object that he'd found lying in his back yard. Gives me the willies just to recall it. At any rate, when poor McDoon saw Remlap approaching (he had been clinging to the slim hope that the man might have been struck by a train), he immediately took out his wallet and handed all of his cash to Peterson.

"Here, take it," he said. "You're going to get it in the end anyway."

Arnold said nothing to his opponents as he stepped onto the tee; he just turned to Charley and scowled, "Let's hope you have a decent day, McDoon. I can't carry you for the entire eighteen."

Being two heads shorter than Remlap, Charley bit his tongue while Peterson and O'Maley raised their brows at the audacity of the statement. They knew perfectly well that McDoon would thoroughly outplay Arnold, yet the bigger man would somehow manage to make each lost hole appear Charley's fault, and even have him apologizing by the round's end.

O'Maley hit first—a nice play down the middle. Then McDoon followed with a crushing drive that sailed down the left side of the fairway. Peterson's shot was not as long, but it still put him in good shape. When Arnold's turn came he reached into his bag for the driver and came away with the niblick. He goggled at the old club in astonishment for a moment, then placed it back into the bag and pulled out the wood, which he used to hook the ball sharply into the rough.

Peterson and O'Maley each laid their ball safely on the green, but McDoon pulled his approach slightly off line and into the bunker. Remlap reached for his five-iron and again wound up with the niblick. This time he slammed the club back, retrieved the five, and angrily swung at the ball, chunking the approach shot with authority.

This sequence of events more or less repeated itself on the next two holes, both won by the team of Peterson/O'Maley. Arnold would carefully watch as his hand closed on the club he needed, but no matter how much caution he took, he would inevitably find himself in possession of the niblick. Sometimes it took three or four tries to produce the desired result. Finally, on the par-three 6th, Remlap sealed the offending club into his bag's zipper pocket. Satisfied, he grabbed his seven-iron and took a practice swing. Herk...jerk...the clubhead buried into the grass, bending the shaft in two. Remlap returned with his six-iron: Herk...jerk...the shaft of the club separated from the grip and sailed down the course, almost impaling the marshal as he sat napping in his cart. Furious, Remlap wrapped his big hands around his eight-iron. This time he decided to forego the practice stroke and swung at the ball. Herk...jerk...and nothing happened. The clubhead had dislodged from the shaft on his backswing and flown clear into the lake that bordered the tee box. The others watched this uncanny display with considerable unease. Charley later told me that he wondered, at the time, if Remlap was going to go to pieces as well.

Now, Remlap may have been a scoundrel; he may have been a low-down, despicable cad; but he wasn't anyone's fool. He realized what was going on, and he decided to play the niblick while he still had some choice in the matter. Retrieving it from the zipper pocket, he stood over the ball and noticed how the club felt featherlight in his hands. A deep calm descended on him, and when he swung it was a swing for the ages: smooth, compact, carefree. O'Maley said that he had never seen the likes before or since. The ball floated lazily toward the green, struck the pin and fell straight into the cup for a hole in one.

Remlap continued to wield the magic niblick for the remainder of the match. And although he carded no more aces his strokes remained silky smooth, and the ball flew true enough to propel his team to victory over their rivals, their score by far the best of the field. For the first time in his life Arnold Remlap walked away a winner.

In the weeks that followed he maintained this sterling level of play, consistently besting his playing partners and even garnering a tidy sum off the wagers that were, under the circumstances, rather unfairly made. One would have thought that such success might have helped to soften some of the rough edges of Arnold's personality, but it was the contrary that proved true. Ever arrogant, Arnold now had something to be arrogant about. He began to lord it over his playing partners, snickering nastily whenever someone hit an unfortunate shot and even openly jeering as he roundly thrashed his humiliated opponents into submission.

But one day, as he strode off the 18th green with a pocketful of Morgan Simms' hard-earned cash, he stumbled over the niblick and fell headlong into the left-front bunker, receiving a deep gash from the rake that Simms insisted he had placed points down only moments before. Simms also later swore (to the great amusement of the boys at the 19th hole) that Arnold didn't stumble over the club, but that the club had actually *jumped* into the air and tripped its owner into the sand!

So off goes Remlap to the local hospital, where he is made to simmer for two hours in an emergency procedure room with nothing to entertain him but an old poster preaching the evils of tapeworms. All the while his lawyer's mind is busily spinning a web of revenge: how he's going to sue the country club for negligence, Simms for the slander he was surely propagating, the hospital for general inactivity and yours truly for malicious intent by giving him the treacherous club in the first place. But all of these litigious dreams evaporated the moment the young intern entered the room.

My, she was a peach, a real beauty. Remlap was instantly smitten, and he wasn't the only one moved by the meeting. For like beauty, ugliness is also but skin deep. Fortunately for Remlap, his repulsiveness was confined solely to the *other* side of his epidermis. In the flesh he was a rather dashing fellow, the type who'd have women knocking themselves out to get at him if it wasn't for his odious personality.

To disguise her rush of attraction the pretty doctor pretended to study her clipboard. "Hello, Mr....Remlap," she said. "I'm Dr. Stevens."

Arnold sat transfixed, staring at her lovely mouth. He spotted the niblick (he had left it at the club) leaning against the wall behind her. "Please," he said, "call me Arnold."

She smiled warmly and held out her hand. "Deal, but only if you call me Anna."

"Anna," Arnold repeated, taking her hand, which felt warm and small in his.

Anna clutched the clipboard to her chest and stepped to Arnold's side, exploring the cut over his ear. "So tell me how you got such a ghastly wound on such a nice head."

"A golf club tripped me."

"Don't you mean that you tripped over a golf club?" she laughed, stepping to the sink.

As she began to wash her hands, Arnold noticed the club propped up on a nearby chair as if it wanted to get a better view of the proceedings. "No," he said with uncharacteristic truthfulness, "it deliberately tripped me."

Anna stopped scrubbing and turned to search his eyes carefully as her hands dripped on the speckled linoleum. Satisfied with her diagnosis, she flicked her fingers twice into the sink and pulled out a couple of sheets of paper towel. "I hate it when that happens.

"I love the game, myself," she continued as she cleaned the cut and gently shaved the hair away from his torn scalp. "Do you play much?"

"Sure, all the time. How about you?"

"Whenever I'm not too busy playing doctor," she replied, glancing into his eyes before looking away.

The conversation meandered through typical golf talk as she stitched up the wound, and it became obvious to Arnold that she actually liked him. He could not remember the last time he had a fruitful encounter with anyone, especially a beautiful woman. He even made her laugh a couple of times. Yet, there was something amiss about her. The old Arnold would never have noticed in a million years, but with the niblick close by he found himself suddenly open to subtlety.

When she had finished her task, Anna stepped back. "There, good as new. Try and keep the sutures dry and you can come back and have them taken out in two weeks."

Remlap sat in silence as the young woman washed again and jotted down a few notes on her clipboard. She seemed to perform these tasks laboriously, applying much more care and time than was necessary. Clearly the ball was in Arnold's court, and he wanted desperately to ask her out for a date, a cup of coffee or even a simple trip to the driving range. But years of rejection had surprisingly ill-prepared him for intentionally risking more.

"Well," Anna said finally, lingering by the door, "I have other patients to see."

"Yes," he said idiotically.

This made her frown and shuffle her feet. She gave it one last try: "It was nice meeting you."

"Yes," Arnold said, cursing himself silently.

Anna raised her eyebrows and blew out her cheeks slightly. "Well...good-bye."

And then she was gone. Arnold sat and stared at the empty doorway for a long time. When he finally came to his senses he found the niblick lying across his knees. He caressed it gently, consoling himself with the knowledge that he would see her again in a couple of weeks.

* * *

Arnold counted off the days impatiently, returning a fortnight later, firmly determined to voice his true feelings. But instead of the lovely Doctor Stevens, he was greeted by an aging male physician.

"Where's Anna?" he asked in alarm.

"Who?" the doctor asked as he pulled out the sutures.

Arnold felt a sinking twinge in the pit of his stomach. "Doctor Anna Stevens. She was the woman who treated me."

"Don't know her."

"What do you mean you don't know her?" Remlap growled. "You work in the same hospital, don't you?"

"Look, young man," the doctor replied sternly, "there's no one on staff by that name. Perhaps she was an intern volunteering her time in the ER. They do that sometimes, just to get the experience."

Devastated, Remlap checked at the nurse's station and found that this was, indeed, the case. He also found that they steadfastly refused to give him Anna's address or phone number, stating that it was hospital policy not to reveal such information. When he got home he immediately pulled out the yellow pages and searched for Anna among the listed physicians. Nothing. He had similar luck when checking the residential listings. He did find an A. Stevens by dialing up information, but it turned out to be a man named Archie.

Well, the weeks passed and Remlap moped about in self-pity. He still got in his weekly rounds, still swung the magic niblick with accuracy and grace, still won matches and tournaments with ease, but his stride was listless and his shoulders slumped in defeat, even in the midst of victory. His fellow members had never seen him act in such a way. They were used to Arnold feasting on the weakness of others rather than revealing any of his own. Arnold Remlap, they were forced to admit, was human after all.

* * *

Then came a rainy day in March when Remlap, returning home from a washed-out round, came across a broken-down truck on the side of the road. The hood was up and half a body protruded from the mouth of the wounded machine. He drove on past, as he always did, and the niblick, lying on the seat beside him, suddenly said, "Stop and help that person, Arnold."

Yep, that's what I said; the club actually spoke to him. At least, that's what he claims happened. Whether the words were spoken aloud or just to his mind, we'll never know…I don't care if you buy it or not, sonny. No skin off my nose. Now, do you want to hear the rest of the tale or not? 'Cause I got other things I could be doing with my time…All righty, then…

As I was saying, the niblick ordered Remlap to stop, and Arnold, now totally submissive to the club's spell and too distraught to protest, turned the car around and went back to offer his assistance. Popping open his golf umbrella, he shuffled over and leaned into the engine compartment.

"Need a hand?" he asked sullenly.

The man who emerged from under the hood was just as tall as Arnold but much older, perhaps in his mid-to-late seventies. He wore a huge, wide-brimmed hat that drooped over his ears in the rain. A long streak of grease had found its way beneath his left eye, and another ran along the bridge of his nose, giving him the look of an athlete with poorly applied eyeblack. He looked Arnold up and down and gave him a wide grin.

"Here, turn this when I try and start her," he said, giving Remlap a screwdriver and pointing out a tiny screw on some incomprehensible part of the motor. The man then hurried behind the wheel and turned the ignition. When it refused to catch he directed Arnold to make adjustments to another unknown contraption. This time the motor roared to life, and poor Arnold—who had no idea what was going on or why it wasn't he who was attempting to start the vehicle while the owner did the dirty work—jumped when the hunk of metal suddenly came to life beneath him and bashed his head on the underside of the hood.

Arnold rubbed his aching scalp and was preparing to lay into the old man when a startling (to Arnold at least) thing happened. The fellow stepped from the cab and embraced his newfound apprentice in a huge bear hug, laughing and slapping Remlap on the back as they stood in the rain. As you might imagine, this utterly dumbfounded Arnold, who mutely rocked back and forth with the man's affections.

"Thank you, young man," the old fellow said when he released Arnold. "Don't know how long I'd have been out here if you hadn't come along. You're a decent fellow."

Decent was not an adjective anyone had ever used to describe Arnold Remlap. The umbrella listed sideways, and he gaped at the man as the rain ran off the end of his nose and dripped past his open mouth.

"The name's George Witherspoon," the old gent said.

"Arnold Remlap."

"Well, Arnold, you're absolutely sodden. Let's get you out of those wet clothes. Have you had your supper yet?"

Arnold, still reeling and trying desperately to catch up with the proceedings, shook his drenched head.

"Capital! You can follow me home," Witherspoon said happily. "The wife's bound to have something hot on the stove. Least we can do."

Here was another first: Arnold Remlap being asked to dinner. He walked back to his car and numbly climbed behind the wheel. What surprised him the most was, not the invitation, but that he actually wanted to go with this man…to see where he lived, to discover the source of this well of kindness, to meet "the wife" and find out exactly what that something was she had on the stove.

Staying close behind the truck so he wouldn't lose his host in the thickening rain, Arnold followed George off the highway and deep into a maze of backcountry roads, one of which followed beside a swollen creek. The lane kept leaping over the stream as they progressed (or the stream kept ducking under the lane—Arnold couldn't decide which), hopping from bank to bank in indecision, until the road eventually tired of the game and veered sharply away toward a handsome stone house, nestled in the outflung arms of a hardwood forest.

Arnold pulled into the forecourt, shut off his engine, and studied the place through the downpour. The smoke from the chimney struggled out the flue and rolled down the old slate tiles, as if reluctant to leave the happy dwelling. George banged loudly on Arnold's hood and motioned for him to follow. The two men ran for the cover of the porch and stepped through the dark oak door.

As they shed their soaking overclothes, George bellowed, "Mother, we've got company!"

A plump woman soon appeared around the corner and eyed Arnold curiously as she wiped her red hands on an apron. She was much younger than her husband, yet somehow managed to seem the older of the two.

"Becky, this is Arnold," George said, pulling off his boots.

"Good heavens, George," she scolded. "What have you done now?" She quickly wrapped an arm around Arnold and guided him toward the living room fire. "The boy's soaked to the bone. Look, he's shivering!"

"I broke down out on the highway," George explained. "Arnold here was decent (that word again!) enough to stop and lend a much-needed hand."

"He'll catch his death if we don't warm him up some," Becky said. "Run and get him some fresh clothes, George. Go on…off with you!"

George scurried up the stairs while Becky draped a blanket over Arnold's shaking shoulders. Her husband soon returned with a set of thermal underwear and a dark green bathrobe, and in no time Arnold was safely snug in an easy chair by the warm hearth. As George went to change, Becky ducked into her kitchen and reappeared a moment later with a steaming mug of cocoa.

"You'll be stayin' for supper, then?" she asked in what was more of a statement than a question.

Arnold actually smiled at this, stretching rarely-used muscles. "If it's not too much trouble."

"Pshaw!" she exclaimed with a laugh and an odd little kick of her left foot. "Ain't no trouble at all. Plenty of food. Simply have to add another plate, is all."

"Then I'd love to stay," Arnold replied.

Becky retreated into the kitchen and Arnold sank into the soft cushions, trying to grasp the odd emotions that had washed over him since entering the house. It took him a few moments to realize that he was wanted there, that someone actually desired the company of Arnold Remlap. It was a feeling that he had never experienced. Not from his runaway coward of a father or the drunken mother who had abused and then abandoned him at the age of four. Certainly not at the orphanage, or from the long series of foster families that refused to comprehend his hostility. In the end, Arnold eventually became what he feared he was all along—unlovable. So he was left to find his own path through life. Arnold fought his way through public school, bullied his way through college, laid waste to his classmates at Penn State Law, and was currently the scourge of the Millson County Courthouse. He was what they called a self-made man, but his shoddy workmanship was finally rising to the surface. For, just as McDoon had feared, Arnold was, indeed, coming apart. Something large and jagged had broken free inside him to carom around the close confines of his soul, wreaking great havoc, slicing away the years of hatred and spite and resentment and self-loathing.

A subtle change in the air caused Arnold to glance to his left, and he saw the niblick leaning against the stone mantle. *Ah…he* thought, with a mixture of fear and excitement, *there lies the instrument of my undoing.*

As he was gazing at the club a girl of about ten summers entered the room from the kitchen. She was very small, with a bowl of dark curly hair that bounced about her tiny head. Pulling a chair from the dining table, she turned it backwards, sat down, folded her arms over the back, and laid her chin on the cushion of flesh to stare at Arnold with frank curiosity. When she had finished her scrutiny, she nodded and said, "I hear you rescued George today."

"Well, I don't know about that," Arnold said. "I just turned the screwdriver."

"I'm Liz," she said. "Me and my folks help to run the place."

"Run the place?" Arnold asked, unsure want she meant.

"Yeah, it's a maple syrup farm. Didn't George tell you?"

When Arnold shook his head, she mimicked the gesture, "That's old George for you."

The sound of stomping boots echoed from the foyer, and a short, neat-looking man yelled out, "Becky, whatever you got brewing in there smells heavenly! You're an angel, you are. You're…" He stopped when he saw Arnold sitting by the fire.

"Arnold, this is my father, Chris," Liz said. Then turning to her father, she added, "Arnold saved George's life this afternoon."

"I did no such thing…" Arnold began to protest, but Chris must have been familiar with his daughter's gift of exaggeration. "Saved George's life!" he boomed with a wink toward Arnold. "An actual hero come to supper!"

Becky's voice rose from inside the kitchen, "Comfy, Arnold? I take it you've become acquainted with the Lizard. Liz, I hope you haven't forgotten to set a place for Jojo. She'll be here any minute."

"I'm on top of it, Grammy!" Liz called back, adding another setting to the table.

"Who's Jojo?" Arnold asked.

"She's my niece from Philadelphia," Chris said, settling down on the couch.

Becky burst from the kitchen with a plate in each hand. Right behind her was a similarly laden, middle-aged woman who could have been Becky's twin, were it not for the age difference.

"Arnold," Becky said as she arranged the plates on the table, "meet my daughter, Sarah."

"Hello, Sarah."

"Good evening, Arnold," she replied, laying down her burden and giving Chris' cheek a peck.

"Where is that girl?" Becky said, glancing up at the clock on the mantle. "She should have been here a half hour ago." She sighed and looked at the food on the table. "Well, it can't be helped; she'll show when she shows. Everyone, please take at seat. George! Have you fallen asleep up there? Supper's on!"

George fumbled down the stairs and Becky asked him to say the blessing.

"Lord…you've done it again," began George. "Just when we think the hour's grown as dark as it can get, you send a ray of sunshine to light our path and show us the way home." (Arnold lifted an astonished eyelid at George, then popped open the other to peek in wonder at the niblick.) "Thank you for our family, our health, this food, and for Arnold. May we also be a lamp unto his feet. Amen."

"Amen," echoed the company, and Sarah pulled the lid off a huge bowl of chicken and dumplings. Arnold's mouth began to water instantly. He waited patiently for the others to be served, then eagerly shoveled a massive dumpling into his mouth just as a commotion was heard from the vicinity of the front door.

"Sorry, everyone!" called a female voice. "The roads are impossible! How do you all stand it?"

Recognition overtook Arnold an instant later. He leapt to his feet just as Anna stepped into the room.

"Arnold!" she exclaimed, stopping in her wet tracks. "What are you doing here?"

Everyone anxiously awaited Arnold's response, but it refused to show itself, his mouth being basically glued shut by the gooey mass of dumpling. With a great effort he somehow got his jaws moving again and proceeded to chew with as much speed and dignity as possible. Liz giggled into her hand, causing Arnold to blush. He quickly swallowed his pride (but not the dumpling) and continued to toil away in the awkward silence. It was George who eventually came to his rescue.

"Seems you two know each other," he said between bites. "Saves me the introduction."

Becky jumped up and ushered her granddaughter to a waiting chair. "Arnold stopped to help your granddad on the road...."

"Pulled him out from under a burning truck," interjected Liz as she passed around the corn.

Anna placed the napkin in her lap. "That was very kind of you, Arnold."

"You're Jojo?" Arnold asked, managing to sneak a few words past the blockage.

"My full name is Joanna," she replied, "but I figured that going by Dr. Jojo was not the best way to instill confidence in my patients."

The whole family laughed, but all poor Arnold could do was stand and stare at Anna while the others waited politely for him to return to his seat. He showed no sign of budging and Becky said, "If you're going to stand and eat, Arnold, I can always get you a tray from the kitchen."

When he realized how he must appear, standing in George's borrowed long johns and robe, Arnold reddened further and plopped back into his seat. But he refused to take his eyes off the young doctor now that he had found her again, fearing that she might not be there when he looked back. Anna, too, kept sneaking glances at her former patient between bites and snippets of the conversation.

Sarah watched this silent exchange with bright eyes. "How did you two meet, anyway?"

"Arnold fell and cut his head at the golf course a few weeks ago when I was volunteering at the emergency room," Anna answered, peering at Arnold's scalp. "How has it healed, Arnold?"

"Just fine, thanks."

"So, you're a golfer, Arnold?" Chris asked, reaching behind him and holding up the niblick. "Then this must be yours."

George dropped his fork and hurried around the table to examine the old iron. "It's a real beauty, Arnold," he whispered. "Must be a hundred years old."

"Three hundred, actually."

"Is that the same one that tripped you?" inquired Anna.

"Yep," Arnold nodded, "that's the culprit."

"What's this?" Chris asked. "You say the club tripped you…on purpose?"

"That's right," replied Arnold with a weak smile. He proceeded to tell them the tale of how he came to possess the niblick and its strange powers. When he had finished, the company sat in deep thought.

"Magic, you say?" George pondered. "Has it worked?"

Arnold glanced at Anna. "Oh, yes…like a charm."

"Well, I would say that young Arnold's adventures give credence to our theories," George said. "Wouldn't you, Christopher?"

"You bet they do," agreed Chris.

"What theories?" Arnold asked.

"We've been talking lately about how much the game of golf acts like a metaphor for life," Anna said.

"Dear me, here you all go again!" moaned Becky. "You talk as if it were a religion."

"Hush, Mother," said George sternly, "the Lord's listening."

"I will not hush! I happen to think that you're all taking the game way too seriously. Don't you agree, Arnold?"

"I'm not sure," Remlap answered cautiously, "I have yet to hear their ideas."

"Well, first off," Anna began, "golf, like life, is a journey. In fact, they're both a series of journeys comprised of beginnings and destinations—goals, if you will. Some of the journeys are long; some are shorter. All of them differ in ways from the one before and the one to follow, each posing a unique set of challenges that must be met and conquered if we are to succeed."

"And this success is measured against a given scale—some might even say an inequitable one—just as it is in the real world," Sarah chimed in.

"In both, it's necessary to consciously choose the path one wishes to take before one acts," Anna continued, warming up to the task, "to carefully weigh the pros and cons. For each shot directly impacts the next and, indirectly, the ones to follow."

"Hazards and pitfalls abound," Chris pointed out. "Competition is intense. Risks are regularly taken, accompanied by proportional rewards or consequences."

"Just look at how we spend our lives," Anna said, waving her hands in a circle around the table. "Days or even weeks can go by with nothing much happening, but every now and then we're required to make a decision or take some action. The same thing happens on the links. The actual time we spend striking the ball is quite small when compared to the time it takes to progress from shot to shot, and it's what we do with that in-between time that makes all the difference."

"That's why it's so important to enjoy the moments we spend walking to the ball," George said emphatically, "to take the time to look around us and breathe in deeply as we go. All this rushing around in carts and stamping of feet in impatience as we wait to play—it's unhealthy, I say! If we can't embrace the lulls in life, then how can we expect to fully appreciate its higher moments?"

"George thinks that the powers-that-be should banish carts altogether," Liz said, "even though he himself can barely make it around on foot."

"They're the scourge of Western civilization," the old man insisted, leveling a finger at his granddaughter. "And the day I can't walk the course is the day I hang up the clubs forever."

Everyone hooted at this proclamation, and Anna, watching Arnold closely, asked, "Something to add to the discussion, Arnold?"

"I was just wearing my lawyer's cap," he said, "thinking that a parallel could easily be drawn between the rules that govern play and our penal code."

"That's the spirit, Arnold," encouraged Chris. "Are there not appropriate penalties for our disobedience? Most of which are far more harsh than some of the sentences they deal out to criminals these days."

"There's even an unwritten ethical code that dictates our etiquette toward one another on the course," George said, "and it has its roots firmly planted in the Good Book's golden rule: treat others the same as you would be treated."

"And when all is said and done," Liz said grandly, rising to stand on her chair and holding her arms over the company, "when we've played our final hole and the ball comes to rest in the cup, the good Lord can tally up our 'score' and judge us accordingly."

Chris smiled at his daughter's theatrics and turned to Anna. "Tell Arnold about your paper."

"Oh, I'm sure that Arnold doesn't want to hear about some stuffy old college thesis," she replied shyly.

George leaned over and nudged Arnold's arm. "Our young doctor has some fascinating ideas about golf and the subconscious mind."

Arnold crossed arms. "Then by all means, let's hear about them."

The family began to clap, and Liz stuck two fingers into her mouth and whistled loudly. "OK, OK," Anna laughed, motioning them to silence. "When I was still in med school, I wrote a psychology paper titled 'The Golf Swing as a Psychoanalytical Tool,'" she said with a toss of her head. "Caused quite a stir at the time. My theory is that an individual's personality and idiosyncratic character traits are revealed in one's swing (this explained Arnold's heretofore her-ky-jerky efforts), and that a simple study of the mechanics can save a psychologist hours of couch therapy."

"The eyes may be the window to the soul," Chris said with a wink of one of his panes, "but the swing is the mirror that reflects all of our inner turmoil."

"Or peace," Sarah added.

Arnold gave Anna a skeptical look.

"Don't buy it? How about a demonstration, then?" She pointed at the niblick in her grandfather's hands. "Give it a go, George."

The old man took the club and waggled it appreciatively. Then he took a wild, vicious swing that just missed scraping the low-beamed ceiling.

"Now," said Anna, leaning back in her chair, "tell us what you can glean from that, Arnold."

"Definitely not a textbook swing," Arnold said after a few moments' thought. "Very undisciplined, very outside-in."

"And what might that tell you about a person?"

"That he's unconventional; he's his own man."

"Very good, Arnold," Anna said with delight. "That's our George all over. Likes to blaze his own trails, and his swing path lends a distinct *push* to his shots, which is how he deals with his world — always pushing the envelope. What else?"

"It's a powerful swing, but he's loose at the top," Arnold responded, "bending his elbows and wrists way too much."

Anna leaned forward, "Meaning?"

"A devil-may-care attitude?" Arnold ventured. "Almost a recklessness."

"I'm impressed," praised the doctor. "Granddad is a man who doesn't spend a great deal of time pondering the consequences, tending to shoot first and ask questions later. His actions have power behind them, but they frequently lack direction. His hands and wrists are quick at impact, showing that he likes to manipulate his environment and put a good spin on things."

George, having heard this many times, shrugged good-naturedly and passed the club to his son-in-law. Chris used it to carve a careful arc through the air of the living room. Then he sat down to await judgment.

"Now, Uncle Chris here is a totally different sort," Anna proclaimed. "Whereas George is quick and wild, Chris is more reserved and deliberate. He holds back part of himself, fearing that events might get out of hand if he ever really lets go. He's more concerned with getting somewhere in one piece than arriving ahead of everyone else. His swing is nice and compact, suggesting a man who is well aware of his limitations. And did you notice how little he shifts his weight? Here again, Chris sacrifices power for control — a strong sense of centeredness is what I call it."

Sarah took her turn with the niblick, and Anna smiled. "Isn't that a sweet swing?" she asked. "Smooth and unruffled, just like Aunt Sarah. See how she gets the maximum range of turn out of her hips and shoulders? That shows a flexible personality. And it's a very upright and flush swing through impact, which speaks volumes about her high moral standards and a desire to remain inbounds at all cost."

When Liz stepped up to demonstrate her form, the analysis was obvious to all. Everything about the stroke was over-exaggerated, from the take back that brought the clubhead close to her left knee, to the graceful follow-through that had her arching at a seemingly impossible angle.

"OK, Arnold," Liz said as she waved the niblick in front of him, "now it's your turn."

Arnold swung the niblick and the room grew suddenly still.

"Holy cow!" said Liz breathlessly.

"My word..." uttered Sarah.

"Capital," George whispered.

"Lord, have mercy!" Becky said as she rapidly crossed herself.

"Pretty," said Chris, "very pretty. What do you think, Dr. Jojo?"

Anna didn't speak right away. She asked Arnold to demonstrate it a few more times and then offered her conclusion. "It's a lovely swing, Arnold, no doubt about that. In fact, I can't say that I've ever seen one that's more...well-adjusted. But there's something not quite right about it. To tell you the truth, I'm having a hard time reconciling it with the man before me."

She paused and chewed on her lower lip before continuing. "It's almost as if it doesn't fully belong to you."

This would have infuriated the old Arnold Remlap, who firmly believed in possession being nine-tenths of the law, but the new version looked down at his shoes. "It's kind of a new swing."

"Ah...that explains it!" Anna exclaimed, looking around the room. "Couldn't you all feel the newness of it?"

"You're right, dear," Becky said. "It has a sort of new-car smell to it. Like he's just out taking it for a spin."

"That's because it's a young swing, a swing in transition," Anna said, "still flexing its muscles and getting a feel for the place. The kind of swing a butterfly might have after it escapes from the chrysalis. You can sense a sharp danger in it, like a razor poised on the brink between joy and sorrow." She paused and gave Arnold a sad look. "But either way it falls, it cuts just as deeply."

Anna let this statement hang in the air for a moment before turning to Becky. "What's for dessert, Grandma?"

"Wait," Arnold said. "Don't we get to see your swing?"

"And who's going to analyze it?" Anna asked in amusement.

"I am," he answered.

"Very well," she said, taking the club and producing a slow, graceful effort.

"There," Anna said, handing back the niblick and returning to her seat. "What can you make of that?"

Arnold held the old club tightly and considered his response. As he did so, the disconcerting vibrations he had picked up during their first meeting flooded back stronger than ever.

"At first glance, the swing is almost flawless," he began. "Confident, good tempo, fine form—a swing of someone who knows where she wants to go and just how she's going to get there."

Anna grinned, and the others nodded their agreement.

"But a closer look reveals a certain rigidity," Arnold added, "a stubbornness evident in the way you refuse to break your elbow and wrists on the backswing. There's a minute hitch in your swing right at the apex, as if you're hesitant to continue. And just before you reached impact I sensed an ebbing of the force behind the shot, a half-heartedness that reveals a general fear to follow through on things."

The smile disappeared from Anna's face, and an air of discomfort passed around the table as Arnold pressed on

"Your head remained fixed on the tee long after the club had passed, which suggests that you're searching for something, something that's no longer there."

Sarah gasped, and George muttered, "Good Lord…"

Anna had visibly paled by this point, and Chris said protectively, "That'll be enough of that, young man!"

"No," Anna said weakly, staring at Arnold, "let him finish."

Arnold didn't want to finish. For once in his life he had the power to hurt another and wished no part of it. But the niblick hummed in his hands, dragging the words from his mouth.

"The truth is, there's a hole in your swing, Anna, a yawning gap right in the middle that you don't know how to fill. You try and make adjustments as best you can: a slight change of stance here, a modified grip there. But you can't make it go away, can you? Can you, Anna?" This last sentence was issued in a raised voice that startled everyone in the room, including Arnold.

Dead silence followed. Then, with a small cry, Anna pushed away from the table and stood in front of the fire with her back to others. Becky rose and tried to put an arm around the girl, but she pulled away to face her antagonist.

"You missed your calling, Arnold. You would've made a fine analyst," Anna said, wiping large tears from her eyes with the back of her hands. "I had no idea I was so transparent." She looked with desperation at the expectant faces around the table, as a huge sob escaped her.

"Funny, I thought I had covered up the major damage fairly well, but then again, how does one bury a hole?" Another sob racked Anna's body, and she leaned against the mantle for support.

"Three years ago, my *fiancé*," she began, biting off the word and spitting it across the room, "the man I dated all through high school, the man I ached for and stayed true to during my undergraduate work, the man who my next glimpse of was all that I lived for, the man I loved more than anything I've ever known…left me." She finished in the barest whisper as if afraid to hear what she herself had to say.

She clung to the warm stone as another wave of sorrow passed through her. "Three years ago, the man I was going to marry, the man I was going to sleep with every night for the rest of my life, the man whose children I was longing to bear and raise, the man I was going to share my every thought with, grow old with, gladly die with…repeatedly slept with another woman."

She was weeping openly now, with a grief that issued not only from her eyes and mouth, but seemed to gush out of her skin and hair and nails, as well, flooding the room with her pain.

"Three years ago, the man who held my hand on long walks through the snow, the man who knew just how to cheer me up with mint-chip ice cream, the man who promised to love me forever and ever…ran off with my best friend—and *married* her!" Anna screamed the words, raging at the walls, and ceiling, and furniture.

"Yes, I have a hole in me, but it can't be filled!" She paused briefly and tilted back her head, gulping in a deep breath before continuing on, more calmly. "Lord knows I've tried. I've thrown everything I can think of into it: school, work, men, food, exercise, pets, hobbies. But it refuses to be gratified, I tell you. It's bottomless!"

She staggered to the middle of the hearth, and Arnold wondered briefly whether she was going to rend her clothing in anguish. He stood just in time to catch her in his arms as she completely broke down and buried her face in George's old robe.

Arnold gently stroked her hair and awaited the wrath this poor girl's family would surely loose upon the catalyst of this fiasco, but when he looked up he was met with warm smiles, and even tears of joy.

Becky came over and laid a hand on her granddaughter's trembling shoulder. "God bless you, Arnold. We've been trying to get her to open up about it for years, but she refused to let us in, claiming that it didn't matter—plenty of fish in the sea and similar nonsense. But we knew it was eating away at her, hollowing out a home suited only for corruption." She looked down and a bright tear fell on the girl's dark hair. "She's going to be all right now. Come, Sarah, Liz. Let's see how those pies are doing and I'll put on a pot of coffee."

They followed Becky into the kitchen while Chris and George retired to the den, leaving Arnold alone with the now quiet Anna. She leaned heavily against him as if trying to deposit her burden, then pulled back her head and said, "Thank you, Arnold."

"For what?"

"For playing the exorcist," Anna said, giving him a fierce hug. "I know it sounds crazy, but I really feel much better. Who knows, maybe that mad rush of words let some fresh air into my soul," she said, laughing and clapping her hands in delight. "After all, they say nature does abhor a vacuum."

The change in her was nothing short of miraculous. She was actually giddy with relief. "Come on," she said, taking his hand. "I want to show you something."

Anna led him to the back door and opened it. The rain was still coming down in buckets as she pulled him over the threshold.

"What about our jackets?" Arnold protested.

"We won't need them; it's not far."

She bolted into the storm with Arnold in tow, dodging among the scattered trunks of tapped maples trees, their sap buckets protected from the rain by homemade rubber hoods. Directly ahead was a low-roofed building, and Anna ducked under its dripping eave. Inside it was dry and sweet-smelling, and in the dim light Arnold could make out rows of stainless-steel tanks.

"This farm has been in my family for eight generations," Anna said as they stood in the doorway, "ever since my great-great-great-great-great-grandfather won it from General Gates in a card game at Valley Forge."

She let go of Arnold's hand and started to move slowly around the edges of the room. "This was my favorite place to come as a kid. It's called the collection room; it's where they collect and store the sap before distillation. I always fancied that the sweet air helped me collect my thoughts."

"Did you live here?" Arnold asked, shaking the rain from his pant legs as he watched her progress.

"When I was very young, before my folks moved to Philadelphia," she said. "But I still love it here, and I try to get out to the country as much as possible, although I don't get here as often as I'd like."

"That explains why I couldn't find you," Arnold said.

Anna stopped her tour of the room and peered at him through the gloom. Then she began to walk again, running her open hand over the cool surface of the tanks as she approached Arnold. She stopped in front of him and leaned her face close to his, wearing a coy smile.

"Well, now you've found me again, haven't you?"

Arnold was about to kiss her when a bell sounded from the direction of the main house. "Coffee's on," she said. "Race you back."

She was out the door and into the rain before Arnold had a chance to reach for her, forcing him to chase her back to the kitchen, where Sarah was just pulling a steaming apple pie from the oven. Over dessert and coffee the talk turned to life on the farm, Anna's work at the hospital, and Arnold's lucrative law practice. When the clock chimed nine, Becky rose. "I don't know what it's like in a law-yer's world, Arnold, but we Witherspoons have to be up before the sun. The sap may run slow, but it's always running, and we have to be there bright and early to catch it."

"And I need to be on the road to Philly by seven," Anna added.

Arnold changed into his dry clothes and they all saw him to the door.

"You'll come see us again, I hope?" George asked as he held out Arnold's coat.

"Oh, yes," Liz insisted. "Please, do!"

"Of course, I will," Arnold replied happily.

"Wonderful!" Becky said. "How about next Friday? I'll put on a roast."

"I'll be here," Arnold said.

Anna smiled and said, "So will I."

As he slipped on his boots, Arnold said, "I'm playing in the club championship this Sunday. Will you come and watch?" The invitation was meant for the whole family, but he was looking at Anna as he tended it.

"I'm sorry, Arnold," she said, "but I have the rotation on Sunday."

"Oh," Arnold said, clearly disappointed. "Well, how about the rest of you, then? I could use the support."

"We'll be there, son," George said.

"With bells on," Sarah promised.

"Wouldn't miss it for the world," Chris proclaimed.

"It'll be better than the Masters," Liz exaggerated.

"I'll pack a picnic," Becky added sensibly.

Arnold looked at the happy faces surrounding him in the foyer and raised his brows at Anna. He wanted to ask how he could reach her in Philadelphia, but the knowing looks made him uncomfortable.

"Good-bye," he said, "and thanks."

"It's we that have you to thank, Arnold," Becky said, wrapping her arm around Anna.

The rain had still not let up, falling in fat drops on the flagstone drive to bounce and scatter in the darkness. Arnold dashed for his car and had just started the engine when he saw someone running toward him between swipes of the wiper blades. It was Anna, wearing her grandfather's big yellow slicker. He lowered his window and she ducked her head into the opening.

"Here's my number in Philly," she yelled over the downpour, handing him a slip of paper. "I know you didn't ask for it, but you're gonna get it anyway." Then she kissed him hard on the mouth, digging her fingers into his wet hair. "Good luck on Sunday!" she cried, then ran back toward the house.

As Arnold drove home in the storm, he was surprised to find that he was crying.

*   *   *

What's that? No, our friend wasn't quite out of his dark woods yet. True, the niblick had worked wonders on his soul, and for the first time in his life he felt that maybe the rest of the world wasn't out to get him after all, that perhaps there was a place for him among humanity. But there was almost thirty years of damage and rot to repair—a tall order for a golf club, even a magical one.

* * *

So the big day of the club championship arrived and, as luck would have it, Arnold's newfound virtues were to be sorely tested. For opposing him that day was none other than his most hated courtroom rival, a woman considered almost as loathsome as Arnold himself: Wanda "the Witch" Hazelton. Arnold felt an overwhelming urge to strike the woman when saw her standing on the tee, and I believe he might have done so had it not been for the timely arrival of the Witherspoon family.

"Ho, Arnold!" Liz called from the gathering crowd.

A murmur of surprise echoed through the modest gallery as they realized that Arnold Remlap actually had a well-wisher present.

"Hi, gang," he said, smiling and walking over to where they stood in the shade of Becky's brightly-colored sun umbrella. "Thanks for coming."

"Capital idea my boy, glad we came," George said, sporting his floppy hat. "What's the competition look like?"

Arnold shot a withering glance at Witch Hazel. "Couldn't be worse," he said. "She's the club's best golfer and the bane of my existence. I don't know if I'll be able to concentrate."

"Just let the club do the work, Arnold," Chris said with a wink and a nod toward the niblick.

"I'll try."

Wanda and Arnold were the clear favorites with the odds makers, and for the first nine holes the match went according to form. At the turn the two were dead even at three under, with the rest of the field wheezing out of contention. Arnold's swing was sweeter than ever, but the Witch's constant badgering began to wear on him. He went so far as to play his shots on the opposite side of the fairway in order to stay well clear of her machete-like tongue.

"You the man, Arnold!" Liz shouted on the 10th tee. "You're looking better than Hogan!" Arnold cracked a smile and loosened up a bit, but on the next hole his opponent strategically coughed during Arnold's backswing, causing him to pull his drive badly off line.

"Hard luck, Remlap," Hazelton chortled. "Why don't you try using a club fabricated in *this* century? They make 'em out of metal these days, you know."

The gaffe cost him a precious stroke, and then the Witch *really* began to bear down on him. Rattled and off balance, Arnold began to mutter to himself and curse under his breath, slamming his clubs back into his bag after each errant shot. He dropped two more shots and started to press matters, which only made things worse.

Hate seeped back into his patchwork heart, and the Arnold of old could be seen lurking behind the hard gaze he gave his worsening lies. Even his newly-found swing was affected, showing a hint of a *herk,* much to the dismay of the Witherspoons.

But fortunately for Arnold, Hazelton's underhandedness did not go unnoticed by the gallery, which had been trying unsuccessfully to make up its mind which of the two evils to root for. Noting the Witch's lowly tactics, they eventually began to pull for Arnold, and with the crowd behind him he managed to put a stop to the bleeding and remain three strokes back, with four holes yet to play.

But Wanda Hazelton was notorious for closing out both her cases and her matches. Give the Witch a lead going home, it was said, and it was all over except the plea bargaining. Yet Arnold refused to panic. He sensed that something was about to happen, and as he was cleaning his spikes on fifteen he heard a familiar voice call from the gallery: "Go get her, Arnold."

"Anna!" he cried joyfully, rushing over to give her a big hug (as another ripple of shock passed through the crowd). "I thought you couldn't make it."

She shrugged. "I coaxed a colleague to switch shifts with me and came as fast as I could." She knit her eyebrows together in a look of concern. "Granddad says you're having a rough time of it."

"Yeah," he answered, glancing back at Hazelton. "What does the Lizard say?"

Anna laughed. "She says your wheels have come off completely, and that we should call a tow truck."

Arnold laughed with her, and Wanda called out shrilly from the tee, "Hey, Remlap! You gonna play or make time?"

Arnold gave Anna a wink and stepped up to his ball. He studied the lake that dominated the fairway, its nearest shore lying some 250 yards from the tee, with the far bank at well over 300.

Wanda followed his gaze. "Don't be a fool, Remlap. Nobody's ever cleared the lake."

Arnold ignored her and used the niblick to club a staggering drive. It was still rising when it reached the lake, clearing the obstacle with ridiculous ease to fall safely in front of the green. The gallery roared to life, and a clearly shaken Wanda sent her tee shot into the trees. Arnold won the hole and took the next with a brilliant fairway wood. On seventeen he evened the match by sticking a beautiful niblick four feet from the pin and sinking the putt for birdie.

By this point Arnold was so enraptured that he wasn't sure whether it was his ball or his soul that went soaring down the middle of the 18th fairway. Nor did he register the Witch's pathetic duck hook as it skittered deep into the rough. He floated down the course, embraced by his fellow man, encouraged by his newfound friends and quietly supported by the woman he was now sure he loved.

Arriving at his ball, Arnold looked across the fairway to see how his rival had fared. It was utterly hopeless. Wanda's ball had come up hard against the bole of a large beech tree, leaving her with no opportunity to advance. The best she could hope for was to hit it backward and into play, but with Arnold in perfect position and already seventy yards past her lie, the prospects looked bleak at best.

As the gallery openly relished her predicament, Wanda cursed loudly, glaring alternately at the ball and the tree, as if trying to decide which she hated more. And in those hard eyes Arnold recognized the desperation, the longing and the loneliness that had been his constant companion for almost thirty years. Right then and there Arnold Remlap knew what he had to do, and to his credit he did not falter or tarry for an instant. He marched resolutely into the Witch's private screening of hell and loudly cleared his throat.

Wanda wheeled on him immediately. "Buzz off, Remlap," she said venomously. "I'm finished, OK? You've won the bleeping match, so just run along and grab your trophy and spare me the gloating."

"I didn't come over to gloat," Arnold said gently. "I came to help."

"Help!" Wanda roared. "I don't need your help, Counselor."

Arnold looked at her ball. "Yes, you do, Wanda. Here," he said, holding out the niblick, "I suggest you use this."

"What kind of fool do you take me for, Remlap?" she hissed. "How can that piece of junk be any help?"

Arnold glanced at the pensive gallery and lowered his voice, "It's magic."

The Witch threw back her head and roared with laughter. "Have you lost your mind?" she cackled. "What are you drinking, boy? Whatever it is, give me some, 'cause I could sure use a belt right about now."

"Listen to me, Wanda," Arnold said earnestly. "Who was the club's worst golfer as little as a few months ago? Who left a trail of ugly divots wherever he went? Who couldn't hit the broad side of a barn from 100 yards with a wedge and a bucket of range balls? Who, Wanda?"

"You," she replied thoughtfully.

"And now, here I am on the verge of beating you in a head-to-head match for the championship. And it all started when I got this old niblick. How do you explain that?"

"I can't."

"Then take it," Arnold said, holding the niblick out again. "What have you got to lose?"

Wanda shrugged and took the club. "Why are you doing this, Arnold?" she asked in confusion. "I thought you hated me."

Arnold looked up at the clear blue sky, then shifted his gaze to the Witherspoons, to Anna, and finally back to the niblick. "I've come to learn that hate is just something you do when you don't know how to love."

As Arnold turned back to his ball, he saw Anna give him a big smile and a thumbs-up. She knew what that sacrifice had meant to him, as did George in his floppy hat, and Chris, and Sarah, and Becky, and even little Liz, who found the gesture so heroic that she let it stand on its own merits without the benefit of magnification.

Arnold didn't watch as Wanda took her shot; he didn't have to. He kept his eyes on Anna's as the ball caromed off the trunk of the beech, flew deeper into the woods, ricocheted off another tree, shot up the fairway, bounced off a broken sprinkler head, sailed high into the air, skipped off the rake lying next to a greenside bunker, rolled onto the putting surface and carved a long, graceful arc right into the heart of the cup.

*   *   *

So that's my tale, lad, and you know the rest. From that day forward Arnold Remlap was changed for good. He became a community hero, a pillar of society, an elder of the church and, eventually, our beloved town mayor. He married Anna, of course, and they've raised two smashing children who have since taken over the reins of the old Witherspoon farm, now that Chris and Sarah have retired to Florida, and Liz decided to lend her special gifts to the *National Enquirer*. As Anna likes to put it, she and Arnold are in the process of happily, but very slowly, dying together.

What became of the niblick, you ask? Well, Wanda, who, by the way, experienced her own remarkable metamorphosis, gave it to her new sister-in-law the day Wanda wed (to her delirious joy) Judge Lewis, whom she had loved from across the bench for years. The sister-in-law passed it on to a friend, who lent it to a man from Billingsport, who then bequeathed it to a total stranger, and that is where the travels of the club pass from my knowledge. It's out there somewhere, passing from hand to hand, soul to soul, healing as it goes. Perhaps someday it'li turn up again in these parts, and who knows, maybe you'll be the next benefactor of the magic niblick.

Now scram...I've got a customer!

Four
For
Fore

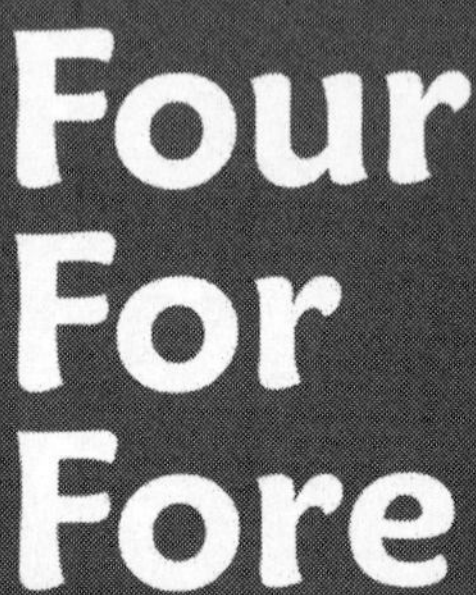

G. Guilford Barton

Completing the Series

GOLF IS NO
ORDINARY GAME!

One of the most galvanizing events of the 20th century, at least for Americans of my generation, was the assassination of JFK. I can still remember exactly where I was and what I was doing when I heard the news. The tragedy has spawned much controversy and speculation and will probably always remain something of a dark mystery. It has also spawned the story that follows.

Four For Fore

"**D**id ye hear what happened to MacAndles?" asked the first from the end of the bar. A tired sun half-heartedly cast its last rays over the open windowsill to dance along the row of aging bottles that lined the wall. After a long pull on his dark bitter the second man wiped his mouth with the back of his hand.

"Nae," he replied.

"He was struck by a ball on the 8th green."

"Ye don't say!"

"Aye," responded a third as he lowered his considerable girth onto a stool scarred and weathered by decades of nicks and wood smoke and errant toasts. "Never knew what hit 'im."

The second looked up from his foaming pint in horror. "Did nae one bother to call *fore*?"

"Nae," hissed the first disdainfully and spat into the fire as if it had somehow committed the mortal offense.

"Ah, what's the world coming to?" lamented the second. "Is he all right, then?"

"We don't know," replied the third. "He was still insensible when they carried 'im off the course."

"Good Lord!" bellowed the first. "Do they know who struck the wicked blow?"

The third shook his bearded head. "Only that the ball seemed to sail in from the 8th tee, nice and low and hard. Ye should have seen it carom off the back o' MacAndles' head and bounce t'ward the pin. If it was nae such a tragedy I would have tipped me cap ta such a stroke o' luck."

"So ye were there, then?" asked the first.

"Aye, I was waiting to drive off on the 9th when I heard a sickenin' sound from behind me and turned just in the nick o' time to see MacAndles spinning to the ground like a wounded gull."

The second twisted on his stool. "I heard that the shot came in from the 15th and struck 'im on the brow."

"Who told ye that?" demanded the third.

"Angus Reed, that's who. He was caddying for another member o' the foursome, Reggie O'Riley. Claims that he caught a glimpse o' something white flying over that grove o' spruce trees and the next thin' he knows MacAndles is lying there with 'is eyes rolled up inside 'is head."

"And *I'm* telling ye that the ball came from the 9th tee," protested the third. "I saw it with me own eyes, man!"

"It could nae have been the shot ye saw," the first said. "O'Riley swears that it ricocheted off o' MacAndles, struck Fergusen flush on the thigh and *then* bounded away. So it had to come from the front."

"Maybe there were two balls?" offered the second.

"Are ye daft, man?" laughed the first. "Do ye know the chances o' separate shots simultaneously felling the same golfer?"

"Besides," said the third, "only one ball was found at the scene."

They sat in silence for a time, staring deep into their glasses as the fire crackled and sputtered its contribution to the conversation. Finally the second stirred on his stool. "What make o' ball was it?"

"A Slazenger five," answered the first.

The second looked up sharply with eyes narrowed. "Farcourt plays a Slazenger five and he despises MacAndles!"

"Aye...he's on the carpet now being questioned by the rules committee."

"I hope they pull his membership," growled the third. "Serve 'im right, the bloody sod."

The first wagged a gnarled finger at his companions. "Word is that he has an alibi. Claims he was mired on the 12th at the time, playing six shots out o' that nasty pothole bunker near the green."

"Does he have any witnesses?"

"Aye, although nae one could actually see 'im down in the hole, both Sir Bruce and McHenry reported seeing geysers o' sand and hearing someone that certainly sounded like Farcourt cursing from the bunker."

"That does sound like 'im," the second admitted reluctantly, "and if Farcourt *was* on the 12th then he could nae have been 'im that played the fell stroke."

"Why not?" asked the first. "It's reachable with a strong drive."

"True, it is in range but it would have taken a prodigious hook ta get it around the pines that line the fairway, and everyone knows that Farcourt plays nothing but a fade."

"Aye," said the first glumly.

"Bloody shame, that," said the third. The fire had just begun to die away when the fourth walked into the clubhouse and tossed a fresh log on the flames.

"Are ye talking about MacAndles, then?" he asked.

"Aye, we can nae decide if the shot came from the 15th fairway or the 8th tee box or both."

"That's because it came from neither, lads."

The other three sat up and took sudden notice. "Then where *did* it come from?"

"From that hill full o' gorse out t'wards the sea."

"Ye mean the gorsey knoll?" asked the first.

"Aye, that's the one; the ball flew from there fer sure."

"Says who?" demanded a skeptical third.

"Says Andy Cartright. He was MacAndles' playing partner and they were up by three before the calamity. He said he clearly heard a ball struck from that direction just before he lost MacAndles—and consequently the match, I might add."

"Are ye suggesting that there was deliberate foul play involved?" asked the second.

"I'm nae suggesting anything, but there *was* a good number of pounds riding on the outcome."

"How much?"

"A hundred."

"A hundred quid!" roared the first. "Who were they playing against?"

"MacGregor and Samuels."

"But they're a couple o' saints," declared the second. "Never knew either o' them to so much as step on another man's line."

"Maybe," said the fourth darkly, "but a hundred pounds sterling has a way o' bringing out the devil in any man."

The third slammed his glass to the bar and scowled at the fourth. "I don't believe it—I will nae!"

"Believe what ye will," shrugged the fourth, "but Cartright also said that he saw someone leaving the knoll."

"Who?"

"He did nae get a good look at 'im, only that he was wearing a black MacIntosh and carrying a mashie."

"Did they nae go after 'im?" asked the second.

"Aye, but he disappeared into the dunes," reported the fourth, leaning forward with a whisper. "And neither MacGregor nor Samuels wished to press the chase, claiming that they was already late for supper."

"It all smacks o' a conspiracy," said the first to a chorus of nods.

"Do ye think we should call for an investigation?" asked the second.

"Nae," said the fourth, "let it be."

"But we must," protested the third. "It's our duty ta the game!"

The fourth shook his head and pushed back his cap. "Look 'ere, lads. Ye've got men with raincoats and mashies vanishing into thin air. Ye've got mortal enemies with left to right swings and iron-clad alibis. Ye've got balls flying in from all points o' the compass and bouncing off skulls like they was wickets. And ye've got a pair o' angels with enough motive ta hang the whole lot. It's a muddle, lads, and it always will be. There's evil in the world sure as the night is black," he said, draining his glass and placing it carefully on the ancient wooden bar. "Sometimes it's best to just let things be."

"Aye," said the first.

"Well said," said the second.

"Bloody shame," said the third.

The fourth rose and tipped his cap as his shadow flickered across the wall and slipped out the door to mingle with the night.

G. Guilford Barton grew up outside of Detroit and is a graduate of the University of Michigan. He enjoys camping, fly fishing and, of course, golf. G. Guilford discovered his passion for writing later in life and now lives a blessed existence with his wife and two sons.

Write me at Twitter @TheGolfingBard or
www.Facebook.com/GolfIsNoOrdinaryGame

http://thegolfingbard.wordpress.com/

MORE GREAT READS
FROM BOOKTROPE

Rainbow Curve **by Michael Boylan** (Fiction) Fans of baseball's history will appreciate this compelling tale about race, politics, corrupting power and one man's courage to stand up against it.

Home Field – Writers Remember Baseball **by John Douglas Marshall** (Memoir - Sports) Nine great writers, including two National Book Award winners, reminisce about their own experiences with America's national pastime.

OFFSIDE: A Mystery **by William P. Barrett** (Mystery) At the height of the L.A. real estate bubble in 2006, the murder of a referee of youth soccer in a ritzy suburb is blamed on a coach angry about a call.

Running in Darkness **by James Daly** (WW II Fiction) American artist Jack Martin finds himself joining a fledgling resistance group to combat Hitler and the Nazi party. But is he capable of doing what's needed? A fast-paced World War II thriller.

GOTU **by Mike McNeff** (Action Thriller) When a drug cartel attacks a cop, the rules apply. When they attack a cop's family? There are no rules. An action-packed thriller written by a 40-year law enforcement veteran.

Learning to Float **by Allan Ament** (Memoir - Caregiving) When his wife suffers a debilitating stroke, Allan Ament begins a transformation from criminal defense attorney to caregiver. The couple's journey toward their "new normal" will amuse and inspire.

Discover more books and learn about our
new approach to publishing at **www.booktrope.com**.